Pictu
Hoisin Chicken (pg. 86-87)
Gyoza Potstickers (pg 32-33); Orange Chicken

gourmet food with all of the flavor and none of the guilt

THE GUILT FREE GOURMET

Low Calorie, Low Fat Cookbook of Awesomeness... Numero Cinco

Cookbook Volume 5
ASIAN CUISINE

Follow me online at:

The Web: www.theguiltfreegourmet.net
Connect: @dhallakx7
Facebook: The Guilt Free Gourmet LLC.
Instagram: TheGuiltFreeGourmet ... No, seriously... Follow me on Instagram.
Youtube Channel: The Guilt Free Gourmet ... Subscribe please! I upload all of my Connect cooking vids.
Amazon: You can find all of my cookbooks on my website, as well as on Amazon.
(not to *be* confused with the old, vegan, gluten free, hippie dessert book of the same name... that's not me!)

Copyright 2023 by Daniel Hallak
Updated: 02/07/23
Book design by: Daniel Hallak
Edited by: Mary Geiler
Nutritional Information by: Sarrah S. Settarra, of '*Sashi Makes Stuff* ... www.sashimakesstuff.blogspot.com
Photography by Daniel Hallak

LEGAL MUMBO JUMBO

The Guilt Free Gourmet® 2023

Weight Watchers International & WW ®

Dedicated to Mary Geiler. The lady who has been dealing with my ramblings for 3 years now. She's dealt with my constant barrage of typos, bad grammar, run-on sentences, venting... my, ridiculously, excessive, use, of, commas,... horrific use of punctuation' marks;! and my inability to spell the words 'resteraunt' or 'collander' correctly, even after 3 years of waving her fists at me in frustration.

If I ever strike it rich, like Jed Clampett... I am seriously going to foot the bill for all of the therapy you deserve for putting up with me and my shenanigans. I guess a BevMo membership would also be appropriate, in lieu of the non existant 401k and PTO here at The Guilt Free Gourmet.

Best part, because this is dedicated to you and I didn't want you to see it... you never got a chance to proof read it first. Now yOu have 2 deal with all th3se typoz, on yer dedicatiun' page... forevur! MUAHAHAHAH!!!!

But, on a postive... you can't be too mad at me, because, here's a pic of Jesse. Yes.... I played the Jesse-card. Thank you for everything... Inga :)

- Daniel
07-06-2021

Korean Bulgogi Beef Stir Fry - pg. 66-67

Thai Basil Chicken - pg. 128-129

Chinese Mushroom Chicken - pg. 104-105

Filipino Chicken in Adobo Sauce - pg. 54-55

TABLE OF CONTENTS

2023 | *Cookbook: Volume 5: Second Edition*
Low Calorie, Full Flavor Asian Cuisine

Singapore Noodles - Pg. 118-119

Why Asian Food?

Trying to help you all understand the reasoning behind why I cook the way I do, as well as what made me decide to try and branch out to Asian food ...

How To Use QR Codes

Showing you how to use your mobile device's camera app, to scan the "QR Codes" on each recipe ...

Free Cookbooks?

Yup, you aren't crazy. I actually DO let everyone have all of my cookbooks for free, digitally ...

Important Gadgets

Pointing out a couple of important gadgets and gizmos that are used throughout the book's recipes ...

Highlighted Ingredients & Substitutions

Now we're getting into the nitty gritty. Six pages of suggestions, tips and ideas for food substitutions, as well as some of the ingredients that might not be familiar to you. A lot of these ingredients were exotic for me, at first, which is why I'm highlighting them ...

Foundations & Cooking Tips

Most of my 'foundation recipes' are covered in Cookbook 1, but I did want to carry over my 2 breading recipes, Asian meat mix, as well as add a couple tips ...

Sauces & Dips

Recipes for 15 low calorie, mostly fat free, low sugar Asian sauces & dips. They're great for dim sum, as well as being versatile enough to be used on entrees ...

Dim Sum & Soups

Recipes for 12 low fat, low calorie 'skinnied-down' Asian appetizers (Dim Sum) and soups. I have everything from homemade shumai dumplings, potstickers and satay chicken skewers, to fresh spring rolls, meat-filled Bao, to hot and sour soup ...

Main Dishes

And now, the reason you're all here. A boat-load of low calorie, low fat, mostly sugar free Asian food. Everything from platters of noodles to meat entrees and fried rice. The recipes in this section aren't just your usual Panda Express copycat recipes either. I have food from multiple regions of Asia, including:
Cambodia, China, Japan, Korea, The Philippines, Taiwan, Thailand & Vietnam ...

Closing Thoughts & Acknowledgements

My final ramblings, hopefully not toooo incoherant, as well as shout outs to some of the folks that helped get this crazy train rollin' down the tracks. ...

Nutritional Info. & Macros

The nutritional numbers for everything ...

Recipe Index

Even though I like to make you folks wave your first in the air, trying to find recipes... I figured I'd try to be helpful this time around ...

WHY ASIAN FOOD?

I remember exactly when I decided that my 5th cookbook would be focused on Asian food, it was Summer 2020. A member in Connect was commenting about how unhealthy Panda Express' Orange Chicken was, followed by there weren't any low point copycat recipes online, that were breaded and under 5 points per serving. So I looked at a few popular recipe sites and yup, theirs were all coated in flour and fried in oil, then coated in a syrupy uber-sweet sauce with gobs of honey, sugar and orange juice. Then, the skinny bloggers would proudly tout their 'light/healthy' version. After a few days of looking up various recipes, I decided to switch gears. Rather than only looking up 'copycat' recipes of "Chinese Fast Food" dishes, I started looking up TRADITIONAL Chinese recipes, from actual Chinese Chefs, who own Chinese restaurants. You know... the real deal. I found a few good sites from actual Asian Chefs, took note of what they all had in common, then used the 'recipe builder' to hack down their traditional Asian recipes, with non-traditional ingredient substitutions.

That got me thinkin', "I wonder if there's ever been a legit, full-fledged WW-Friendly cookbook devoted to Asian food?" After searching online, I saw that there was only 1, and it was published 26 years ago. So, I decided to challenge myself and make an Asian cookbook of my own. I figured it'd be a great way to challenge myself, because, well... I didn't know how to cook Asian food. 😂

That started a 10 month process of researching different regional recipes from different Asian countries. A big problem is my wife and I never, ever get to go out, (2 special needs kids will do that). We hadn't actually gone out to get Asian food in years. Other than Americanized wannabe-Chinese fast food, which is NOT real Asian food, I had absolutely no idea what to make, let alone what any of it is supposed to taste like. So, I turned to my 'tribe'. I asked people in Connect, the private social media forum for Weight Watchers members, for suggestions.

I was flooded with requests for Asian dishes that I'd never heard of before, but, at least I had a list now. I spent MONTHS watching youtube videos, reading Asian cooking blogs, looking through websites devoted to various Asian cuisines... heck, I had to learn how to use all new ingredients that I'd never even heard of, much less purchased before. It was pretty intimidating, but it was honestly a TON of fun as well. I love trying new things in the kitchen. Plus, as a stay at home dad... this is my creative outlet that lets me feel like I'm more than just a diaper changin' chauffeur.

I honestly hope that you all come to enjoy these recipes, as much as I enjoyed trying to make them. I know that a lot of these dishes are going to be extremely intimidating for you to try. Trust me, I completely understand. I've included TONS of notes, all over the place, as well as an entire section explaining 'exotic' ingredients that may not be familiar to you. My hope is to make this as accessible as possible. I even go out of my way to try and avoid requiring you to purchase tons of crazy ingredients. I use ingredient substitutions EXTENSIVELY throughout this book, hoping to make it as easy as possible for you.

So, enjoy your skinnied-down journey through Asia... at least you won't need a passport for this trip.

Understanding My Listed 'Point' Values

For this newly revised version of my cookbook, for the 2023 plan, I'll be providing point values in 2 ways. Traditional AND a QR code you can scan. In this example, under 'points', you'll see a blue text bubble with 2 numbers. The **LEFT** number is points on the *'regular'* plan, while the **RIGHT** number is the point value for the *diabetic* plan. Easy peasy.

R = Regular 0 point foods list
D = Diabetic 0 point foods list

R   D

1-3

So in this case, the first serving is 1 point for folks on the 'Regular' plan and 3 points for people on the 'Diabetic' plan.

USING 'QR' CODES

Have you ever seen those crazy looking, square shaped code-thingies on a menu, flyer or in a magazine and wondered what they are? Well... they are the exact same as a 'link' you'd find on a webpage, which you can click to go somewhere. But, these links are printed onto paper. You use a mobile device's Camera to scan (click) them.

So you don't have to "take my word for it", with my listed recipe's points, I wanted to provide you a way to check them for yourself, while also giving you the ability to track them. For all my recipes, if you scan the codes in this book, they'll open a link on your mobile device. Once clicked, the link will open up my recipe in YOUR app's recipe builder. This will let you see the accurate points on your plan, as well as letting you adjust servings and TRACK WHAT YOU ATE!!

Step One:

Open your phone's "camera" app, ya'know, the one you take pictures with. Open it, then point the camera at the square code-thingie you want to look up.

Step Two:

When you see 4 little yellow brackets around the corners of the code you want, a pop up that says *"Open QR.IO in Safari"* will appear at the top of the screen. Click that banner.

Step Three:

When you click the recipe's picture, it will instantly load up my recipe into YOUR WW app (if on a mobile device). If you're on a desktop, there's no need to scan a code. Just go to the 'Point Values' page on my site and click the recipe.

Your App will show you the points for my recipe, based off of YOUR 0 point food settings. Then, simply 'track' the food, adjust the servings, etc.

Give It A Try

Want to give it a quick try? Use your mobile device's camera to look at, then open the link for this QR code. Go ahead.... I'll wait. If you get it right, you get to see me and and my buddy *@chiafullo*, hangin' out in Lederhosen.

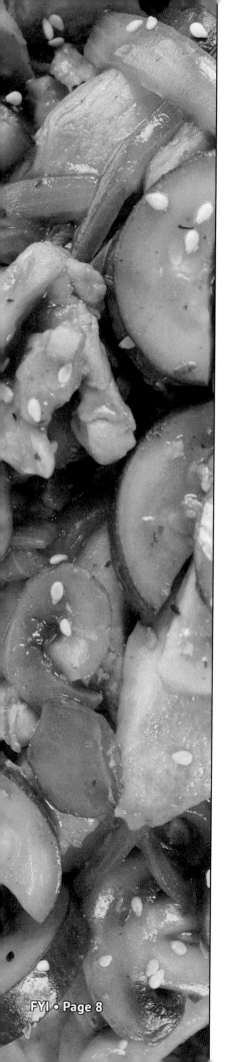

REALLY? FREE COOKBOOKS?

Though all of my cookbooks are available in printed format, on Amazon.com, you can open, view, save, print and share ALL of my cookbooks for free, at absolutely no charge whatsoever on my website: *www.theguiltfreegourmet.net*

I allow everyone access to my Cookbooks for free, in digital format. My website has no ads, promotions, pop ups, or links begging you to use my discount code and save 10% on something so I get a kickback. This is my ministry. Yeah, a coupla bucks is nice, but at the end of the day, the most important thing is feeling like I get to help people. For a guy who's stuck at home cleaning house and changing diapers all day... it's a pretty nice feeling.

The Guilt Free Gourmet Cookbook Volume 1
(Newly Revised for 2023)
- Guides & Tutorials
- Ingredient Swaps
- Meat Seasoning Recipes
- Foundation Recipes
- Sauces
- Extra Snark

The Guilt Free Gourmet Cookbook Volume 2
(Newly Revised for 2023)
- Dips & Spreads
- Salad Dressings
- Appetizers
- Assorted Snazzy, Yet Surprisingly 'Light' Desserts

The Guilt Free Gourmet Cookbook Volume 3
(STILL BEING REVISED for 2023)
- Dressings, Spreads & Condiments
- Gourmet Burgers & Sandwiches
- Side Dishes
- Salads
- Desserts

For most of you folks that cook a lot and have spent years trying new things in the kitchen, these Gadgets & Gizmos are nothing new to you. But this particular page is directed more towards people who aren't as comfortable in the kitchen yet and what some of the gadgets are that I use a lot, while making the various recipes in this book.

1. WHAT THE *@#!? WHERE'S THE WOK!?!?

This is probably the first Asian cookbook in history where a Wok will not be used, period. Why? Because, I'll bet 99% of the people who bought this book, don't own a Wok. However, most everyone has a large pan. My goal is for my cookbooks to be as accessible as possible. I've made 5 cookbooks now, using a simple, cheap, *3 Quart 'high walled' saute pan*, I got for $20, at Walmart. However, if you want to use a Wok, go ahead.

2. Oven Thermometer

If you don't have one... buy it. I got mine at the 99 cent store and it's served me for years. You know when you set your oven to 400 degrees and it beeps to tell you it's ready? It's lying.... it's lying, big time. Ignore the beep and look at the thermometer. Chances are your oven is still 150 degrees colder than what you set it for. You THINK you're baking your chicken for 20 minutes at 400 degrees, when really, you put it in at 150 and it isn't going to hit 400 for another 15 minutes. Wait till your oven is actually at the right temperature, then proceed.

3. Bamboo or Steel Steamer Baskets

You can go 1 of 2 ways with this. You can spend a lot of money and buy expensive stainless steel steamer insert baskets for a regular stock pot. Or... you can go the less expensive, yet more traditional route. If you want to make any of the dim sum dumplings, you'll need to steam them. I spent $20 on amazon and bought a *10 inch, 2 layered bamboo steamer set*. You pretty much fill a 10" pan or pot with some water, bring it to a boil, and set this thing on top of it. Boom, steamed stuff.

4. Fine Wire Mesh Strainer/Sieves

In this cookbook, I actually use these babies to lightly dust meat with a 0 point amount of flour, before dredging it in egg wash and breading it. In typical recipes, nearly every single Chef and blogger in the world dumps a boat load of flour into a bowl and sets their chicken into it, coating both sides. It's completely unecessary to use that much. Plus, it adds a lot of carbs, calories and points, which aren't needed. If done correctly, you can can actually "dust" both sides of 4 chicken breasts, with a good coating of flour, using only 1-1/2 tsp... which is 0 points.

5. Food Processor

In this book, I only use a food processor in... I believe... 2 or 3 recipes. Primarily I use it to process together the fillings for my potstickers, shumai dumplings, Vietnamese meatballs, the marinade for my chicken satay skewers and.... well, ok. I guess I do use it for a few things. If you don't own one, you can simply chop and chop and chop the heck out of things, by hand.

6. Digital Kitchen Scale

This is an optional one, but it needed to be pointed out. Some of my recipes in this book will request for you to use a specific amount of things, such as "7oz ground turkey mixed with 5oz of ground shrimp", or "233 grams of wonton wrappers". Of course, you can always eyeball and guess the measurements, but c'mon.... if you're already "in-system", you know how very important it is to own one of these anyways.

And yes... in keeping with my frugal nature, I have a cheap one I bought at Big Lots, years ago. It works just fine.

INGREDIENTS & SUBSTITUTIONS

You want me to buy WHAT?!?!?!

If you're like I was before making all of these dishes... there's a good chance you'll have no idea what the heck you're going to need, or why you need it, for a LOT of these dishes. These next few pages will highlight the ingredients that might seem exotic now, but you'll consider them old friends after cooking a few recipes. AS WELL AS how I recommend substituting them out, for lower point substitutions.

'DARK' SOY SAUCE

Ok, to answer the obvious question on everyone's minds... 'DARK' soy sauce **IS NOT THE SAME THING** as regular soy sauce. Don't feel bad, I was scratching my head too, when I first started seeing it listed in Asian recipes. Yes... 'regular' soy sauce iiiiiiiis dark, but it isn't daaaaark. ;-)

Regular soy sauce is thin, like water and packs an extremely savory and salty flavor punch. Wonder why Asian food at restaurants has such deep, dark, colors for the sauces? Yup, it's the **DARK** soy sauce. Dark soy sauce is a little thicker, a little less salty, has a slight sweetness, but more than anything, it's used to deepen and darken the color of ANYTHING you add it to. If a bottle of black food coloring had a baby with a bottle of soy sauce, the offspring would be 'Dark' soy sauce. **Different brands have different point values.** The generic listing for 'dark soy sauce' lets you have up to 2 Tbsp for 0 points. *'Sushi Chef'* brand lets you have 3 Tbsp for 0 points. *"Lee Kum Kee"* brand actually has 1 point at 1 Tbsp... *"Chin-Su"* brand gives 'ya 3-1/2 Tbsp for 0 points... but the champ, *KA ME* Dark Soy Sauce lets you have up to 10 Tbsp for 0 points. Sadly, it's very hard to find, even on Amazon. Also, as a warning... **DO NOT BUY 'MUSHROOM FLAVORED' DARK SOY SAUCE!** Don't do it! Mushroom Flavored Dark Soy Sauce is gross, with a very pungent flavor. Also: **Dark Soy Sauce CONTAINS WHEAT!!!!**

REDUCED SODIUM & GLUTEN FREE SOY SAUCE

Mitigate the Sodium-Bomb, & Avoid de'Gluten!

Look, we all know that most all Asian food has a TON of sodium. I've tried to use as little soy sauce as I can in my recipes, because I know a lot of folks have sodium restrictions... but there's only so much we can do. I highly recommend using lower sodium or reduced sodium soy sauce. These dishes are still going to have a TON of sodium, but it'll be lower than using regular. Another thing to note: If you're allergic to gluten, you can use *'TAMARI'* style soy sauce. It's available in all major grocery stores, in the Asian food aisle. Tamari is a little darker and a little thicker than regular soy sauce. **You can also make a gluten free dark soy sauce substitute,** by adding a little molasses to the Tamari. Also, you can use *'soy free'* soy sauce, and *'liquid aminos'*, as soy sauce alternatives.

OYSTER SAUCE & VEGETARIAN OYSTER SAUCE

OMG, is it really made out of oysters? Bleh!

Get over it, Nancy... the stuff is awesome! It's not made FROM oysters... rather from the liquid leftover from cooking them. It's an extremely thick, dark, salty and earthy tasting sauce with a hint of the ocean. It's used eeeextensively in Asian food. But Daniel, I'm vegetarian!!! Well don't worry, you can find vegetarian, gluten free 'oyster' sauce at the store too. It's made from mushrooms. It has a slightly different flavor, but will work just fine.

Chinese Cooking Wine - Shaoxing Wine

HOW TO Substitute It Out!!

This is one of those areas where ingredient substitutions really shine. TONS of Asian recipes call for this wine. It's a heavily seasoned 'Rice Wine'. It's dark in color, is very salty and well... it's wine. It's also very high in points. In EVERY RECIPE that traditionally calls for it, I use my go-to 0 point substitution. Rather than using this high point rice wine, I use 1 Tbsp of white wine, with 1-2 tsp rice vinegar and(or) 1 tsp balsamic vinegar.

Sugar Free Syrup Instead of Honey

How To Swap Out Bee Puke.

As delicious and complex a flavor as honey is, it is also very high in points and sugars. There are a few options for getting around it though.
#1, *Sugar Free Pancake Syrup.* The flavor profile is different, but it is sweet, thick and a lot lower in points. *#2, Sugar Free Imitation Honey.* You can purchase it online, pretty cheap through Walmart. However, it is barely lower point than real honey and only has 10 less calories per Tablespoon. However, it's still a good option for diabetic folks.

Fermented Red Pepper Paste (Gochujang)

Wait... I'm buying what??

This stuff is found in the Asian food aisle. You've probably walked by it a million times and haven't noticed it. It might say 'fermented red pepper paste', it might say 'gochujang paste'... same thing. It's used extensively in Korean food. In my recipes, I used it for the sauce of my Korean 'Bibimbap'. Different brands have different points.

Bamboo Shoots & Water Chestnuts

Sounds Weird... But You Need 'em

These are two of the unsung heroes of Chinese food. Not as sexy as Dark soy sauce, not as flashy as Sriracha hot sauce. These babies are textural dynamos that clock in every day, do their job and don't care for accolades. Both can be found in the Asian food aisle. When you do use them, you want to drain them from the liquid in the can. Also, I highly recommend purchasing 'sliced' water chestnuts. Don't make the mistake I did of buying the canned 'whole' ones. It's a huge time saver.

Wonton Wrappers

Potstickers & Steamed Dumplings

If you plan on making my 3 recipes with dumplings, Shumai, Potstickers & Wor Wonton Soup, you'll have to buy wonton wrappers. You can find them in major grocery stores. You can find them in the refrigerated area where they sell tofu or other Asian products. For my recipes, you'll be purchasing small, 3-1/2" square shaped wonton wrappers. They might come in a rectangular package. It's ok, those packages have 2 square stacks, laid down next to each other. The point values for my recipes were made with 'Twin Dragon' brand wonton wrappers.

Asian Noodles

Calculate using DRIED noodles

We all know what linguine and spaghetti are, but if you're like I was, most of you have probably never used or bought Asian noodles before. They differ greatly from the 'regular' Italian style pastas you might be used to, but don't be intimidated. It ain't no thang. First things first, all the noodle recipes in this book, regardless of what type of noodles a recipe calls for, the measurements given are for DRIED noodles. IE: "8 oz wide rice noodles" means, 8 oz of dried, uncooked wide rice noodles. You can find Asian noodles in most major grocery stores, in 2 places. In the Asian food aisle, as well as the refrigerated section where they sell tofu. If you have a local Asian market nearby, they are MUCH cheaper there. As a last resort, you can always order them online. Different brands call for you to prep the noodles in different ways (boil vs soak), so follow the package directions, then use the noodles for my recipes.

THIN 'VERMICELLI' RICE NOODLES

These are ultra thin rice noodles. I'm not joking, they are thinner than angel hair pasta. You MIGHT find them in Asian markets as 'vermicelli' rice noodles, or, you can find them labeled as 'rice sticks'. They are the same thing. If you can't find them, you can swap them with regular angel hair pasta. However, the dish will have a very different texture. It's still good, just different. But, use what you have.

WIDE RICE NOODLES

These are by far my favorite type of rice noodles. They are used in my Thai 'drunken' noodle recipe. They're about twice as wide as fettuccini, with a slightly bouncy/chewy texture. It's the best way I can describe it. They are fantastic. However, if you can't find them, use pappardelle. It won't be the same, but it's better than nothing.

UDON & SOBA NOODLES

I use 'soba' noodles for my chow mein and udon noodles for my yaki udon dish. Though they DO sell soba noodles, already cooked and vacuum sealed, near the tofu at your grocery store... Those are in 7-8 oz bags of already cooked noodles in pouches. Don't buy those! My chow mein calls for DRIED noodles. Also, don't worry when you see different 'types' of soba noodles at the store. It doesn't matter if the package says "chuka soba" or "buckwheat soba", or whatever-soba. As long as it's a package of DRIED noodles that says 'soba', then you're good. Same goes for Udon noodles. Udon noodles, once cooked, can kind of be described as thicker, slightly rounded, chewy linguine noodles.

SWEET POTATO (GLASS) NOODLES

These noodles look really cool, have a very interesting texture (no other way to put it) and are used a good deal in Filipino and Korean noodle dishes. In my book, I use them in the Korean Japchae noodle dish, though I've also seen them used in Filipino Pancit. They are made from sweet potato starch and you'll usually find them in the Asian food aisle, along with the other noodles. They'll either be labeled as 'Glass Noodles', 'Japchae Noodles', or 'Sweet Potato' noodles. Also, great news for folks who want a 0 point alternative. You know those 0 point pouches of 'Shirataki' noodles in the store? The noodles in a sealed bag of water? Well, they are 1000% perfect substitutions for these noodles.

Asian Vinegars & Substitutions

RICE VINEGAR

Rice vinegar is EXTREMELY important in my recipes. I not only use it as-is, but I also use it as a base for ingredient-swaps, in place of other high point vinegars and wines used in traditional Asian recipes. One thing to note REGULAR rice vinegar is 0 points for a good amount of it. However, make sure not to purchase 'seasoned' vinegar.

RICE WINE VINEGAR SUBSTITUTION

The WW database lists 2 types of rice wine vinegars, one has points, the other doesn't. I've NEVER found a bottle of 0 point rice wine vinegar, so as a rule, I left it out of all my recipes and chose to do a substitution. Whenever a recipe called for rice wine vinegar, I used regular rice vinegar with up to 1 Tbsp of white wine (chardonnay) and then I add some sweetener. Vinegary rice flavor, wine, and sweet. Done.

CHINESE BLACK VINEGAR SUBSTITUTION

Again, Chinese black vinegar is hard to find, unless you have a nearby Asian market, so I use an easy substitute to make my recipes more accessible. I use regular rice vinegar with up to 2 tsp of balsamic vinegar added. It's a great, viable substitution, using an ingredient everyone already has.

Hoisin Sauce

A Delicious Umami-Packed Sauce

Hoisin is a classic Chinese BBQ sauce. It's dark, thick, sticky, and brown. You usually find it slathered on the super red and tasty barbecue ribs at Chinese restaurants. Hoisin is made with sugar, fermented soybeans, vinegar, garlic, salt, chili, and other spices. It packs a tremendous flavor punch. Unfortunately, it's also crazy high in points.... like, stupid-high in points. I try to limit its use and stretch the flavor. It's used in my Beijing and Hoisin chicken recipes.

Fish Sauce

The Hard To Find Ingredient

Get your nose plugs ready folks, we're about to get funky!! For a lot of you, fish sauce will be your first truly exotic ingredient for these recipes. So let me start off by saying, yes... it IS fish sauce. Technically, it's anchovy water. As gross as that sounds, it packs so much deep, oceany pungent flavor to Asian food. It is utterly essential in Thai and Vietnamese cuisine. Heck, I even add it to ground turkey to make it instantly have a deep, rich, 'Asian' ground meat flavor.

Black Bean Sauce

No, It Isn't Just Pureed Black Beans

No... it's not just pureed black beans. Chinese black bean sauce is an extremely savory, salty and thick paste-like sauce. It's made with fermented black beans, chiles, garlic, brown sugar, Chinese cooking wine and more. It adds a tremendously pungent and rich flavor to dishes. I highly recommend 'black bean garlic sauce'. It has all the flavor of regular black bean sauce, but with added garlic savoriness.

Asian Chili Sauce

This Is An Important One

Almost all traditional Asian recipes I looked up, which called for 'heat'... used either dried Asian chiles, or 'Sweet Chili Sauce'. No, no and no. #1. I am not going to ask some little grandma in Arkansas to go find dried Asian chiles. #2. 'Sweet' Asian chili sauce has points. Know what doesn't? Regular chili sauce, with a little bit of sweetener added to it. See? It's that easy to drop points and calories. Ingredient swaps, baby. In every single recipe that normally calls for dried chili peppers, instead, I add 1-3 tsp of 0 point chili sauce. My personal preference is 'Huy Fong' Chili Garlic Sauce. It's the most widely available. You can find it in most all major grocery stores, unlike dried Asian chili peppers. You can also use sriracha, but it's a little hotter.

Flavored Cooking Sprays Instead of Oil

Obvious, but deserves a shout-out

I personally use a lot of butter flavored cooking spray. When seasoning raw meats, I hit both sides with butter flavored or olive oil flavored cooking spray to help flavor the meat. You can also use the butter spray on popcorn. In this book, I use the coconut flavored spray in a few of the Thai dishes, such as Panang Curry.

Powdered Peanut Butter

Dehydrated Peanut Butter

Powdered peanut butter, regardless of the brand, is freaking awesome. You can mix it with water to rehydrate it for use as regular peanut butter or you can add the powder to recipes and baked goods to give a PB flavor without all the added mass, points, or stickiness. It's great in everything from smoothies to satay sauces, baking mixes or mixed with pudding or yogurt. The best part being that it's a fraction of the points of regular peanut butter. Don't like peanuts? There's powdered Almond butter.

Fat Free Chicken & Beef Broth

This Has To Be Mentioned

Look, broth seems like a total no-brainer of an ingredient. "Why is this here, Daniel?" Because I have to. 99% of recipes simply say to use beef broth or chicken broth. Guess what, Fat Free broths are a good deal less fat, calories & points. Use fat free broths for these recipes. It's how the points were calculated.

Food Allergy Substitutions

GENERAL Allergy Info.:

I've mentioned before that regular soy sauce, vegetarian oyster sauce, Asian rice noodles and sweet potato noodles are usually gluten free (check the labels to be safe!), while 'dark' soy sauce has gluten. However, there are a few others allergy things I get asked a lot, which are pretty common sense. But every time I post a new Asian recipe I'm them. So... If you're allergic to pineapple and want to make a dish that asks for it... use a similar fruit YOU CAN HAVE! Allergic to shrimp but want to make one of the shrimp dishes? Use a different protein! Allergic to onion? Use more celery. Swap out ingredients, folks. It's fun and simple.

Asian Noodle Textures & Substitutions

Asian Pasta vs. 'Regular'

If you're a full-on Gringo, like I am, buying and preparing Asian rice noodles can seem very intimidating, as silly as it sounds. Don't worry though, it's not a big deal. "Rice Noodles" are simply noodles made with rice flour, in place of wheat flour. Rice noodles have a slightly firmer, kind of springy texture. They have a little bit more tooth to them. As such, there is a HUGE difference in texture if you try using 'regular' noodles, instead of Asian noodles, in Asian dishes. You can find them in the Asian food aisle at the grocery store. If you're unable to get them, you can use the following substitutions, in their place.

* Vermicelli 'Thin' Rice Noodles:
- Use regular Angel Hair pasta. The finished texture of your noodle dish won't be the same, but it will work ok.

* Wide Rice Noodles:
- Use WIDE pappardelle noodles, as a substitute. Boom, done.

* Soba Noodles:
- Use whole wheat spaghetti noodles. Soba noodles are made with wheat flour, so... whole wheat spaghetti noodles are an ok alternative, though not perfect.

* Glass/Sweet Potato Noodles:
- Use 0 point shiratake 'shaped' spaghetti noodles, also known as 'magic spaghetti'. However, remember to rinse them off very, very, very well.

Regular vs. Toasted Sesame Seeds

Now, Use Whichever You Want

In previous plans, toasted sesame seeds were less points than untoasted. That isn't an issue anymore, because that ridiculousness has finally been fixed. Now, though they are both the same points (1 tsp for 0 points), you can make the sesame seeds in your dishes have a slightly more intense flavor by toasting them for 2-3 minutes in a hot pan, till just smoking and fragrant.

Mirin, Sweetened Rice Cooking Wine

Obviously Easy Substitute

Mirin is one of the most simple and straight forward substitutions you can do. It's simply a slightly sweet rice wine used for cooking. It's also pretty high in points. Whenever a traditional recipe I was hacking down called for Mirin, I simply used 1 Tbsp of white wine (0 points) with some rice vinegar and sweetener.

Daikon Radish & Substitutes

Convenient Substitutions

Daikon radish is a common ingredient in Japanese cuisine. Daikon is a root vegetable similar in shape to a large white carrot, with a flavor that's similar to a mild red radish. Though common in some areas of the US., not everyone has access to them. So, here's some alternatives, though the flavors and textures aren't identical, they are still viable options, in a pinch. Jicama, regular Red Radish, White Carrots and Parsnips are all options which might be easier to find.

DIY Low Point Brown Sugar Substitute

A Little Molasses Goes a Long Way

First off.... YES... I know that you can buy 0 point brown sugar substitutes. Popular ones are Lakanto brand "golden" monkfruit, Swerve 'gold', Sukrin Gold, among others. There's a lot of variety out there. However, I can't always find them in the grocery stores by my house and I don't want to order them online... because I'm cheap.

Luckily, there's an easy fix. Real brown sugar is simply regular sugar mixed with a little molasses. Well, if you have molasses and any type of sweetener, you can sub it in recipes. 1/4 tsp of molasses is 0 points. If I'm making a dish that calls for 1/4 cup or less of brown sugar, I'll use that much sweetener, then add the 1/4 tsp molasses to the dish. It tastes good and is a simple hack. Feel free to use more, but adjust your points accordingly. Or... go the easy route and simply buy the 'brown sugar replacement'. Boom, done.

Low Calorie & Fat, Coconut Milk

Momma says Whaaaaa?

If there's one thing that I am known for, more than anything, it's low fat & calorie ingredient substitutions. One of the most obvious, to me anyways... is a low fat/calorie alternative for canned 'light' coconut milk. C'mon, let's face it... there ain't NOTHIN' 'light' about canned, light coconut milk. 1 cup of 'light' coconut milk has 151 calories and 15 grams of fat, with 8 points. Ya'know what's better than that, if you're trying to watch your weight? 'Silk' or 'Almond Breeze' UNSWEETENED coconut beverages. You can find them in your grocery stores, in the same area where they sell almond milk. 1 cup of these babies has only 35-40 calories, and between 3.5 to 4.5 grams of fat. They are thick, work great as the base for a sauce... and they don't coat your mouth (OR HIPS) with a thick layer of fat. You don't feel like your curry sauce is a liquid brick, sitting at the bottom of your stomach. The only downside is that because they have virtually no fat, curries made with these beverages are hotter than if you were to use regular fatty coconut milk. You'll also want to add a little cornstarch, to help them thicken, if used in a hot sauce/dip.

Breaded & Baked Chicken Pieces, Instead of Frying With Oil

Ok, this is going to be a big point of contention for some of you. Namely, when a dish calls for crispy pieces of chicken, I choose to bread and bake the chicken, rather than coat it all with flour, then fry it in oil. All traditional recipes, as well as all of the 'skinny' bloggers cook their Asian dishes the traditional way. Well, though the regular way does taste great... it's also VERY HIGH IN POINTS AND CALORIES!

My low point breading recipe can coat one and a quarter pounds of bite sized chicken pieces for only 4 total points on all 3 plans. I use it to bread the chicken in my sweet fire chicken, orange chicken, beijing chicken and sesame chicken recipes. Rather than frying chicken in oil, I bake the pieces in the oven, till crispy and set them aside. I then make my sauce/glaze in a hot pan, and toss the baked, breaded chicken chunks with the hot/sticky sauce. The only drawback is, you need to serve the dish immediately. Just like chicken parmesan, the breading is crispy at first, but after about 5-8 minutes, the breading starts absorbing the sauce. It's a trade off, as far as I'm concerned. Lucky for you, my dishes are so low in Points, you can choose to forgo my breaded/baked method and still use the flour/oil method if you want. But, adjust your points. *AIR FRYER:* If you have an air fryer, you'll need to lower my suggested baking temperatures.

Stevia, Truvia, Monkfruit & 'Natural' Sugar Replacements

Whether people agree with me or not about using them... I have absolutely no problem whatsoever with using Sweeteners. "But, but... they aren't natural!" Wrong, Susie. There are plenty of natural sweeteners that are NOT white sugar. My personal favorite is Lakanto brand monkfruit. I have to warn you about one brand though... "Monkfruit In The Raw" brand is mixed with multidextrine and has the worst artificial aftertaste ever, in my opinion. Honestly, it's gag inducingly horrible. If you see it, run away like a citizen of Tokyo, running from Godzilla.

My primary reason for using sweetener is calories. I'm most concerned with using anything I can to cut calories from my recipes, without cutting flavor or portion sizes. Using sweeteners instead of sugar, if you have no food sensitivities to them, is a no brainer. 1 cup of sugar has nearly 800 calories. By contrast, an entire cup of most sweeteners has 0 calories.

Much to my surprise, when I started making this book, I quickly realized just how much sugar is utilized in Asian cuisine. Seriously, nearly every sauce or dish seemed to have at least 1 to 2 Tablespoons of sugar, whether white or brown, some had up to 1/2 cup in their sauce.

IMPORTANT NOTE:

My recipes don't demand that you use one specific type of sweetener. In the ingredients for recipes that call for sweetener, I list *"0 point sweetener 'o choice"*. However, use a 1 to 1 sugar replacement. Make sure the package you buy states it's a sugar replacement. Meaning... 1 tsp of 'this sweetener' is the same as 1 tsp of regular sugar, in a recipe. You have NO IDEA how many times I get people saying they made a recipe and it's insanely sweet. When I ask what type of sweetener they used, they typically respond "sweet and low packets". So, they used 1/4 cup of those little coffee packets, which are super concentrated. Use a sugar replacement. However, some brands of sweetener are NOT 'true' 0 points. If your brand gains points after a certain amount, you will need to adjust the listed point values for my servings.

Tenderizing Meat With Baking Soda Instead Of Cornstarch

This is the one that I get asked about, more than anything else. "Why in the heck do you put baking soda on your chicken, Daniel!?!?" Well, because of science:... and points.

#1. Traditional Asian cooking recipes tell you to 'silk' your meat by coating it all with cornstarch, let it sit for a bit... then cook it in oil or boil it in water. Presto! You have chicken that's super crispy or super tender, depending on how you cook it. Well, 1-1/2 tsp of cornstarch is 0 points. After the 1-1/2 tsp, it starts gaining points. I would prefer to use that 1-1/2 tsp of 'free' cornstarch to thicken a sauce. I'd rather get the most 'bang for the buck' with my points.

#2. Baking Soda actually DOES tenderize meat a whole heck of a lot more than cornstarch. I'm not talking about dusting meat with a pound of baking soda... that'd taste horrible. However, by making a solution of a little baking soda with a little water, then rubbing it all over the meat and letting it sit for 20-30 minutes, the baking soda actually begins to BREAK DOWN the outer protein walls of your meat. This results in EXTREMELY tender beef, chicken and pork. It also helps make meat brown better and stay juicier. It's a common technique in French cooking. You can cook the meat longer without it drying up and it's a lot more tender. Science, baby! However, be advised... though the baking soda makes the meat much more tender, use it sparingly. If you go crazy and add too much, it tastes like yuck. 😬

Low Carb Bread Crumbs

How to Use Low Calorie, Low Carb Bread to Make Low Point Breadcrumbs

When I first made my cookbooks, there WAS no widely available Keto bread. Now, you can find it in most major supermarkets and Walmarts. Because of its wide availability now, I decided to revise this cookbook to include its use. Though a lot of brands are available at 1 point per slice, you'll need to experiment to find the brand(s) you like best.

Ingredients:

- 5 slices of ANY BRAND "Keto", sliced bread. I personally love the 'Signature Select' brand, which is available at most Albertsons, Vons, Kroger, Ralphs and other Kroger 'family' stores. (Signature Select is 5 slices for 4 points)

Things You'll Need:

- An oven
- Baking sheet pan(s).
- Food processor OR a gallon ziplock bag with a rolling pin
- A 10" or 12" pan, to toast the crumbs

Serving Info:

Yield: 1-1/4 cups crumbs. Makes enough breading to coat a 1964, Mint Green Buick Skylark

R D
4-4
Points shown are for the ENTIRE BATCH

- last checked 12/06/22 -
Use your mobile device's 'Camera' App to look at this code for nutritional info.

Directions:

1. Take 5 slices of your preferred "Keto" bread. Slice them into squares and lay the cut pieces onto a foil-lined baking pan. Arrange them in a SINGLE LAYER. Use more than 1 pan if you don't own 1 large pan. Having the bread in a single layer is important.
2. Preheat your oven to 250 degrees. Once it comes up to temperature, bake the bread for 20 minutes, then remove from the oven and let cool for 15 minutes.
3. (2 options). **Option 1:** Place the cooled bread into a food processor, pulse a few times, then process till they are broken down to crumbs. Or.. **Option 2:** Place the bread into a bag and use a rolling pin to crush it all into crumbs.
4. Heat a large pan over medium heat for 1 minute, then add the crumbs. DO NOT MOVE THE PAN!! Let the crumbs sit in place and cook. EVERY 30 SECONDS, stir and toss the crumbs around, then leave them alone for another 30 seconds, then toss again. Repeat till they take on a slightly uniform golden hue, like in the bottom left picture. *(Mine took 7 minutes)*
5. Pour the hot crumbs back onto the foil of the baking pan and spread them out. Let cool to room temperature. Once cooled, store in an air tight container. Done.

NOTES:

1. You can use ANY brand of 1 point per slice bread you want. *I used Signature Select, Premium Keto Bread, which is 5 slices for 4 points.* If you use a different brand, adjust your recipe's points accordingly. This brand is my favorite. It can be found at Kroger-family stores.
2. Going forward, I will still be using "Breading 2.0" as my default breading in recipes, because not everyone has access to 1 point per slice, sliced bread.

BREADING 2.0

Snap! Crackle! Pop! Rice Breadiiiiiiing

If I already show you how to make bread crumbs with Keto bread, why show you how to make crumbs with Rice Krispies?? Simple. Not everybody across the US has access to 1 point per slice Keto bread (that doesn't suck), but everyone has access to Rice Krispies... I'm helpful like that.

Breading:
- 1-1/4 cup crispy rice cereal (like rice krispies). Place it in a ziplock bag and <u>lightly crush it</u>, don't pulverize it.
- 1-1/2 tsp plain breadcrumbs
- 2 tsp panko breadcrumbs
- 1/4 tsp salt
- 1/4 tsp cracked black pepper
- 1/4 tsp garlic powder
- 1/4 tsp onion powder

Egg Wash:
- 2 large eggs
- 1 tsp baking powder
- 1 Tbsp dijon mustard
- 1 Tbsp water

Additional Ingredients/Equipment: (optional, only needed if you're breading meat)
- 1-1/2 tsp all purpose flour
- fine mesh wire strainer/sieve.

Servings Info.:

Yield: about 2/3 cup breading
Servings: Depends on how you use it. It can bread 4 good sized chicken breasts, around 30 chicken chunks, or a whole tray of onion rings.

R   D
1-1

- last checked 11/14/22 -
Use your mobile device's 'Camera' App to look at this code for nutritional info.

Bread Up To 30 Pieces

'Dusting' Meat with Flour

Directions:

1. Add all the listed 'breading ingredients' into a large ziplock bag. Lightly crush the breading until it has the same texture as panko breadcrumbs (coarse crumbs, pictured to the right).
2. Heat a pan over medium heat for 1 minute, pour in the coarsely crushed breading. Heat for 3-4 minutes, tossing every 30 seconds, till the dry ingredients take on a uniform and lightly golden hue. Set aside to cool.
3. **_If using to bread a protein_**, place the 1-1/2 tsp of flour into a wire mesh strainer. In the same way you'd dust powdered sugar over a dessert, tap the mesh a few inches over the meat, to lightly dust both sides with flour. You can 'flour' 4 chicken breasts in this way for 0 points.
4. When ready to use the breading, prepare the egg wash: Whisk together the 2 eggs, set aside. In a small dish, stir together the baking powder, dijon mustard and water into a smooth, thick paste. Whisk into the beaten eggs. It will slightly thicken the egg wash.
5. Use according to your recipe's directions. Which usually involves coating the protein in flour, dipping it into the egg wash, then coating it with crumbs. Bake as directed by your recipe.

Toasted vs. Untoasted Breading

UNTOASTED

TOASTED

FROZEN DUMPLINGS NEED LUV TOO

Yes, fresh, homemade Asian dumplings and potstickers are AWESOME... but making them isn't always practical.

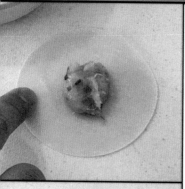

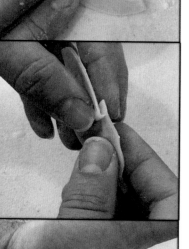

We all know that homemade dumplings, just like homemade pasta... tastes better than the packaged stuff you'd buy at the store. We also know that if you make dumplings exactly like I show you in the Dim Sum recipes section, they are pretty low in points, compared to packaged dumplings. But you know what the frozen dumplings are better for? NOT HAVING TO MAKE THEM YOURSELF!

Honestly, 99% of the time, you get home from work and making handmade dumplings is the last stinkin' thing on your 'to-do' list... and that's fine. Thankfully, there are some low point, time saving options for replacing fresh dumplings with frozen ones. Do they taste the same? No. Will they save you a ton of time and energy?... Heck, yes, they will!!!

So... I wanted to touch on a couple brands I've found in my local stores, while encouraging you to look for your own available in-store options, for if you need to use them in a pinch.

Trader Joe's: Chicken Cilantro Mini Wontons

These little chicken dumplings are awesome. They are great on their own, as an appetizer... or when used in a soup in place of handmade dumplings. They can be used as stand ins for mini potstickers, by cooking them in a pan. Cooked in broth to make a simple and quick wonton soup, served over rice, or cooked in a steamer. to give them a more traditional steamed dumpling texture. Best part... you can have up to 4 of them for 1 point and up to 8 of them for only 2 points. You can't beat that.

Bibigo: Mini Wontons
(Available at Costco & Sam's Club)

These are on par with the Trader Joe's frozen dumplings, in respect to taste and texture. But, Bibigo has a big advantage over the Trader Joe's brand. Namely, they are available with more than just one flavor of filling. These are also extremely low in points.

NOTE: Obviously, these aren't the only 2 brands of frozen low point dumplings. Search your local stores (including Walmart) for other options. Combining frozen dumplings with my dipping sauces is an awesome, time saving appetizer.

Serving Info:

Seasoned Mix
Servings: 8
Serving Size: 2oz

Ingredients:

- 1 pound extra lean ground turkey
- 1 Tbsp Asian "fish sauce"
- 1/2 tsp ground black pepper (coarse ground, preferably)
- 1/2 tsp ground ginger (or, 1 tsp minced, fresh ginger)
- 3-4 medium garlic cloves, minced
- 2 Tbsp reduced sodium soy sauce
- 1 tsp 'dark' soy sauce
- 1/4 tsp baking soda dissolved in 1/2 tsp water
- 1 tsp lime juice
- 1/2 cup green onion, finely chopped (not the white part)
- 3/4 tsp sesame seeds, toasted in a hot pan for 2-3 minutes.
- 2 tsp chicken or beef flavored bouillon (granules)

Directions:

- Combine all ingredients in a mixing bowl, until well mixed. Allow to sit for 20 minutes, covered.
- Cook as desired, though I do NOT recommend over direct, high heat. For info. on burger patties, see Cookbook 1 & 3's meat seasoning & tip sections.

ASIAN MEAT MIX

Ground turkey or chicken LOADED with asian flavors

This mix is so delicious and flavorful, it could easily pass for ground pork when used for Asian dumplings or burgers. I came up with this mix while trying to make a Vietnamese Banh Mi burger, a few years back and I couldn't believe the texture and flavors. I actually LOVE making this into meatballs, with my sweet & sour sauce, or as already stated, for 'Asian' burgers.

BAKED WONTON STRIPS

These are usually deep fried, served at Chinese restaurants with a small dish of ultra syrupy, goopy, jarred 'Duck Sauce', for dipping. These are definitely a healthier snacking alternative.

Ingredients:

- Store bought, packaged Wonton wrappers.
- cooking spray

POINTS:
Slice your wonton wrappers into the halved strips,
then weigh them in grams to determine
how many you can have for a certain amount of points.
Mine were 22 strips for 1 point and 42 for 2 points

Directions:

1 Begin preheating oven to 375. USE AN OVEN THERMOMETER!
2 Slice the squared wonton wrappers into 1/2 inch wide, long strips.
3 Slice the long wonton strips in half, making shorter strips.
4 Arrange the strips onto a foil lined baking pan, making sure they don't touch. Spray all over the strips with cooking spray, coating them. Flip the strips, then coat the tops again.
5 When the oven IS AT 375 (check the thermometer!), place the pan into your oven and bake for 5 minutes. Check at about 3 minutes. If one side is starting to get too brown, rotate the pan.
6 When they are all a mostly uniform golden brown, remove from oven and let cool to room temperature. Done.

Notes:

- Wonton wrappers are 3.5" squares. You can make (7) 1/2 inch strips from each square. Then, when you slice those in half (2nd pic) you can get 14 baked strips per wrapper.
- If you make any of my soup & dim sum recipes that ask you to trim down the packaged wontons, this is a great way to use those discarded strips of sliced wontons.

Soy Glaze & Dipping Sauce - Page 23

Vietnamese Ginger Chili Sauce - Page 25

Thai Sweet Chili Sauce - Page 25

Sweet & Sour Sauce - Page 23

Katsu Sauce - Page 22
on crispy baked Chicken Torikatsu - pg. 132-133

Thai Peanut Sauce - Page 24

Page 20 • Sauces & Dips

Condiments & Dips

A small collection of Asian inspired, low calorie, low fat dips and condiments.
These recipes are perfect for use with dim sum, appetizers, or even to be used as sauces.
You can also use these condiments as sauces for entrees and cooked meats.
Note: Some of these make a small 1/4 cup batch. Those are meant to be served
in a small dish, where everyone shares it for dipping.

Reminder, all of these dips have a LOT of sodium, so be mindful of it, if you're on a sodium restrictive diet.
Drink lots and lots of water to help flush out the sodium and don't be in shock if you
experience a weight gain after eating high sodium food. Water retention is real.

Also, a few of the dips in the coming pages are small yield recipes, which make only around 1/4 to 1/2 cup
of sauce. You know how when you order potstickers or dumplings at a Chinese restaurant
they give you a small bowl with some dipping sauce, for the entire tray? Same thing. Those are
communal dips, meant for everyone. My entire 1/2 cup may have 1 or 2 points, but if you are only dipping
dumplings in them and have less than a couple Tablespoons, you should be good to count your serving as 0.

CAMBODIAN PEPPER LIME DIP

This very simple dip makes just enough to fill a small condiment dish, which you'd normally see served with dim sum or meat, for dipping. It has a very acidic and bright pop of lime, with the umami of soy sauce and fish sauce. Then, it gets kicked up with red pepper flakes.

Serving Info.:
Yield: 1/4 cup
Serving Size: n/a
Servings: *It's a communal dip*

R D
0-0

- last checked 12/16/22 -

Ingredients:
- 3 Tbsp lime juice
- Zest of 1 lime, minced
- 2 tsp reduced sodium soy sauce
- 1 Tbsp water
- 1/2 tsp coarse ground black pepper
- 1/4 tsp salt
- 1 tsp fish sauce
- 1/8 tsp crushed red pepper flakes

Directions:
1 Mix all ingredients together until well combined.
2 Marvel at the fact I finally posted something that only really has one step. It's a Christmas miracle!

HOISIN DIPPING SAUCE

A lower calorie take on a classic Chinese dipping sauce. Hoisin can be considered 'Chinese BBQ sauce'. This is a thinned dip that has the same flavor, while stretching the points.

Serving Info.:
Yield: 1/2 cup
Serving Size: 1/4 cup
Servings: 2

R D
1-1

- last checked 12/16/22 -

Ingredients:
- 1-1/2 Tbsp hoisin sauce
- 1-1/2 Tbsp sugar free 'light' syrup (pancake syrup)
- 1 Tbsp no sugar added ketchup
- 1 tsp lime juice
- 1/4 cup water
- 1 Tbsp 0 calorie brown sugar replacement o' choice
- 1 Tbsp reduced sodium soy sauce
- 1 garlic clove, minced
- 1-1/2 tsp cornstarch, dissolved in 2 tsp water

Directions:
1 Bring all of the ingredients to a boil, over medium heat. Simmer for 1 minute. Remove from heat, set aside and cool to room temperature.

'DUCK' SAUCE

This sweet, fruity and tart sauce is traditionally used to complement rich or fatty appetizers and entrees, like fried egg rolls or cooked pork. It's essentially a tangy plum sauce. The color of your finished sauce will depend on how ripe your plums are.

Serving Info.:
Yield: 1-1/4 cup
Serving Size: 1/4 cup
Servings: 5

R D
0-1

- last checked 12/16/22 -

Ingredients:
- 3 medium plums, halved, with skin and pit removed
- 1 Tbsp water
- 1 Tbsp 0 point sweetener o' choice (I used lakanto monkfruit)
- 1/4 cup unsweetened applesauce
- 4-1/2 Tbsp sugar free apricot preserves
- 2 tsp reduced sodium soy sauce
- 1 tsp rice vinegar
- 1/8 tsp salt
- 1-1/2 tsp cornstarch, dissolved in 1 Tbsp water

Directions:
1 Heat plums, water, sweetener, applesauce, preserves, soy sauce, vinegar and salt to a boil in a small pot.
2 Simmer for 4 minutes at a low simmer/boil, then use a whisk to break down the plums and mix all the contents, till smooth.
3 Add the dissolved cornstarch and simmer for 3-4 minues. Remove from heat, cool to room temperature.

KATSU SAUCE

Japanese Katsu sauce is tangy, sweet and savory. It's traditionally served alongside 'Tonkatsu', Japanese breaded pork cutlets. However, I use it for my 'Torikatsu', or breaded chicken. In essence, it's a type of Asian BBQ sauce, with rice vinegar and soy sauce. Traditional recipes have a looot of ingredients. Mine is simplified, comes together in minutes, with a similar flavor profile, at a fraction of the points.

Serving Info.:
Yield: 1 cup
Serving Size: 1/4 cup
Servings: 4

R D
1-1

- last checked 12/16/22 -

Ingredients:
- 1/2 cup canned tomato sauce
- 3 Tbsp unsweetened applesauce
- 3 Tbsp PLUS 2 tsp worcestershire sauce
- 3 Tbsp low sodium soy sauce
- 1 Tbsp 'dark' soy sauce (optional, for a darker color)
- 3 Tbsp rice vinegar
- 1/4 tsp onion powder
- 1/4 tsp coarse ground black pepper or 1/8 tsp finely ground
- 1 Tbsp PLUS 1 tsp 0 calorie sugar replacement o' choice
- 1-1/2 tsp cornstarch, dissolved into 1 tbsp water

Directions:
1 Mix everything together in a small pot. Bring to a low boil. Simmer for 3 minutes. Remove from heat, set aside and cool to room temperature.

- If you don't use the 'dark' soy sauce, it won't affect the flavor of the sauce. However, it will have a more reddish hue.

Korean Gochujang Sauce

Gochujang sauce is FREAKING FANTASTIC!!! This sauce is spicy, sweet, tangy, savory and tastes great slathered on just about anything imaginable. The regular stuff is 5 points for 2 Tbsp. Boom.

Serving Info.:
Yield: 1-1/2 cups
Serving Size: 1/4 cup
Servings: 6

R D
1-1

- last checked 12/18/22 -

Ingredients:
- 10 Tbsp water
- 1-1/2 tsp cornstarch, dissolved into the water
- 3 Tbsp lower sodium soy sauce
- 2 Tbsp 'dark' soy sauce
- 6 Tbsp 0 calorie sugar replacement o' choice
- 3 Tbsp rice vinegar
- 1-1/2 Tbsp sugar free syrup (pancake syrup)
- 2 garlic cloves, crushed and minced
- 1/2 Tbsp fresh ginger, minced
- 1/2 tsp salt
- 2 tsp sugar free strawberry or peach preserves/jam
- 2 Tbsp 'no sugar added' ketchup
- 4 Tbsp fermented red pepper paste (see pg. 11 for more info.)
- 1/4 tsp sesame oil

Directions:
1 Mix all the ingredients together in a small pot. Bring to a boil.
2 Simmer for 4 minutes, till thickened. Remove from heat, set aside and cool to room temperature.

Orange Ginger Dipping Sauce

This dipping sauce is actually used as the glaze/sauce for my 'Orange Chicken' recipe. However, it ALSO makes for a fantastic dipping sauce.

Serving Info.:
Yield: 1-1/4 cup
Serving Size: 1/4 cup
Servings: 5

R D
0-0

- last checked 12/18/22 -

Ingredients:
- 1/3 cup orange juice
- 7 Tbsp water
- 4 tsp cornstarch, stirred into the water, till dissolved
- 2 Tbsp PLUS 2 tsp reduced sodium soy sauce
- 1-1/4 tsp 'dark' soy sauce
- 4 Tbsp 0 calorie sugar replacement o' choice
- 3 garlic cloves, crushed and minced
- 1 tsp fresh ginger, minced
- 1 Tbsp orange zest, finely chopped
- 2 tsp Huy Fong Asian chili garlic sauce
- 1 Tbsp PLUS 1 tsp sugar free syrup (pancake syrup)
- 1/4 tsp cracked black pepper

Directions:
1 Bring all of the ingredients to a boil, over medium heat.
2 Simmer for 2-3 minutes or until thickened to desired consistency. It will thicken slightly when removed from heat.

Soy Glaze & Dip

This simple, but absolutely delicious sauce is perfect for use as a dip for dumplings, cooked meat, or even drizzled on vegetables. It has a tremendously flavorful depth of flavor from the ginger, garlic sesame oil, rice vinegar...and well... pretty much everything.

Serving Info.:
Yield: 1/2 cup
Serving Size: n/a
Servings: It's a communal dip!

R D
0-0

- last checked 12/16/22 -

Ingredients:
- 3 garlic cloves, minced
- 1 tsp ginger, minced
- 1 Tbsp PLUS 2 tsp sugar free syrup (pancake syrup)
- 3 Tbsp PLUS 1 tsp reduced sodium soy sauce
- 1-1/2 tsp 'dark' soy sauce
- 3 Tbsp rice vinegar
- 1/4 tsp sesame oil
- 1/4 tsp honey
- 1/8 tsp crushed red pepper flakes (optional)
- 2 tsp 0 point sweetener o' choice (I used Lakanto monkfruit)
- 1-1/2 tsp cornstarch dissolved into 2 tsp water

Directions:
1 Heat all ingredients in a small pot, till boiling. Cook at a low simmer for 1-2 minutes, or until sauce starts to thicken. Remove from heat, set aside, cool to room temperature.

Sweet & Sour Sauce

My recipe for sweet & sour sauce takes a traditional recipe and WW-erizes it. This recipe has a large yield because it's used in my sweet & sour chicken recipe, on pages 122-123. You could easily halve the recipe, if you'd like a small 1 cup batch.

Serving Info.:
Yield: 2 cups
Serving Size: 1/4 cup
Servings: 8

R D
0-0

- last checked 12/16/22 -

Ingredients:
- 1-1/8 cup water (1 cup, plus 2 Tbsp)
- 2-1/2 Tbsp cornstarch, dissolved into the water
- 1 cup rice vinegar
- 1 cup 0 point sweetener/sugar substitute (stevia, monkfruit, swerve, etc)
- 2 Tbsp no sugar added ketchup OR canned tomato sauce
- 3 garlic cloves, crushed and chopped
- 2 tsp fresh ginger, finely chopped

Directions:
1 Mix all the ingredients in a small pot, till well combined. Bring to a rolling boil for 5-7 minutes, or until the sauce has the thickness of warm maple syrup.
2 Allow to cool to room temperature, stirring occasionally. It will continue to thicken as it cools.

SZECHUAN PEPPERCORN SAUCE

For this recipe, you WILL need a very specialized ingredient, which you'll most likely have to order online. Szechuan peppercorns are NOT spicy. When toasted, they have an extremely aromatic aroma. In fact, once toasted, Szechuan peppercorns smells like fragrant tea leaves. They also have a cool after-effect. They give a very slight tingly-numbing effect to your tongue. It's pretty cool.

Serving Info.:

Yield: 1-1/4 cup
Serving Size: 5
Servings: 1/4 cup

R D
0-0

- last checked 12/16/22 -

Ingredients:

- 3/4 tsp szechuan peppercorn powder ***
- 1 cup water
- 1 Tbsp <u>PLUS</u> 1 tsp cornstarch, dissolved/stirred into the water
- 3 Tbsp <u>PLUS</u> 1 tsp lower sodium soy sauce
- 3 Tbsp rice vinegar
- 1 Tbsp lime juice
- 1/4 tsp sesame oil
- 1 tsp fresh ginger, finely diced/minced
- 2 garlic cloves, crushed and minced
- 7 Tbsp 0 calorie sugar replacement (such as Lakanto monkfruit)
- 1/4 tsp black pepper
- 1/8 tsp ground coriander

Directions:

1 Whisk together all of the ingredients, till smooth. Bring to a low boil in a small pot.
2 Cook for 2 minutes, or until thickened. Set aside and let cool.

Notes:

- You can order the Szechuan peppercorn powder on Amazon, or you can find it at Asian or International markets. Though, honestly, it's cheap and saves you the hassle if you just buy it online.
- Again, Szechuan peppercorns are not hot. They aren't spicy. People think they're cool because of their slightly 'tea-like' aroma and their tongue-numbing ability. It's a pretty unique sensation, to be honest..

TERIYAKI SAUCE

This sauce is truly awesome and comes together really fast. Is it authentic? No. Is it tasty and does it fit the flavor profile? Yup.

Serving Info.:

Yield: 1 cup
Serving Size: 1/4 cup
Servings: 4

R D
0-0

- last checked 12/16/22 -

Ingredients:

- 3/4 cup water
- 1-1/2 tsp cornstarch
- 2 Tbsp 0 calorie brown sugar replacement
- 3 Tbsp PLUS 1 tsp low sodium soy sauce
- 1 Tbsp sugar free syrup (pancake syrup)
- 1 medium garlic clove, chopped
- 1/2 tsp fresh ginger, minced
- 1/8 tsp salt
- 1/8 tsp red pepper flakes (optional)

Directions:

1 Add all ingredients into a small pot, stir till well combined.
2 Bring the sauce to a boil for 4-5 minutes. Remove from heat, cool to room temperature.

THAI PEANUT SAUCE & DIP

This recipe has 10x the depth of flavor you'll find in regular 'skinny blogger' recipes. It also has a fraction of the calories and fat.

Serving Info.:

Yield: 1 cup
Serving Size: 1/4 cup
Servings: 4

R D
0-0

- last checked 12/16/22 -

Ingredients:

- 3/4 cup water
- 1-1/2 Tbsp cornstarch (dissolved into the water)
- 1/2 tsp asian chili sauce (I used Huy Fong chili garlic sauce)
- 1/2 tsp asian "fish sauce"
- 2 tsp reduced sodium soy sauce
- 1 tsp lime juice
- 1/4 tsp red curry paste, to taste (optional)
- 6 Tbsp Powdered Peanut Butter *(that's 1/3 cup + 1 Tbsp)*
- 1/4 cup "Silk" unsweetened Almond/Coconut blend beverage, or any unsweetened Almond or Cashew milk or low point 'Coconut Beverage', such as from the "***So Delicious!***" brand.
- 1-1/2 Tbsp 0 point sweetener o' choice (*stevia, monkfruit, etc.*)
- 4 peanuts, crushed as garnish (yes.... just 4 single peanuts)

Directions:

1 Whisk together all of the ingredients, till smooth. Bring to a low boil in a small pot.
2 Cook for 2 minutes, or until thickened. Set aside and let cool.

- Though my recipe calls for a 'coconut flavored beverage', if you don't use one, it'll still taste fine. Or, sub it out for unsweetened almond milk and a little coconut extract from the baking aisle.

THAI SWEET CHILI SAUCE

Think of this Thai dip as a savory and pretty spicy version of traditional Chinese sweet & sour sauce.

Serving Info.:
Yield: 1 cup
Serving Size: 1/4
Servings: 4

R D
0-0

- last checked 12/16/22 -

Ingredients:
- 1/2 cup water
- 7 Tbsp rice vinegar *(1 less Tbsp than a 1/2 cup)*
- 1 Tbsp lime juice
- 1 Tbsp reduced sodium soy sauce
- 2 tsp sugar free peach jam or preserves
- 1/2 cup 0 point sweetener o' choice (I used lakanto monkfruit)
- 1 Tbsp tomato sauce OR no sugar added ketchup
- 2 garlic cloves, minced
- 1 tsp ginger, minced
- 2 tsp red pepper flakes
- 1-1/2 Tbsp cornstarch

Directions:
1 Mix all the ingredients in a small pot, till well combined. Bring to a rolling boil for 5-7 minutes, or until the sauce has the thickness of warm maple syrup.
2 Allow to cool to room temperature, stirring occasionally.

VIETNAMESE DIPPING SAUCE

This extremly tart, sweet, spicy and pungent sauce is a classic Vietnamese staple. Of all of the dips and sauces in this small collection... this one is my favorite, for dipping the spring rolls, pot stickers and shumai dumplings.

Serving Info.:
Yield: 1 cup
Serving Size: 1/4 cup
Servings: 4

R D
0-0

- last checked 12/16/22 -

Ingredients:
- 1/4 cup fish sauce
- 1/4 cup 0 point sweetener o' choice
- 1/3 cup water
- 2 Tablespoons lime juice
- 2 teaspoons rice vinegar
- 1 garlic clove, minced
- 1 Tbsp Asian chili sauce (I used Huy Fong Chili Garlic sauce)
- 1 Tablespoon finely diced/minced carrots

Directions:
1 Set the carrots aside.
2 Add the remaining ingredients in a bowl and whisk together until the sweetener dissolves.
3 Stir in the minced carrots, right before serving, for garnish.

- This is honestly my favorite of all the dipping sauces. I love this stuff, despite the 'dead sea' level of sodium in it.

VIETNAMESE GINGER CHILI SAUCE

This sauce is similar to the Vietnames Dipping Sauce, BUT it's a little less sweet, has a deep garlic flavor and a slight fruitiness.

Serving Info.:
Yield: 1/2 cup
Serving Size: 1/4 cup
Servings: 2

R D
1-1

- last checked 12/16/22 -

Ingredients:
- 1/4 cup fish sauce
- 2 Tbsp 0 point natural sweetener o' choice
- 1-1/2 tsp ginger, minced
- 5 garlic cloves, minced
- 2 Tbsp lime juice
- 2 tsp Asian chili sauce
- 2 tsp sugar free peach preserves/jam
- 1 Tbsp water

Directions:
1 Whisk all ingredients together, till the sweetener and peach preserves have dissolved. Set aside.

- This is meant more as a 'communal" sauce. The entire 1/2 cup has 1 total point. This sauce is meant more as the type that's served in a small dish, next to appetizers, with a small spoon in it. People can drizzle small amounts onto their food for 0 points.

YUM YUM SAUCE

Yum Yum Sauce is a staple at Japanese Hibachi restaurants, although it isn't actually a traditional Japanese sauce. It's as American as Pineapple Pizza, baby! (Get over it, haters!) Yum Yum sauce is a sweet, tangy and slightly spicy creamy mayo sauce. It's usually loaded with so much mayonnaise, you need bypass surgery after 2 Tbsp. MY version is light, delicious and incredibly full of flavor.

Serving Info.:
Yield: 1 cup
Serving Size: 1/4 cup
Servings: 4

R D
0-1

- last checked 12/16/22 -

Ingredients:
- 3/4 cup plain fat free Greek yogurt
- 1 Tbsp low fat mayonnaise
- 2-1/2 Tbsp no sugar added ketchup (or canned tomato sauce)
- 1-1/2 Tbsp rice vinegar
- 1 tsp paprika (for color)
- 1 tsp garlic powder
- 2 tsp 0 calorie sugar replacement o' choice
- 1/4 tsp salt
- 1/4 tsp pepper
- (optional) pinch of cayenne pepper, or more, to taste

Directions:
1 Whisk all ingredients together, till smooth.

- The cayenne pepper is optional, but it does add a nice little hint of heat. Add more, to taste, if desired.

Gyoza Potstickers - Page 32-33

San Choy Bow - Page 36-37
Minced Meat filled Lettuce Cups

Char Siu Bao - Page 28-29
Asian Steamed Buns

Vietnamese Meatballs - Page 43

Egg Drop Soup - Page 44-45

DIM SUM & SOUPS

A small collection of low calorie, low fat, low sugar Dim Sum appetizers and Soups. When combined with the sauces and dips in the previous pages, you'll never have to go out for Dim Sum again
Well... unless you want to give your kitchen a break for the day.

DIM SUM (SMALL BITES)

SOUPS

Hot & Sour Soup ... pg 46-47

Reminder, all of these Appetizers & Soups have a LOT of sodium, so be mindful of it, if you're on a sodium restrictive diet. Drink lots and lots of water to help flush out the sodium and don't be in shock if you experience a weight gain after eating high sodium food. Water retention is real.

CHAR SIU BAO

A Lightened Up Version of Steamed, Stuffed Asian Pork Buns...Using Minced Teriyaki Chicken instead of Pork!?

One of my aaaaabsolute favorite appetizers (or dim sum items) to eat at a Chinese restaurant is soft, tender ultra moist... bbq pork filled steamed buns. "Char Siu" means 'fork roasted'. It's most commonly associated with pork. Char Siu Baos are usually filled with roasted bbq pork that's chopped up. For MY version... I'm chopping/mincing some of my Teriyaki chicken. Now now, don't get your knickers in a bunch. It's got great flavor, texture and a similar color, for a lot less points.

Servings Info.:

Yield: 8 buns
Serving Size: 1 bun

R D
3-3

- last checked 12/09/22 -
Use your mobile device's 'Camera' App to
look at this code for nutritional info.

Ingredients:

- 1/2 batch (2 breasts) of my Teriyaki chicken recipe, pg 126-127, chopped/minced into small pieces. Set aside.

- 2-1/2 tsp active dry yeast
- 2-1/2 tsp granulated sugar (yup, **REAL SUGAR!**)
- 2/3 cup water, divided into (2) separate 1/3 cup portions.
- 1-7/8 cups all purpose flour (measure 2 cups, remove 2 Tbsp)
- 2 Tbsp 0 point natural sweetener o' choice
- 1/4 tsp oil (vegetable or canola)
- Cooking Spray, 8 second spray
- 1/4 tsp salt
- additional warm water, as necessary (1 tsp at a time)
- (for dusting) Baking powder.... instead of flour. Trust me.

Directions:

1. Scoop the active dry yeast and sugar into a tall container or cup. I know it sounds food-snooty, but it's VERY important... stir in 1/3 cup of 100-110 degree water. Use a thermometer if you have one, you <u>need</u> it to be between 100-110 degrees. Stir the water gently till mixed, then allow to sit, untouched, for 15 minutes.

2. While the yeast is slowly frothing and 'blooming', it's a great time to take your cooked chicken (or other preferred filling) out of the fridge. Chop and mince it up into small pieces. Add sauce to make it moist, but not wet. You don't want the filling runny. Set aside.

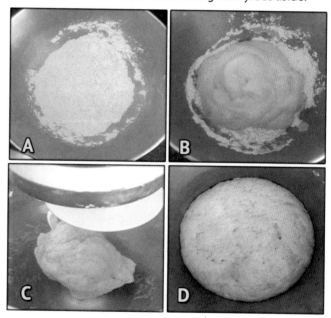

3. **(A)** While the yeast is 'blooming', add the flour, sweetener, oil and salt into a mixing bowl. Spray cooking spray into the bowl for 6 to 8 seconds. **(B)** After the yeast has 'bloomed' for 15 minutes, pour the yeast-liquid over the flour. **(C)** Begin mixing the dry and wet ingredients together. The mixture will be dry, but that's ok. Use a rubber spatula to scrape down the sides and continue mixing. Pour in the 2nd 1/3 cup of water and mix. Add more water, <u>1 tsp at a time</u>, if needed. You want to make it the consistency of very soft 'Play Doh'. **(D)** When the dough reaches the soft play dough feel, quickly spritz the sides of the bowl with cooking spray, then walk away for 1 hour. It will double/triple in size.

- *GLUTEN FREE OPTION:* Bob's Red Mill makes a very good "1 to 1 Baking Flour" that is 100% certified gluten free. It works pretty decent for these, though obviously not 100% as well as all purpose flour.
- *FILLINGS:* Though extremely non-traditional, I had to use chopped up Teriyaki chicken for my recipe... because I ran out of space on the left page. I didn't have space to add a bunch more ingredients for a unique Asian BBQ chicken filling. However, this is still extremely tasty. If you'd like to watch how to make these, look on youtube for 'how to stuff Asian steamed buns'. Don't forget to type 'STEAMED' in your search, or your spouse is going to question your browsing history.
- *SNAZZY DESIGNS:* There are neat patterns and designs that you can make on the top of your steamed buns. Again, look online for simple video tutorials. I'm lazy, sometimes.
- If you make these as unstuffed steamed buns, slice them across when finished. They make great burger buns for snazzy Asian-themed burgers (think Banh Mi burger).
- *STEAMER:* I used a big pot with metal steamer inserts, because at the time of this recipe, I didn't own a bamboo steamer basket yet. Use what you have, like MacGyver.
- *LAZY BUNS:* If you don't want to go through all the 'yeast' trouble, you can make these using 2 ingredient dough. Make a 1-7/8 cup batch of 2ID, adding an extra 1 Tbsp baking powder. The buns won't puff up as much and won't be as soft or delicious... but it'll knock 1 hour off your prep time.
- *RICE FLOUR:* If you want to go full tilt AMAZINGLY traditional texture... you can use rice flour instead of the all purpose flour. However, while 2 cups of AP flour is 26 points... 2 cups of Rice Flour is 35 points. Whiiiiich is kinda why I'm not using it.. My goal was to keep these at no more than 3 points.

4. Fill a large pot (that comes with steamer inserts) with a few inches of water. Bring to a very low boil, cover with lid. Cut (8) 2.5" squares of parchment paper and set aside. **(A)** Instead of flour, sprinkle some baking powder onto a cutting board, then scrape the dough onto the board. Sprinkle more baking powder, to tighten the dough up, if needed, and gently knead/fold it for 1 minute. **(B)** Form it into a ball, then **(C)** Cut into 1/8 sections, then fold each one again for 30 seconds. **(D)** Flatten one of the little dough balls into a palm sized 'round', then place a 1 to 2 Tablespoon scoop of filling into the center. **(E)** Carefully stretch the dough up and over the meat filling, then roll it around in your palm to make a smooth ball shape. One of the sides might still have a visible seam, that's ok. **(F)** Place each ball onto a square of parchment, seam side down. Place the balls into the top and bottom of your steamer inserts and let rise for 20-30 minutes. **(G)** Place inserts into the pot. The boiling water at the bottom should NOT touch the inserts. Cover with lid, turn heat up to High and steam for 12 minutes. **(H)** Remove buns from heat....Done.

CHICKEN SATAY

A Healthy Version of Thailand's Most Popular Chicken Skewers

Chicken Satay is pretty much the most popular appetizer in all of Thai cuisine. Traditionally, it's long strips of chicken thighs, pounded thin and marinated for a looooooooong time with a mixture of oil, tons of turmeric or curry powder and other spices, depending on which region's recipe you're following. In this case, I'm using chicken breast and instead of mixing all of the spices with oil for the marinade, I'm using a low calorie coconut milk beverage. Because not everyone has a grill, my recipe calls for using your oven's broiler. Also, because not everyone has access to lemongrass, I'm using lemon juice. I'm accommodating like that.

Servings Info.:

Yield: 42 skewers**
Servings: 42**
Serving Size: 1 skewer

R D
0-0

- last checked 11/16/22 -
Use your mobile device's 'Camera' App to look at this code for nutritional info.

Ingredients:

- 2 pounds boneless, skinless chicken breast

Marinade:
- 2 Tbsp lemon juice
- 4 medium garlic cloves
- 1/2 pound shallots, peeled, chopped**
- 1-1/2 tsp ground turmeric
- 1 tsp ground coriander
- 1/2 tsp chili powder
- 1-1/2 tsp salt
- 1/4 tsp baking soda, dissolved with 1/2 tsp water (trust me)
- 1-1/2 Tbsp 0 point natural sweetener of choice (stevia, truvia, monkfruit, etc)
- 2-1/2 Tbsp reduced sodium soy sauce
- 2 tsp 'dark' soy sauce, for color
- 1/4 cup Coconut Milk Beverage, unsweetened** (located near the almond milk in your grocery store. You might find the brands "So Delicious" or a blend of almond milk or soy milk with coconut milk)

Additional:
- Wooden Skewers
- 0 point cooking spray

**Chicken Note:*
Though my instructions show me slicing up THICK chicken breasts, you can purchase 2 pounds of thin cut chicken breasts. It will allow you to skip over step 1A.

Directions:

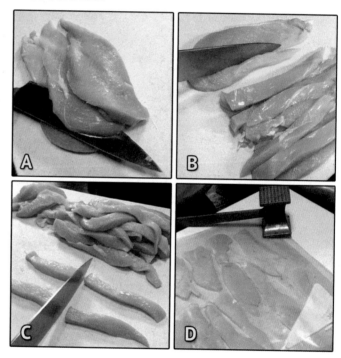

1. **(A)** My grocery store had THICK chicken breasts on sale, so that's what I used. I wanted the strips to be just shy of 1/2 inch thick, so I sliced the chicken breasts, horizontally, in 1/3's. **(B)** Slice all of your breast cutlets into long strips, there will be a LOT of them. **(C)** These are appetizers, so cut all of the really long strips in half. Hey... you're entertaining, so the more skewers you can get out of that 2 pounds of chicken the better. **(D)** Place a handful of the sliced chicken strips between 2 separate gallon sized plastic bags and using a mallet, play whack-a-mole with them. You don't want to tear them apart, just flatten them a little bit. If you need to let out more aggression, might I suggest using ***Talk Space*** in the WW app?

2A | 2B | 2C | 2D

2. (A) Put all of your marinade ingredients together for a cool picture. **(B)** Place all of the listed marinade ingredients into a food processor or blender and **(C)** process until smooth. In a large mixing bowl, **(D)** coat all of the chicken with the marinade. Cover with plastic wrap, allow to marinate overnight. Be warned, all those blended shallots are veeery pungent. Your eyes will water more than at the end of 'Old Yeller'.

3. The next day.... Soak your wooden skewers in a pan of water for 30 minutes. Line 2 baking sheet pans with foil, then spray with cooking spray. Position 1 of your oven racks onto the 2nd position from the top, then preheat your oven to 425 degrees.

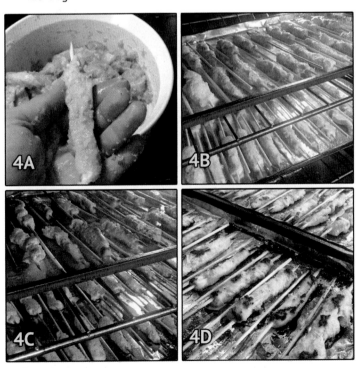

4A | 4B | 4C | 4D

4. (A) Carefully skewer each chicken strip and place onto the foil lined pans. **(B)** Your oven should be heated to 425 degrees. When you're ready to start cooking, turn on the BROILER setting to HIGH, spray the chicken with cooking spray, then place into the oven. **(C)** After about 6-7 minutes, the chicken on the top rack should start getting some slight char, that's what you want. Swap the pans, moving the top pan to the bottom rack and the bottom pan to the top rack. Cook for an additional 5-6 minutes. These are thin skewers, they cook quickly. **(D)** When the tops of both pans of chicken have a little bit of black char on them, remove from the oven. **Serve with my low point & calorie Thai Peanut Dip, recipe found in the "Dips" section, pg 24.** Finish by squeezing a lime over the skewers, then sprinkle with either fresh chopped cilantro or green onion.

NOTES:

- I was able to get 42 thin sliced chicken strips from the 2 lbs of chicken, HOWEVER, you may get less. Adjust your points per serving accordingly. To help with that, know that there is only 1 single ingredient point in this marinade.
- If you want to add a little bit more yellow coloring and flavor, add a little 0 points-worth of yellow curry powder.
- Keep an eye on your skewers when they are under the broiler, once they start to char, they can burn quickly.
- If time heals all wounds, why don't belly buttons fill in? 🤔

GYOZA - POTSTICKERS

A Healthy Recipe for Meat Filled, Pan Fried & Steamed Asian Dumplings

In case you're wondering what "Gyoza" is... it's the Japanese version of a Chinese potsticker. Where the Chinese version usually has a slightly thicker and larger wrapper, as well as having a filling that's a mix of ground pork and minced shrimp, the Japanese Gyoza has a smaller, thinner wrapper, with no shrimp in the filling. For mine... I'm using thinner, store-bought wonton wrappers, for convenience (hence, we're making Gyoza)... but I'm using a Chinese-ish filling. Because... texture.

Servings Info.:

Yield: 41 dumplings
Servings: 41
Serving Size: 1 dumpling

MY PLAN

R D
0-0

Only the 1st dumpling is 0 points. You can have up to 3 for 1 point

- last checked 12/09/22 -
Use your mobile device's 'Camera' App to look at this code for nutritional info.

Ingredients:

Meat Mixture:
- 1/3 lb. extra lean ground turkey
- 1/3 lb. uncooked shrimp, any size. Peeled, deveined, tail off.
- 1/4 tsp baking soda, dissolved in 1 tsp water
- 1 tsp rice vinegar
- 1 Tbsp low sodium soy sauce
- 1/4 tsp fish sauce
- 1 tsp ginger, finely chopped/minced
- 2 garlic cloves, chopped
- 1 tsp 0 point sweetener o' choice (I used lakanto monkfruit)
- 1/4 tsp salt
- 1/4 tsp black pepper
- 1/4 cup green onion, thin sliced
- 1/2 cup onion, diced

Additional Ingredients:
- Cooking spray
- Store bought wonton wrappers. IDEALLY you want to buy 'gyoza' wrappers... however, because not everyone can get those, in my recipe, I'm using regular, 3-1/2 square wonton wrappers. They are more commonly available.

Wonton wrappers can be found wherever they sell the refrigerated 'Asian' groceries, like tofu, at your local grocery store. I used 'Twin Dragon' brand wonton wrappers.

Directions:

1. **(A)** Add all of the meat mixture ingredients into a food processor. **(B)** Process till well mixed and smooth. Spoon mixture into a large bowl, cover, set aside. **(C)** Remove the store bought square shaped wonton wrappers from the packaging. Find a mug or other round object in your house that JUST fits inside the square shape. Place the 'mug' down onto the wonton, then use a knife (on a cutting board) to trim all of the square wrappers into round wrappers. **(D)** TADA!!!!! Congrats! You've just made circular 'Gyoza' wonton wrappers! You could have saved yourself a lot of time and BOUGHT gyoza wrappers... but, this was for folks who can't' find them. After you are done shaping them, set them aside.

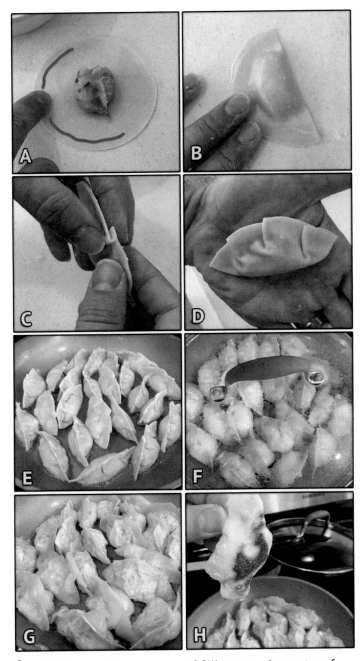

NOTES:

- **WONTON WRAPPERS:** I purchased square shaped wonton wrappers. Not big round ones, or big sheets you'd use for egg rolls. These are 3-1/2" square wonton wrappers. The reason I'm trimming them is that we are SUPPOSED to be using 'GYOZA' wrappers. However, as mentioned, I wanted to show how you can make these with regular, square wrappers. It makes the recipe more accessible to more people.
- **WONTON POINTS:** This recipe makes 41 dumplings. If I were to just build the recipe using 41 wrappers... that'd be 26 points, for the 41 full sized, 3-1/2 inch wrappers. HOWEVER... we aren't using 3-1/2 inch square wrappers sheets, we're trimming them down to circles, which removes a fair amount of wonton. So, I trimmed them, weighed the final 41 round wrappers, in grams, and looked up how many points they were, by weight. It dropped them down from 26 points to 20 (235 grams). Ironically... if you BUY regular 'gyoza' wrappers, 41 of them are 22 points... so my way is a good alternative for folks that can't find those. Remember... different brands might cause your points to vary.
- **I HATE SHRIMP! WAAA!:** If you don't want to have the slight shrimp flavor in the filling, swap it for more ground turkey.
- **FOOD PROCESSOR:** If you don't own a food processor, you can still make this filling. But you'll have to bust out a knife, a cutting board, and chop/mash the bajeezus out of the meat mixture... while trying not to lose any fingers.
- **STEAMED DUMPLINGS:** Instead of potstickers, you can steam these for 8-10 minutes. They come out great, when steamed.
- **PLEATING:** Though the pleated design looks nice, it isn't mandatory. You can skip it. Even with plain, flat edges, your potstickers will cook just fine.

2. **(A)** Place 1-1/2 teaspoons of filling onto the center of each wrapper. Dip your finger into a bowl of water and wet 1/2 of the wrapper's edge (red area). **(B)** Fold one half of the wrapper over the other side, making a half circular pocket. While folding, try and gently press out any large air pockets before you close it up. Press the edges together, pushing down on the edges, to seal the dumpling. **(C)** Lightly wet the outside edges of the wrapper, then fold a little bit of the wrapper back over itself and press together. Repeat the process to create a couple more 'pleats'. **(D)** Once you've created your 'pleats'... set each wrapper aside on a large tray, lined with parchment paper. It'll take a bit to prepare them all. **(E)** Once they are all ready... heat a large pan over medium heat for around 2 minutes. Spray the pan with a good 0 point layer of cooking spray, then add as many dumplings as you can (you'll need to cook them in 2 batches). Cook for 3 minutes, without moving them. **(F)** Add 1/2 cup water, cover the pan and steam for 5 minutes. **(G)** Remove cover and cook for 2-3 minutes, till the water evaporates. **(H)** Remove when the bottoms are browned.

SAN CHOY BOW (CHINESE LETTUCE CUPS)

Traditionally made with minced pork, my version ground turkey, loaded with veggies and coated in a savory sauce

Minced chicken lettuce cups are a pretty standard staple at most casual Asian restaurants nowadays. The filling can be as simple or as complicated as you want. I was inspired to make these Chinese lettuce cups after seeing them on the Asian food website, recipetineats. This is my skinnied down version.

Ingredients:

Meat: *(mix the meat together, set aside for 20 mins.)*
- 1lb xtra lean ground turkey breast
- 3/8 tsp baking soda, dissolved into 1 tsp water
- 1/2 cup fat free chicken broth (yup, into the raw meat)
- 1/2 tsp salt
- 1/4 tsp black pepper
- 1 tsp 'dark' soy sauce

Veggies: *(highly customizable, see notes)*
- 2 medium garlic cloves, crushed and chopped
- 1/2 tsp finely diced ginger
- 1/2 cup onion, finely diced
- 1/3 cup carrots, finely diced/chopped/shredded
- 1/2 cup canned water chestnuts, drained, finely diced
- 1/3 cup canned baby corn, diced/chopped
- 1/2 cup finely chopped mushrooms
- 1/2 cup green onions, thin sliced, loosely packed

Sauce:
- 3 Tbsp fat free chicken broth
- 1/4 tsp sesame oil
- 2 Tbsp lower sodium soy sauce
- 2 tsp 'dark' soy sauce
- 1 Tbsp PLUS 2 tsp oyster sauce
- 1/2 tsp fish sauce
- 1 Tbsp red wine
- 1-1/2 tsp <u>EACH</u>: balsamic vinegar & rice vinegar
- 1-1/2 tsp 0 calorie sugar replacement o' choice
- 1-1/2 tsp cornstarch, dissolved into 2 tsp water

Additional Ingredients:
- Lettuce, any variety with well shaped, semi-firm leaves
- *(garnish)* 1 tsp sesame seeds
- *(garnish)* thin sliced red and/or green chili peppers

Servings Info.:
Yields: 4-1/4 cups
Servings: 22
Serving Size: 3 Tbsp scoop

MY PLAN

R D
0-0
Entire Batch

- last checked 12/13/22 -
Use your mobile device's 'Camera' App to look at this code for nutritional info.

Directions:

1. Mix together the batch of ground meat, set aside. Yes, it WILL be a wet batch o' meat. Roll with it.

2. **(A)** Chop and prep all of the veggies, as well as mixing together the sauce. Set aside. **(B)** After the meat has rested, heat a large pan over medium-high heat for 1 minute. Spray with cooking spray, then add the meat. Cook until it's mostly cooked through, breaking it into smaller and smaller pieces, for 4 minutes. Then, add all of the veggies. Coo for 3 minutes. **(C)** Re-stir, then add the sauce to the pan and use 2 kitchen spoons to stir repeatedly. **(D)** Cook till the sauce has reduced, thickened, and the meat is coated in a rich, dark sauce.

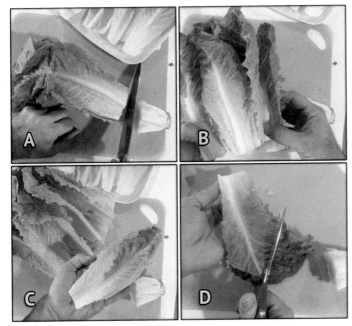

3. (A) ROMAINE: Remove your romaine lettuce from the packaging. Then, pretending you're a Rabbi, cut off the ends. *MAZEL TOV!!* **(B)** Now's the easy part, separate the individual leaves **(C)** Ta daaa! You now have romaine lettuce 'cups'. Rinse and pat them dry, then set aside to use as a vessel for your meat filling (you can serve it hot or cold). **(D)** Now, ideally you want to use the medium sized leaves. However, the outer leaves of the romaine head are HUGE, practically like green elephant ears. If you want to use those huge ones, there's an easy fix to make them more in-line with the size of the rest of your cups... trim the loose, flappy, excess leaf with scissors. Those leftover lettuce scraps can be used later, for a salad.

Fill the lettuce cups with 3 Tbsp of filling, then garnish with sesame seeds and thin sliced red and green chilis, if desired.

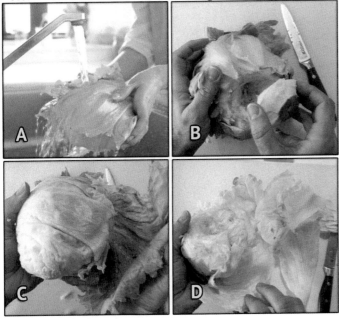

4. (A) ICEBERG: Rinse off the head o' lettuce. **(B)** Use a knife to cut out the core. **(C)** Peel off the 1 or 2 big, thin, outside layers of lettuce. **(D)** Pound the lettuce down on your cutting board 2-3 times, to help loosen it up. Then, start pulling leaf sections off, from the back side. Ta Daaaaa.

NOTES & SUGGESTIONS:
- *LETTUCE TYPES:* Ok, this obviously has to be mentioned. There are a few types of lettuce which are typically used to make 'cups' for these types of appetizers. I'll mention the most popular. Look them up on youtube, as well as videos showing how to clean them and how to make lettuce cups with 'em:
  - Iceberg, Romaine, Butter Lettuce, Bibb, Radicchio and Baby Gem.
- *VEGGIES:* These are 100% customizable. Swap out any of the veggies in this recipe for an equal amount of a different vegetable that you want. Easy peasy.
- *RAW MEAT MIX:* You might be wondering why in the heck we are adding 1/2 cup of broth to our ground turkey (or chicken) breast. Anybody who has cooked 98 or 99% fat free ground turkey knows it is dry as sand and doesn't break into 'fine' crumbles when cooked, unless prepped right. Adding all this liquid is the way to fix it. Yes, it's a watery/loose mix, but when you cook it, it breaks apart into finer bits. Check out my chili cheeseburger in cookbook 3, there's nearly 3/4 cup of liquid in that chili mix, so it'll replicate the fine 'ground' of Tommy's Chili, using ground turkey breast.
- *CHILI PEPPERS:* I only used them for color. Leave them out if you'd like.
- *CHICKEN:* Want to use chicken instead of turkey? Go ahead! Simply replace the ground turkey with chopped up chicken breast. Then, you won't need to add all that extra 1/2 cup of broth to the meat. I'd pour in 1/4 cup with the chicken as it's cooking.

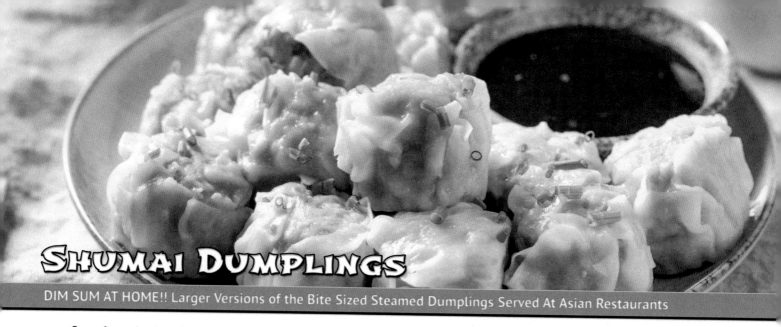

SHUMAI DUMPLINGS

One of my absolute favorite appetizers from Chinese restaurants are the meat filled, steamed dumplings you normally only get while they are serving 'Dim Sum'. Mine are larger, leaner and are still packed with a ton of flavor. Though most people are used to a Chinese filling of ground pork mixed with minced shrimp... I'm using a Japanese style filling, which is ground pork without shrimp. I'm doing a riff on the Japanese style, but using ground turkey instead of ground pork.

Servings Info.:

Yield: 22 dumplings
Servings: 22
Serving Size: 1 dumpling

R D
1-1

- last checked 12/09/22 -
Use your mobile device's 'Camera' App to look at this code for nutritional info.

Ingredients:

Meat Mixture:

- 1 lb extra lean ground turkey
- 1/4 tsp baking soda, dissolved with 1 tsp water
- 2 tsp chicken flavored granules (such as Knorr brand)
- 1 tsp fish sauce
- 2 tsp reduced sodium soy sauce
- 1-1/2 tsp 'dark' soy sauce, optional, for coloring the meat
- 1 garlic clove, crushed and minced
- 1/2 tsp ginger, minced
- 1/2 tsp coarse ground black pepper
- 1/2 cup onion, finely diced/minced
- 2 Tbsp green onion, finely chopped

Additional Ingredients:

- 22 wonton wrappers, square shaped, any brand. The ones I purchased were 3-1/2 inch square sheets. They can be found wherever they sell the refrigerated 'Asian' groceries, like tofu, at your local grocery store. (see notes for points) I used 'Twin Dragon' brand wonton wrappers.

SPECIAL EQUIPMENT:

- You will need either an Asian bamboo steamer, like I'm using in this recipe... or you can use any standard metal pot, with steamer inserts. A small countertop rice cooker with a steamer insert won't work well for this.
- Parchment paper

Directions:

1. Mix all of the meat/filling ingredients together. The mix will be (it's supposed to be) a bit sticky/wet/tacky. Rinse your hands with water while mixing it, to make it easy to handle. Set aside in the fridge for 30 minutes.

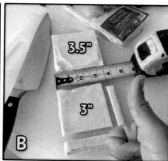

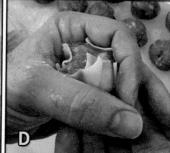

2. **(A)** Use measuring spoons to scoop out 1-1/2 Tbsp portions of meat. Roll each into a ball, set aside. **(B)** Remove the store bought square shaped wonton wrappers from the packaging. Slice them down to be 3 inches, squared, rather than the original 3-1/2 inches. **(C)** Touch your thumb and index fingertips together, making an "O". Place one of the 3 inch square wrappers over the 'hole', then push a meatball down into it. **(D)** Open the 'hole' up a little wider, pushing the meat and wrapper further down. Rotate it around in your palm, shaping it to be more tall than rounded, with flat sides.

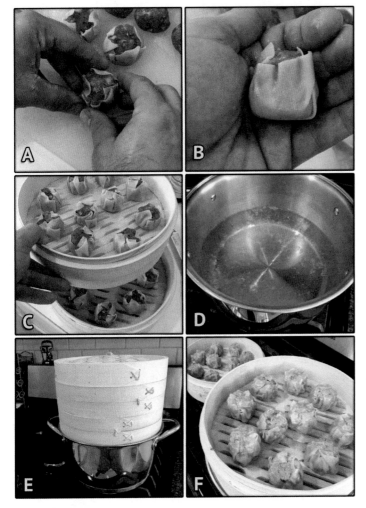

- **WONTON WRAPPERS:** I purchased square shaped wonton wrappers. Not big round ones, or big sheets you'd use for egg rolls. These are 3-1/2" square wonton wrappers. The reason I'm trimming them is these are meant to be appetizers, not big, baseball sized dumplings. I'm trimming them down to 3 inches squared, because that's the standard size of smaller Japanese style dumplings. Another plus, it saves points... see the next note.
- **WONTON POINTS:** This recipe makes 22 dumplings. If I were to just build the recipe using 22 wrappers... that'd be 12 points, for the 22 full sized, 3-1/2 inch wrappers. HOWEVER... we aren't using 3-1/2 inch sheets, we're trimming them down to 3 inches. So, I trimmed them, weighed the 3 inch wrappers in grams and looked up how many points they were, in grams, using the Weight Watchers mobile app's listing. It dropped them down from 14 points to 12 points (141 grams). Points may vary, depending on brand. Scan and check your points.
- **CHINESE FILLING:** Typical Chinese-style filling for Shumai is a 50/50 mixture of ground pork and chopped up/minced raw shrimp. You can definitely use a similar filling here by simply replacing 1/2 of the ground turkey with 1/2 pound shrimp. Boom, done.
- **DUMPLING POINTS:** You can have 2 of these dumplings for 1 total point. 4 dumplings for 2 points, 6 dumplings for 3 points, etc, etc, etc.
- **STEAMER BASKET:** You don't have to use a bamboo steamer basket like I did. You can use any large metal pot, with steamer inserts. Though, I still recommend using parchment paper. If you do want a bamboo steamer, get a 10 inch, 2 tiered one. I got mine for $22 on Amazon.

3. **(A)** Your dumplings are almost there... but, they have rounded bottoms. Press the dumplings down onto your work surface, to flatten the bottoms. **(B)** Your finished dumplings should look similar to mine. A little taller than they are wide, fairly straight side-walls... and with a nice, firm, flat tushy. **(C)** Place parchment paper down into your steamer o' choice, making sure to poke some holes into the paper, so steam can travel up into the top basket. Place the dumplings onto the parchment paper, set aside. **(D)** Bring some water to a rolling boil in a large pot. **(E)** Place your steamer basket, covered (obviously), over the boiling water. **(F)** Steam the dumplings for 8-10 minutes. If you steam them too long, the meat will be very firm. They'll still be tasty.... but the meat won't have a soft texture.

4. There are a lot of different ways to garnish these babies. Typical Japanese presentation would have you pressing a pea into the top center of the dumplings, right before you steam them. Chinese dumplings might be topped with very finely diced, nearly minced carrot. Look up 'Shumai Dumplings' in a google image search, you'll see a wide range of toppings and presentations. I opted for the super simple garnish of sprinkling thinly sliced green onion on top of mine.

FUN FACT:
For the folks wondering how these compare with the little Trader Joe's cilantro dumplings. Those are 4 for 1 point. 4 of those little dumplings weigh 36 grams.... ONE of my dumplings weighs 37 grams. These are appetizers, those are cute lil iddy biddy baby dumplings. Though, those lil guys are great in soups.

SPRING ROLLS (STEP-BY-STEP GUIDE)

An ultra light, fresh & healthy version of traditional deep fried egg rolls, loaded with fresh herbs and veggies

First thing's first... this is not a true recipe. Instead, the following 3 pages are going to be a picture guided, step-by-step guide, showing you the process for assembling and rolling spring rolls. I'll also include lots of suggestions and tips, as well as ideas for 3 regional variations. Use these pages as a guide to teach you the process, then you can create your own rolls, customized with any filling you want. If the thought of making these seems a bit intimidating, think of it like this: If you've EVER rolled up a burrito, you can make these. Yeah... I went there!! The only difference is fresh veggies and herbs, with rice wrappers instead of tortillas.

Servings Info.:

Yields: However many you make.
Servings: However many you eat.
Serving Size: 1 spring roll.

R D
1-1
SEE NOTES

- last checked 12/13/22 -
These listed points are ONLY for the wrappers.
Fill them with 0 point awesomness

WHAT YOU'LL NEED:

- Asian Rice Paper "***Spring Roll Wrappers***", round shaped, 22cm in size. They sell 3 different sizes, you want 22cm ones. (see notes)

Filling:

- The filling is 100% customizable. For purposes of this guide, I'm showing you the assembly for the 'Vietnamese Spring Rolls'. Ingredients listed on pg. #40

2. **(A)** Unlike bloggers, who care about how fancy and color coordinated their gear is, I'm practical. Not everyone has a <u>really</u> wide bowl, so.. let's use a pan!! Fill a 10-12" pan with warm water, take out **ONE** of your (still hard) spring roll wrappers, then **(B)** submerge it in the warm water for 3-4 seconds.

Directions:

 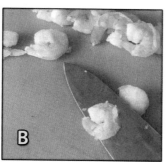

1. [DO AHEAD] **(A)** Make sure to prep/slice your vegetables and herbs ahead of time. Get them all organized and ready. **(B)** If you are using shrimp, have them cooked in advance. <u>If using large sized shrimp</u>, slice each one into 2 thin halves.

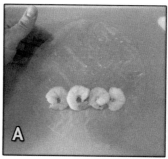 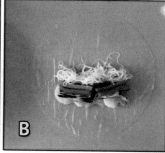

3. **(A)** Spread a little water onto a cutting board, then lay the rice wrapper down onto it. It'll start softening up as you assemble it. Arrange 4 slices of shrimp onto the bottom 1/3rd of the wrapper. **(B)** Over the shrimp, place a layer of carrots, red cabbage, red bell peppers, cucumbers and some rice noodles (or shiratake).

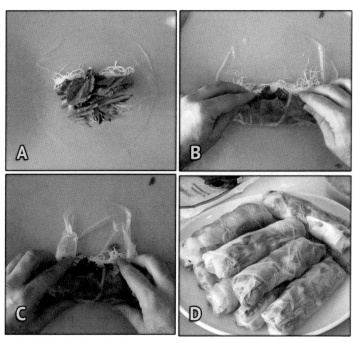

4. **(A)** Now, spread some of the fresh cilantro leaves across the top of the veggies, followed by a couple of fresh mint leaves. You don't want TOO much mint, because it has such a strong flavor. You want a hint of it. **(B)** Now, let's get rolling! Fold the bottom of the wrapper up and over the filling. At this point, the wrapper may be starting to get a little 'tacky'. Do your best. You can always use your finger to rub a little water onto the wrapper if it folds onto itself and sticks, by accident. **(C)** Fold the 2 'side' portions of wrapper, up and onto the filling. Yup… Just like making a burrito. Sorry, food purists! **(D)** Now, simply roll up the spring rolls, trying to compress the filling in as tightly as you can, so it gets a nice, somewhat uniform egg roll shape. Ta Daaaaa! See, easy peasy.

NOTES & SUGGESTIONS:

-   *SPRING ROLL WRAPPERS:* None of the grocery stores near me sold "rice paper spring roll wrappers". You need to buy "spring roll wrappers"! They are round and the size of a full sized, regular tortilla you'd use for #TacoTuesday. I ended up having to purchase them off of Amazon. They were $10 for a pack of 32 of them, which actually isn't bad, because they last forever. Very important… Make sure you buy ones that are "22cm" in size. Though 99% of brands are 1 point per wrapper, some aren't. So make sure to buy a 22cm sized package, scan the barcode, or, 'create food' and enter the nutritional information, to get accurate points.
-   *GO FOR A SWIM:* Rice paper wrappers feel like a paper thin sheet of plastic when you take them out of the package. To use them, you need to dip them under water for 3-4 seconds, then place them onto your work surface. Also, slightly wet your cutting board, or… lightly spray it with cooking spray. The added moisture helps them not to stick to the work surface.
-   *RICE NOODLE SUBSTITUTE:* A lot of spring roll recipes call for vermicelli rice noodles. They are high in points and hard to find for a lot of folks. I have used "shiratake" noodles, aka: 0 point 'magic spaghetti' noodles in these. They are a totally fine substitute. But, you need to rinse them off and pat 'em dry.
-   *FILLING:* Make sure meats are already cooked and cooled, and vegetables are sliced thin and/or uniform-ish in shape/size.

SPRING ROLL VARIATIONS

Three very simple, basic ideas you can use to make different fresh spring rolls, which coincide with the cuisine of 3 different Asian countries. The process of making them is identical, the only slight difference is what combination of veggies and herbs you use. Even with that... the differences between them all is virtually nonexistent. Note: Though some of these three list chicken or shrimp.... use whatever protein you want (shrimp, chicken, tofu). Or, you can leave out the protein altogether and go full veggie-roll.

CAMBODIAN SPRING ROLLS 'NIME CHOW'

Filling:

- fresh bean sprouts
- 2 cups thinly sliced lettuce (or, simply use 'shredded' lettuce)
- Carrots, thinly sliced into sticks/julienned/matchstick/'shredded'
- Fresh basil leaves. 3-4 medium sized leaves per roll
- cooked vermicelli rice noodles, OR shiratake noodles. (If you use shiratake noodles, rinse them well, then pat completely dry)

Directions:

1 Wet the wrappers, one at a time, then place onto a cutting board.
2 Place some shredded lettuce all over half of the wrapper, leaving it 1/2" from the edges. Yup, all the veggies end up surrounded by lettuce.
3 Onto the center of the wrapper, spread some carrots, noodles, bean sprouts, then the basil leaves. Then, roll it up. Done.

THAI SPRING ROLLS 'PA PIA SOD'

Filling:

- Chicken breast, cooked, sliced into strips. OR, you can use cooked shrimp, sliced as shown on page 38, in picture *1B*
- Carrots, sliced into thin sticks/julienned
- English cucumber, thin sliced into sticks
- Red bell pepper, sliced into thin strips
- Fresh basil (or Thai Basil), cilantro and mint
- (optional) thin rice vermicelli noodles, or shiratake noodles

Directions:

1 Sprinkle water onto your cutting board, then dip your rice wrapper in water and place it onto the board.
2 Place a few slices of chicken, followed by carrots, cucumber and red bell pepper. Cover with some fresh basil, cilantro and mint.
3 Roll it all up like a mini, translucent lil burrito. Done.

VIETNAMESE SPRING ROLLS 'GỎI CUỐN'

Filling:

- Size 15-20 or 16-21 shrimp, cooked, sliced in half to make 2 thin halves out of each shrimp (see picture *1B* on pg 38)
- Carrots, thinly sliced into matchsticks/'shredded'/julienned
- Red cabbage, thin sliced/shredded
- Red bell pepper, thin sliced
- English cucumber, thin sliced into sticks
- Cooked rice vermicelli noodles, OR, 0 point shiratake noodles. Boiled/cooked, drained, rinsed and patted dry.
- Fresh cilantro
- Fresh mint
- Fresh basil

Directions:

1 At this point I shouldn't need to tell'ya. Add the stuff to your wrapper... roll it up... done.

REGIONAL VARIATIONS:

If you've spent a minute or two to look over these 3 different spring roll recipes from 3 different countries, you're probably noticing something... There's no real difference. There really isn't any one major thing that sets Vietnamese rolls apart from Thai rolls, other than an herb. All of the countries use chicken, shrimp or tofu. All countries use the same veggies, in different combinations and all regions pretty much use either fresh cilantro, basil, and/or mint. In Thai recipes, you can use Thai Basil instead of regular basil, but it isn't a 'party foul' if you don't. Some recipes add in some lettuce, some don't. Some add thin rice noodles... some don't. The filling ingredients are all pretty standard across the board. So, mix and match them to your own liking, till you hit your perfect combination.

Common Proteins: (pre-cooked, added cold/cool to the rolls)

- Thin sliced chicken breast
- Boiled/steamed or poached shrimp. Peeled, deveined, tail off.
- Firm tofu, sliced into thin strips

Common Veggies: (sliced thin and uniform, added raw)

- Carrots
- English Cucumber (the thin kind, not the big honkin' cucumbers)
- Red bell pepper
- Red cabbage
- Bean sprouts
- Thin sliced Jalapeno peppers (red or green)
- Any other I didn't' mention, experiment and try what you like

Common Fresh Herbs:

- Basil or Thai Basil leaves
- Fresh Mint (a little goes a LONG way)
- Fresh Cilantro

NOTES & SUGGESTIONS:

- **SPRING ROLL WRAPPERS:** As I mentioned earlier... you do not want to purchase plain ol' "Rice Paper Wrappers". Those are larger and rectangular in shape, causing them to be higher in point .What you WANT to order is: *ROUND* shaped "Rice Paper WRAPPERS". They may say 'Spring Roll' on them, they may not. But.. they need to be round in shape, like tortillas. They also come in different sizes: 22cm (standard), 24cm and 25cm. Obviously, the larger the wrapper, the higher they are in points. Make sure you buy ones that are 22cm in size. As a general rule, 99.999% of the time, those are 1 point per wrapper, for the first few wrappers.

    If your barcode scanner doesn't recognize the package, manually 'create' a new food item. Enter the packages nutritional information, along with the number of servings the package lists. Then, that package will be in your database, letting you pull up accurate points.

ROUND 22cm Wrappers... YES!!!

- **ASIAN MARKETS:** Obviously, if you are lucky enough to have an Asian market near your house, they'll have a nice selection of different wrappers. No need for Amazon.

- **WORKING WITH THE WRAPPERS:** Before you start dipping the wrappers into water and then placing them onto your cutting board... make sure to sprinkle some water onto the work surface and rub it around. If you place the wet wrappers onto a dry cutting board or work surface, you'll find it very difficult to peel them up without them sticking to the surface. I've also spritzed my cutting board with cooking spray, it works just as well.

- **DIPPING SAUCES:** Though Spring Rolls do taste very light and fresh... they are essentially a plain, undressed salad in a wrapper. You really need to eat these with a dipping sauce. This book includes a few low point Asian dipping sauces. However, my personal favorite for Spring Rolls is the 'Vietnamese Dipping Sauce', on page 25.

- **FILLING:** As noted, customize the fillings to whatever you want. As a general rule, any meats are pre-cooked, then added cold. Vegetables added into 'fresh' spring rolls are typically raw. Though, you can also lightly 'dress' them if you'd like.

- **ASSEMBLY:** Make sure all your fillings are organized and ready to go. Also, only wet one wrapper at a time.

SQUARE 22cm Wrappers
NOPE, NOPE, NOPE

"Emperor Shunzhi's 'Plan-Friendly' Picnic" **- painted by:** *Zhu Da*, **early Qing Dynasty (1648)**

SWEET & SOUR MEATBALLS

Tender meatballs packed with garlic, ginger, fish sauce, mint and more

Aside from my Lebanese Kafta meatballs, which I'm putting in Cookbook 7, these are my favorite meatball appetizer. As an added benefit, they are really pretty simple to prep as well. These have tons of classic Asian flavor, with a thick sweet & sour glaze.

Ingredients:

- 1 batch of my Asian ground meat mix, recipe on pg. 19, WITH THE FOLLOWING CHANGES:
  - Add 1-1/2 tsp plain breadcrumbs
  - Add 2 tsp panko breadcrumbs
  - Add 1 egg yolk
- *(for garnish)* thin sliced green onions
- *(for garnish)* 1/4 tsp sesame seeds

SAUCE:

- 1/2 cup EACH: water, rice vinegar & 0 calorie sugar replacement o' choice
- 1-1/2 Tbsp cornstarch, whisked into the liquids
- 2 garlic cloves, finely chopped
- 1-1/2 tsp ginger, finely chopped
- 2 Tbsp tomato sauce (for color)

Serving Info.:

Yields: 31 meatballs
Servings: 31
Serving Size: 1 Meatball

R D
0-0
You can have up to 15 meatballs for 0 points, on both Plans

- last checked 12/04/22 -
Use your mobile device's 'Camera' App to look at this code for nutritional info.

Directions:

1. Mix a batch of the Asian ground meat, with the listed changes Let rest for 20 minutes.

2. Preheat oven to 400 degrees, line a pan with foil and spray with cooking spray. Scoop 1 Tablespoon sized rounds of meat into your palm and form into meatballs. If the mixture gets sticky, dab your fingers into a bowl of water. It'll get rid of the meat's stickiness.

3. Once the oven is up to temperature, bake the meatballs for 9 minutes at 400 degrees. Remove from oven, set aside for 5 minutes. They'll continue cooking. from residual heat. After baking for 9 minutes, my meat had an internal temperature of 168. After resting, it rose up to 172. In case you're wondering, they're going to cook a little bit more in step 5.

4. Whisk all the sauce ingredients together in a bowl, till the cornstarch dissolves. Heat a large pan over medium-high heat for 1 minute, then pour in the sauce. Let it come to a boil and begin to thicken.

5. Once the sauce thickens to the consistency of maple syrup, add the meatballs and cook for 2-3 minutes, or until the sauce has coated them all in a thick glaze. Garnish with thin sliced green onions and 1/4 tsp of sesame seeds. Done.

VIETNAMESE MEATBALLS

Tender meatballs packed with garlic, ginger, fish sauce, mint and more

These meatballs are bursting with flavor. They are loaded with a mixture of ground turkey (instead of beef) and ground shrimp, with garlic, ginger, lime zest, chilis, herbs, brown 'sugar'... though I include a sauce with this recipe, I personally prefer them without it.

Ingredients:

- 1 lb ground turkey breast
- 1/2 lb uncooked shrimp. Peeled, deveined, tail removed
- 4 garlic cloves, chopped
- 1-1/2 tsp ginger, finely chopped
- 1-1/2 tsp lime zest, minced
- 2 tsp Asian fish sauce **PLUS** 1/4 tsp sesame oil
- 1 Tbsp Asian chili sauce (I used Huy Fong chili garlic)
- 2 Tbsp 0 calorie brown sugar replacement
- 3 Tbsp **EACH**: chopped cilantro, mint, green onions
- 1 egg yolk
- 1-1/2 tsp plain breadcrumbs
- 2 tsp panko breadcrumbs
- 1/2 tsp salt
- 1/4 tsp black pepper

- **SAUCE:** 1 Tbsp **each**: soy sauce, lime juice & Asian chili garlic sauce. 1 tsp **each**: fish sauce and 'dark' soy sauce. Finally, add 2 Tbsp brown sugar replacement.

Serving Info.:

Yields: 43 meatballs
Servings: 43
Serving Size: 1 Meatball

R D
0-0
The ENTIR BATCH is
0 points on both plans

- last checked 12/04/22 -
Use your mobile device's 'Camera' App to look at this code for nutritional info.

Directions:

1. Combine the 'meat mixture' ingredients in a food processor. Pulse until the mixture almost becomes completely smooth, but still retains some small chunks of shrimp (2nd picture).

2. Use a 1 Tbsp scoop to form into meatballs. Place onto a large foil-lined pan, sprayed with cooking spray. The mixture will be sticky, so dip your fingers into a bowl of water, while forming the meatballs. It helps remove the tackiness of the meat.

3. Preheat your oven to 400 degrees. Once heated, bake for 10 minutes. Remove from oven, let the meatballs rest for 5 minutes, then move on to step 4.

4. _(SAUCE):_ In a large pan, over high heat, pour in and mix the 'Sauce' ingredients, stir to combine. Once it reduces to the consistency of maple syrup, add the meatballs. Cook for 1 more minute, coating them with a nice glaze. Garnish with fresh chopped cilantro, mint and 1 tsp sesame seeds.

NOTE: Don't like shrimp? Replace it with another 1/2 lb ground turkey. Simple.

Egg Drop Soup

I know this sounds reeeally bleh, to Westerners, but this soup was actually REALLY REALLY GOOD.

I'm going to be up front and say the thought of making and eating this soup totally grossed me out, because... swirly eggs. But seriously, I was completely and pleasantly surprised and how much I really liked it. The broth is ULTRA flavorful and the added creaminess of the delicate eggs really gave this soup a deep, rich flavor. Best part? The entire thing was done, from start to finish, in 15 minutes. It was an amazingly simple soup, but had a huge amount of flavor. Along with a wonderful, silky smooth texture.

Servings Info.:

Yields: 5 cups
Servings: 4
Serving Size: 1-1/4 cup

MY PLAN
R D
1-1

- last checked 12/09/22 -
Use your mobile device's 'Camera' App to look at this code for nutritional info.

Ingredients:

Broth:
- 4-1/4 cups fat free chicken broth
- 1 tsp sesame oil
- 3/4 tsp salt
- 1/8 tsp pepper
- 1 tsp 0 calorie sugar replacement o' choice
- 3/4 tsp ground turmeric (see notes)
- 1/4 tsp fish sauce (yes... I'm serious... see the notes)

Additional Ingredients:
- 3-1/2 Tbsp cornstarch, dissolved with 1/4 cup water
- 3 large eggs, lightly beaten/whisked, in a bowl
- Thin sliced green onions, for garnish

Directions:

1. **(A)** Heat all of the 'Broth' ingredients together in a medium pot, over medium-high heat. **(B)** While the broth's heating, lightly beat the eggs together in a bowl. Set aside. In a separate cup, stir together the cornstarch and water, till dissolved. Set aside. **(C)** When the broth reaches a simmer, add the cornstarch mixture and begin stirring/whisking immediately, to avoid any lumps. **(D)** After about 1 minute, the sauce should be thickened to the consistency of warm gravy. Reduce heat to medium-low. Continue cooking for 2 minutes..

2. **(A)** Use a whisk and begin stirring the simmering broth in a circular motion. **(B)** Once the soup is spinnin', slowly begin pouring in the beaten eggs. Drizzle the eggs into the center at a semi-slow speed, just like you're pouring syrup onto pancakes. While you're pouring in the eggs, continue stirring with the whisk, in the same circular motion. **(C)** Your goal is to continuously break down the silky, feathery tendrils of raw egg, (while continuing to stir in the circular motion) to create fine little delicate particles. **(D)** Continue cooking for 2 more minutes. Remove pot from heat and let rest for 5-10 minutes before serving, letting it cool a bit. Garnish with thin sliced green onion.

NOTES & SUGGESTIONS:

- *TURMERIC?:* The turmeric adds an earthy flavor as well as giving the soup a rich, golden color.
- *FISH SAUCE? WHAT?!?!?:* Yup, you aren't reading that wrong. When I was looking up recipes for Egg Drop soup, I of course found countless recipes which were simply just broth, cornstarch and eggs. Boom, done. Might as well just boil some vegetables in water and call it soup, while we're at it. Later, I started finding recipes for it from Chinese restaurants. One thing they all had in common was the addition of "MSG", which is a very common additive in Chinese restaurants. "MSG" is a very fine chemical powder that imparts INTENSE savoriness, or 'Umami', into Chinese food.

   So, I started looking for alternatives to MSG. There were suggestions on cooking sites, to use added soy sauce, but that would make the soup darker, so that was a no-go. Dried and powdered mushrooms can also be added. Umm, no. I'm not going to make you go buy dried mushrooms, just so you can grind them up for this one single soup. So, I realized that a tiny amount of 'fish sauce' would do the same thing. It's used in Vietnamese and Thai cooking to impart a TON of umami, so... I thought I'd give it a try. Guess what... it works great. It added a tremendous pop of richness, with just that tiny little 1/4 tsp.
- *BROTH:* If you leave out the eggs from this recipe, you end up with an incredibly delicious broth. You can make and serve the broth, without the eggs, for a delicous and simple soup course.

Hot & Sour Soup

My slimmed down recipe for over-the-top, family style Hot & Sour soup. It eats like a meal, baby!

Let's start off by addressing the elephant in the room. If your only experience with Hot & Sour soup is the thin cup of broth they give you as part of your inexpensive Chinese food lunch special... this is nooooot the soup you were expecting. This is a big, hearty pot of soup. It's full of the traditional hot & sour flavor, but also comes loaded with a bunch of veggies, chicken and even tofu. The amount of hot vs. sour in your soup is completely customizable and can be easily adjusted.

Servings Info.:

Yields: 7 cups
Servings: 5
Serving Size: 1-1/3 cup

R D
1-1

- last checked 12/10/22 -
Use your mobile device's 'Camera' App to look at this code for nutritional info.

Ingredients:

Broth:
- 4-1/2 cups fat free chicken broth
- 2 Tbsp reduced sodium soy sauce
- 1 tsp 'dark' soy sauce
- 3-4 Tbsp Asian chili garlic sauce (I used Huy Fong), to taste
- 1/3 cup rice vinegar
- 1 Tbsp 0 calorie brown sugar replacement
- 1 tsp sesame oil
- 1/2 tsp black pepper (or you can use white pepper)

Additional Ingredients:
- 5oz cooked boneless skinless chicken breast. (shredded, diced, cut into strips, whatever...YOUR PREFERENCE!)
- 3/4 cup thin sliced (julienned) carrots, about 2-1/2" long
- 1 medium GREEN bell pepper, sliced into thin 2-1/2" strips
- 1 (8oz) can o' bamboo shoots, drained. Sliced into thin strips
- 2 Tbsp sliced scallions (<u>use the white part</u> of green onions)
- 3-1/2 Tbsp cornstarch, dissolved into 1/4 cup water
- 4 oz FIRM tofu, patted dry, sliced into 2"x1/2" slices
- 1 large egg, beaten, set aside.

Directions:

1. (Do Ahead) Cook chicken breast in whatever manner you want, then shred or chop it up. Set aside.

2. **(A)** Spend some time and chop/prep all of your veggies. It takes a little time, but can be done a day ahead, to save time on cooking day. **(B)** In a medium pot, bring all of the 'Broth' ingredients up to a boil. **(C)** Once boiling, add the cooked chicken and return to a simmer over medium heat. **(D)** Once the soup returns to a rolling simmer, add the carrots, bell pepper, thin sliced bamboo shoots and scallions. Bring back to a simmer and let cook for 2 minutes.

NOTES & SUGGESTIONS:

- **CHICKEN:** This is the only time, in this entire book, where I am NOT going to tell you how you should cook your chicken. You can use shredded chicken breast, diced, chopped, whatever you want. Heck, to make things easier on myself, I simply bought a small bag of pre-shredded chicken breast from my grocery store's Deli section. This is a great recipe to use leftover chicken for, also. Clear out that fridge, baby!

- ***DUDE! THIS ISN'T HOT & SOUR SOUP!?!??:*** Uh... yeah it is. What you're used to getting as a simple little free cup o' soup with your Chinese food, as part of your $5 lunch special at "Uncle Tso's Chinese Take Out" is pretty much just a simple, cheap broth dish. C'mon, they need to make a profit, while giving you a cup of soup with your meal, lol.

    This type of Hot & Sour soup is more of the old-school traditional "full meal" kind of soup. You know how if you're making soup for your family's dinner, you don't give them a pot of broth? Same thing. This is a 'full meal' version of Hot & Sour soup. If you'd like it more brothy, leave out the bell peppers and carrots. Though, you'll be reducing the amount of total servings, due to the decreased yield.

- **CARROTS:** Want to save yourself a bunch of time? Instead of peeling and thin slicing a bunch of carrots or even just trying to thin slice a bunch of baby carrots... simply buy a bag of 'shredded' carrots, or also called 'matchstick' carrots.

- ***CUSTOMIZE THIS BAD BOY:*** You don't' have to strictly adhere to the veggies that I chose to use in this soup. If you don't want to use carrots, try bean sprouts. Don't like bell peppers? Use something else instead, or leave them out entirely. Customize this dish to have whatever you want. Be it the tofu, bamboo shoots... whatever. It'll still taste great.

- ***HEAT LEVEL:*** The delicate dance between how hot or how spicy Hot & Sour soup is, is 100% based on your own preference. Some people like it more sour (more vinegar), while some people like it with more heat. Adjust it to your own liking by adding more or less vinegar, or more or less of the Asian chili garlic sauce, to taste.

5. **(A)** After the vegetables have been cooking at a simmer for 2 minutes, add the sliced tofu. **(B)** After you add the tofu, stir in the dissolved cornstarch/water mixture. Stir and return to a low simmer for 2 minutes. **(C)** Now, slowly pour in the beaten egg. WHILE YOU'RE POURING IT IN, start **(D)** stirring the soup in a circular motion, don't stop! If you don't stir it, you'll get giant clump's o' egg in your soup. What you WANT, is for your stirring action to completely break up the liquid egg in the soup, which will give the soup an incredibly silky, smooth texture with tiny little feathery strands of pillow-soft egg, throughout the soup. Bring back to a low simmer for 2 minutes, then remove from heat. Let the soup rest for 10 minutes or so, before serving. Garnish with thin sliced green onion, if desired. Also, add more chili sauce if you want it hotter.

WONTON SOUP

A deliciously savory ginger, garlic and sesame oil broth, loaded with fresh, homemade dumplings

Wonton Soup is actually an incredibly simple dish, though it can be a bit time consuming, due to making your own homemade dumplings. Though you CAN save time and use store-bought, frozen mini wonton dumplings instead, not everyone has access to those, so I'm showing how to make them. This soup has an incredibly delicious broth you can use as the base for any Asian soup you'd like to make.

Servings Info.:

Yield: 10 cups
Servings: 6
Serving Size: 1-1/3 cups
(including 6 dumplings)

MY PLAN
R D
3-3

- last checked 12/28/22 -
Use your mobile device's 'Camera' App to look at this code for nutritional info.

Ingredients:

Filling Meat Mix:
- 1/2 lb extra lean ground turkey
- 1/8 tsp baking soda, dissolved with 1 tsp water
- 1/4 tsp fish sauce
- 1 tsp reduced sodium soy sauce
- 1 tsp dark soy sauce
- 1/3 cup finely minced onion
- 1/4 cup finely minced green onion
- 1 tsp garlic, minced (1 medium garlic clove)
- 1/2 tsp ginger, minced
- 1/8 tsp coarse ground black pepper

Broth:
- 6 cups fat free chicken broth
- 1 garlic clove, minced
- 1/2 tsp ginger, minced
- 1 tsp sesame oil
- 1/2 tsp fish sauce
- 2 Tbsp lower sodium soy sauce
- 1 tsp salt
- 1/2 tsp black pepper
- 1-1/2 Tbsp cornstarch, dissolved in 2 Tbsp water

Additional Ingredients:
- 36 wonton wrappers, square shaped, any brand... measured and <u>cut into 3 inch squares</u>. (most packages are 3-1/2 inches)
- additional thin sliced green onions, for garnish

Directions:

1. Mix all of the 'filling' ingredients together. Set aside for 30 minutes. While it's resting, start heating a large pot of water, over medium-high heat.

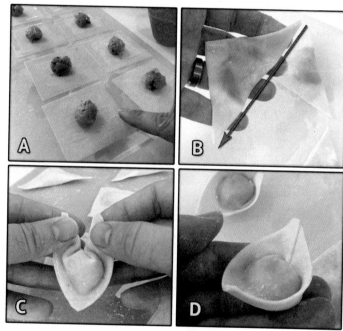

2. **(A)** Take half (18) of the cut wonton wrappers and place 1-1/2 tsp of the meat mixture into the center of each wrapper. Dip your finger in water and wet around the edges of each wrapper. **(B)** Fold each wrapper into a triangle, pressing out as much air as possible. Then wet your finger again and wet the back of the wrapper, along the red arrow in the pic. **(C)** Fold the two side edges of the triangle back, and pinch them against each other. **(D)** When you're done, they should look like a little boat. Holding the 2 pinched edges together for a few seconds helps them to stick together. Set aside. Repeat with the next 18 wrappers. Set aside, while the water heats up.

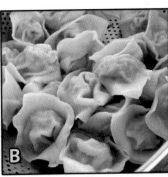

- **WONTON WRAPPERS:** I purchased square shaped wonton wrappers. Not big round ones, or big sheets you'd use for egg rolls. These are 3-1/2" square wonton wrappers. The reason I'm trimming them is to reduce the total ingredient points.
- **WONTON POINTS:** This recipe makes 36 dumplings. If I were to just build the recipe using 36 of the 3.5" wrappers, right out of the package...that'd be 23 points for the 36 wrappers. HOWEVER... we aren't using 3-1/2 inch wrappers, we're trimming them down to 3 inches. So, I trimmed them, busted out my kitchen scale, then weighed all 36 of the NOW 3 inch wrappers, in grams. They weighed 204 grams, which is only 17 points.

  Doing this one extra step removed 6 ingredient points and allowed the soup to be 3 points per serving, instead of 4. (note: different brands of wonton wrappers may be different points. I used "Twin Dragon, all natural wonton wrappers".) If you use a different brand, adjust your points if necessary.
- **DUMPLING-PREP.:** If you don't have time to make this entire recipe all at once, you can prep the dumplings ahead of time. Fill & fold them into their shapes, then freeze and store them in your freezer. When you are ready to make the soup, simply remove them from your freezer. If frozen, you can let them thaw out, oooooor, simply drop half of them into boiling water. Once they start to float, cook for 2 more minutes. Scoop'em out, rinse them off and repeat the process.
- **FROZEN MINI WONTONS.:** You can obviously save time and energy by using store bought, frozen mini wonton dumplings. Adjust your points as necessary, if you do.

3. **(A)** When the water reaches a boil, use a spoon and swirl the water around so that it's swirling pretty quickly. This will prevent the dumplings from sticking to the bottom of the pan. With the water swirling, drop half of the wontons into the water as quickly as possible. Once most of them start floating to the surface, set your timer and cook for 2 more minutes. **(B)** Scoop out the dumplings, place them in a colander and rinse them under cold water. Keep them there. Place the remainder of the uncooked dumplings in the boiling water. Once they begin floating, boil for 2 more minutes, then add them to the colander and rinse them under cold water. Set aside. Every few minutes, rinse them off 1 or 2 more times. This will prevent them from sticking together as they sit.

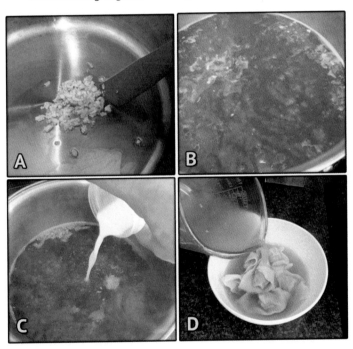

4. **(A)** Take your pot and pour out all of the used, hot water. Wipe it dry, then begin heating the pan on medium heat. Add the sesame oil, minced ginger and garlic. Cook for 1 to 2 minutes, or till they become fragrant, without browning. **(B)** Add the chicken broth, fish sauce, soy sauce, salt and black pepper. Turn up the heat to high and bring to a boil. **(C)** Dissolve the cornstarch into 2 Tbsp of water, then stir it into the boiling soup. Return to a boil and cook for 2 more minutes. **(D)** Take 6 serving bowls place 6 of the cooked/cooled dumplings into the bottom of each bowl. Pour/ladle 1-1/4 cups of the hot broth into each bowl. Let sit for 5 minutes before serving. Garnish with thin sliced green onions, if desired.

WOR WONTON SOUP

Where the vast majority of you might only have ever seen regular wonton soup on a restaurant menu... if you find "Wor" wonton soup... it's truly something special. "Wor" translates to *'Everything'*. So, where regular wonton soup is simply broth with dumplings, WOR wonton soup has broth, dumplings, shrimp, chicken and is loaded with vegetables. This soup eats like a meal.

Servings Info.:

Yield: 12 cups
Servings: 8
Serving Size: 1-1/2 cups

MY PLAN

R D
1-1

- last checked 12/19/22 -
Use your mobile device's 'Camera' App to look at this code for nutritional info.

Ingredients:

Filling For Dumplings:
- 1/3 lb extra lean ground turkey
- 1/8 tsp baking soda, dissolved with 1 tsp water
- 1/4 tsp fish sauce
- 1 tsp reduced sodium soy sauce
- 1 tsp garlic, minced (1 medium garlic clove)
- 1/2 tsp ginger, minced
- 1/8 tsp coarse ground black pepper
- 1 Tbsp green onion, finely chopped

Vegetables:
- 6 oz sliced mushrooms, any variety, though dark topped is recommended (such as baby bella, crimini, brown, etc.)
- 1 cup thin sliced carrot, sliced on a bias, in rounds
- 1-1/2 cup bean sprouts, loosely packed
- 5 oz sliced baby bok choy, (don't use long lengths of stalk)
- 1 garlic clove, minced
- 1 tsp ginger, minced
- 1/2 cup green onion, 1 inch lengths, loose packed

Additional Ingredients:
- 16 wonton wrappers, square shaped, any brand... measured and <u>cut into 3 inch squares</u>. (most packages are 3-1/2 inches)
- 1/2 pound boneless chicken breast, sliced thiiiiiiiin
- 9 cups fat free chicken broth
- 2 Tbsp reduced sodium soy sauce
- 2 tsp fish sauce
- 1 tsp sesame oil
- 1/2 pound shrimp, peeled, deveined, tail off (size 41-50)

Directions:

1. Mix all of the 'filling' ingredients together. The mix will be a bit sticky/wet. Set aside for 30 minutes.

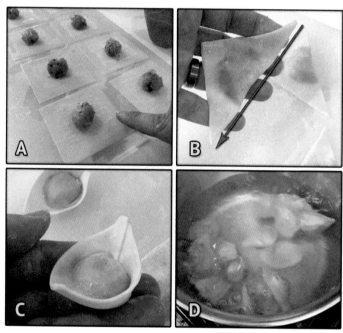

2. **(A)** Take your 3 inch squared wonton wrappers, lay them down 'powdered side' up and place 1 tsp of the meat mixture into the center of each wrapper. Dip your finger into a cup of water and wet around the edges of each wrapper. **(B)** Fold each wrapper into a triangle, pressing out as much air as possible. Then wet your finger again and wet the back of the wrapper, along the red arrow in the pic. **(C)** Fold the two side edges of the triangle back, then fold the two sides together and press till sealed, making a 'boat'. **(D)** Bring water to a boil, then boil the dumplings for 2-3 minutes. Drain and rinse them under cold water. Pat them dry, lay them out on a pan, without letting them touch, set aside for later.

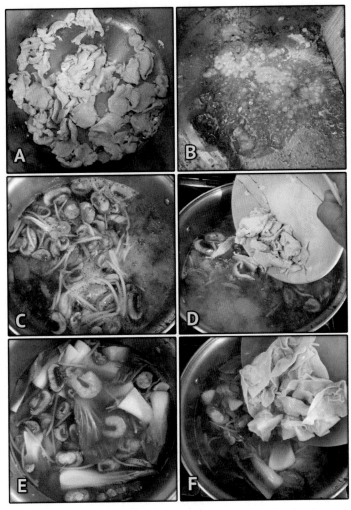

- **_WONTON WRAPPERS:_** I purchased square shaped wonton wrappers. Not big round ones, or big sheets you'd use for egg rolls. These are 3-1/2" square wonton wrappers. The reason I'm trimming them is they are meant to be smaller bite sized dumplings, in a soup, Plus, it saves points.
- **_WONTON POINTS:_** This recipe makes 16 dumplings. If I were to just build the recipe using 16 wrappers... that'd be 12 points, for the 16 full sized, 3-1/2 inch wrappers. HOWEVER... we aren't using 3-1/2 inch sheets, we're trimming them down to 3 inches. So, I trimmed them, weighed the 3 inch wrappers in grams and looked up how many points they were, in grams, using the Weight Watchers mobile app's listing. It dropped them down from 10 points to 8 points (94 grams). <u>Points may vary, depending on brand.</u> Scan your brand and adjust points, as necessary (remember to weigh in grams).
- **_FILLING:_** Using 1/3 pound of ground turkey (approx. 5.3 oz) lets you have enough meat to fill the wontons, but does leave you with a little extra leftover. I tried using 1/4 pound, but it really cut it close... so I'm telling you to use 1/3 pound. On a plus... you"ll have extra ground turkey left over for another dish. Or, season it with my 'Asian' ground turkey mix, cook it into crumbles and add it to the soup. Either way works.
- **_DUMPLING-PREP.:_** If you don't have time to make this entire recipe all at once, you can prep the dumplings ahead of time. Fill & fold them into their shapes, then store them in the fridge or freeze, overnight. When you are ready to make the soup, simply remove them from your fridge/freezer. If frozen, let them thaw out. Then boil them as directed.

3. **(A)** Heat a large pot over medium-high heat for 1 minute. Spray with cooking spray, then add the chicken. Cook for 3-4 minutes, until ALMOST completely cooked through. Remove from pot, set aside. **(B)** Return pot to heat, then add the garlic, ginger and sesame oil. Cook for 1 minute, or until they become fragrant, but don't burn them! **(C)** Add the chicken broth, soy sauce, fish sauce, carrots, mushrooms and bean sprouts. Bring to a boil and cook for 5 minutes. **(D)** Reduce heat to medium, then return chicken to the pot. Return soup to a boil, then **(E)** add the shrimp, bok choy and green onions. Cook for 3 minutes. **(F)** Grats... your soup is done. Add dumplings into the hot pot right before serving. We want to warm them in the broth, not boil them to mush

SUBSTITUTION IDEAS:

- If you don't want to use bean sprouts, you can use whole snow peas, or 1 cup of canned, sliced bamboo shoots or water chestnuts. Preeeetty much use whatever you want. I won't judge. Ok, actually I will... I just won't tell you. I'm passive aggressive like that.
- If you can't get baby bok choy, you can use chopped kale, collard greens, mustard greens, or thin sliced cabbage. You can ALSO use spinach.... but you'll need about 100lbs of it, considering how much spinach cooks down.
- Don't like shrimp? Add more chicken, or heck... leave the meat out entirely and go full-tilt hippie, with some free range, humanely harvested, locally sourced tofu. 😎

Korean Bibimbap with Gochujang Sauce - Pg. 62-63

Singapore Noodles - Pg. 118-119

Orange Chicken - Pg. 106-107

Shrimp with Lobster Sauce - 114-115

Main Dishes

Tired of looking online for low fat, low calorie, low Point Asian recipes, only to be bombarded by entrees that call for 1/2 cup of honey, tons of flour for breading, and enough sugar and oil to give a cardiologist pause? Well, get ready for skinnied-down, LEGIT Asian food. These dishes cover a WIDE range of Asian cuisine, including dishes from:

Cambodia, China, Korea, Japan, the Philippines, Taiwan, Thailand & Vietnam

Korean Chicken Japchae Noodles ... 70-71

Mongolian Chicken ... 100-101

ADOBO CHICKEN

Arguably The Most Popular Dish In All The Philippines. Mine Uses Chicken Breasts Instead of Thighs.

Ok, I have to admit that I have never, ever had Adobo chicken before in my entire life. My Gringo brain always figured that it would be an extremely spicy dish. When I hear the word "adobo", I think of 'canned chipotle peppers in adobo sauce'. I ALWAYS thought adobo chicken was chicken in a spicy chipotle sauce.... oops. Turns out Adobo chicken is actually fantastic and there aren't even any chilis in it. It's pretty much soy sauce, vinegar, bay leaf and black peppercorns. It's sweet, savory, tangy and peppery.

Servings Info.:

Yields: 4 Chicken Breasts
Servings: 4
Serving Size: 1 Chicken Breast

MY PLAN

R D
1-1

- last checked 11/21/22 -
Use your mobile device's 'Camera' App to
look at this code for nutritional info.

Ingredients:

Chicken:
• 4 large chicken breasts, boneless skinless

Marinade:
• 1/3 cup low sodium soy sauce
• 1/3 cup rice vinegar OR regular ol' distilled white vinegar
• 5 dried bay leaves
• 2 medium garlic cloves, minced
• 1/4 tsp baking soda... no questions... trust the science!

Sauce:
• 1-1/4 cups fat free chicken broth
• 1-1/2 tsp cornstarch, dissolved into broth
• 4 medium garlic cloves, minced
• 3 Tbsp 0 calorie brown sugar replacement o' choice
• 2-1/4 tsp paprika (it's not traditional... but just roll with it)
• 1 Tbsp no sugar added ketchup (for color)

Additional Ingredients:
• 1 medium onion, diced
• 4 medium garlic cloves, minced.
• 1 Tbsp whole black peppercorns
• 1/4 tsp cracked black pepper
• green onions, thin sliced on a bias, for garnish
• 1 tsp sesame seeds for garnish

Directions:

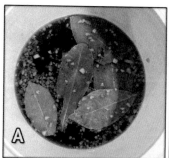 

1. **(A)** Mix all of the marinade ingredients together. Allow the baking soda & vinegar a minute to stop fizzing. **(B)** Pour the marinade over the chicken breasts, smooth sides down. Cover with plastic wrap, let marinate for at least 1 hour, though overnight is preferable.

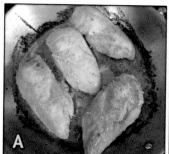 

2. **(A)** Heat a large pan over HIGH heat for 1 minute. Spray with cooking spray, then add the chicken breasts to the pan, reserving the marinade. Cook for 1-1/2 minutes, without moving the chicken. Flip, then cook 1-1/2 more minutes. Remove chicken from pan, set aside. **(B)** Add the onion and garlic. Spray with cooking spray, cook for 4-5 minutes, or until onions are lightly caramelized.

3. While your onions are cooking, mix together the 'Sauce' ingredients. Ok, fine... you can make it ahead of time, too.

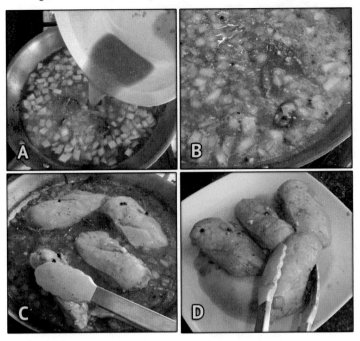

NOTES & SUGGESTIONS:

- **COOK TIME:** The cook times listed in this recipe are based upon the LARGE, thick chicken breasts that I used. Seriously, I used Dolly Parton sized chicken breasts. If you make this dish with thin sliced chicken breasts, you'll need to experiment with reducing the cook-time for the initial pan sear, as well as the 15 minute 'braise'. Otherwise, your chicken could end up dry and tough from overcooking.
- **VEGETABLE BROTH:** "But Daniel... I'm a vegetarian... can I use vegetable broth instead of chicken broth?" Sure, but... umm... this is still a chicken dish...
- **PAPRIKA & KETCHUP!?!?!:** Calm your jets, turbo! Because I wanted the dish to have a reddish hue, I added paprika and one teeeeny tiny Tbsp of ketchup to the sauce. It's completely optional. Leave it out if you want, but your finished sauce will be brown, rather than auburn-red, like my sauce (pictured).
- **PEPPERCORNS:** In the database, black peppercorns gain points, so this recipe gains 1 ingredient point from black peppercorns. However, if you aren't a points-stickler, and are one of those "I don't count points for spices!!!" people, ignore it. Then, your serving of chicken is 0 points on both plans. You do you, Boo.

4. **(A)** When the onions are ready, pour in all of the reserved marinade, as well as the 'Sauce', black peppercorns and cracked black pepper. **(B)** Bring the sauce back up to a boil, reduce heat to medium-high, then simmer for 5 minutes. **(C)** Add the chicken breasts to the sauce, reduce heat to medium-low, then simmer the chicken in the sauce for 15 minutes, turning over occasionally. **(D)** After 15 minutes, remove chicken from the pan and set aside.

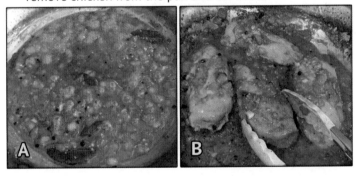

5. **(A)** Let the sauce continue to cook down for a few minutes, so it continues to reduce and thicken. **(B)** When your sauce has thickened, return chicken breasts to the pan. Cook the chicken for another minute or two in the thickening sauce, turning to coat.

6. Place the chicken onto a serving platter, cover with sauce, garnish with sliced green onions and sesame seeds, if desired.

Banh Mi Chicken Sandwich

Good Morning Vietnam!! Chicken Breast, Cucumber Slices, Pickled Veggies, Cilantro and a Spicy, Savory Spread

The unofficial, official chicken sandwich of Vietnam. This light, fresh and flavorful sandwich sports tender chicken on a soft french roll. It's then dressed up with a savory spread, fresh cucumber slices, thin cut pickled carrots, radishes and jalapeños. Finally, it's topped with a heapin' helping of fresh cilantro leaves.

Servings Info.:

Yields: 2 sandwiches
Servings: 2
Serving: 1 sandwich

MY PLAN

R D
0-1

- last checked 11/21/22 -
These points **DO NOT INCLUDE THE BREAD!!**
These are the points for the 'FILLING'. Use whatever bread rolls you want, then add THESE POINTS to your bread of choice.

Ingredients:

Chicken & Marinade:
- 2 medium (3-4oz each) chicken breast, lightly pounded
- (marinade) 1-1/2 Tbsp reduced sodium soy sauce
- (marinade) 1-1/2 tsp fish sauce
- (marinade) 1 tsp lime juice
- (marinade)1/2 tsp paprika
- (marinade)1/8 tsp baking soda, stirred into the soy/fish sauces

Easy Pickled Vegetables:
- 1 cup matchstick carrots (or freshly shredded)
- 1 cup daikon radish, thiiiin sliced, to be similar in size to the matchstick/shredded carrots (see notes)
- 1 jalapeño pepper (red or green), sliced into thin rounds.
- distilled white vinegar... as much as you need (see notes)

Asian Spread:
- 4-1/2 Tbsp fat free plain Greek yogurt
- 1 tsp low fat mayonnaise
- 1 tsp lime juice
- 1/2 tsp sriracha asian chili sauce (or other hot sauce)
- 1/2 tsp paprika, for color
- 1/4 tsp salt

Additional Ingredients:
- Thin cucumber slices
- (2) store bought, french bread hoagie rolls. Scoop bread out of top bun halves. (SEE NOTES)
- 1 bunch cilantro, rough chopped, not packed (about 1 cup)

Directions:

1. **(A)** Peel the daikon radish, then slice it and the jalapeño, removing most of the seeds from the pepper. Add the cut veggies to a small pot and cover with white vinegar. Bring to a simmer, then turn off heat and let cool to room temperature. **(B)** Place the quick pickled veggies into a container, covered with the vinegar. Cover with an air tight lid and set aside in the fridge, to cool.

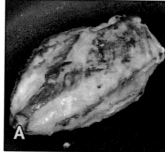
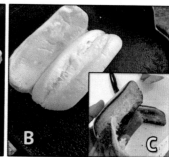

2. **(A)** Mix together the marinade and spread over the chicken. Let sit for 20-30 minutes. Heat a pan over medium-high heat for 1 minute. Spray with cooking spray, then cook chicken for 3 minutes per side. Set aside.
(B) Heat another pan over medium heat, then 'Butterfly' your sandwich rolls. Spray the 'inner' part with cooking spray, then lay them down onto the hot pan. Toast till edges are toasted brown. Remove from heat and let rest till cool. **(C)** Scoop out bread from the top bun, to create a cavity. Set rolls aside.

3. Mix all of the ingredients for the Asian spread together, till smooth and well combined. Set aside.

4. **(A)** Let your cooked chicken breasts rest for 10 minutes, then slice into 1/4" strips. **(B)** Smear a spoonful of the Asian spread onto the toasted bottom buns, followed by a layer of the sliced chicken breast. **(C)** Place thin sliced cucumber rounds over the chicken. **(D)** Take a handful of the pickled carrots and radish out of the vinegar and place onto a paper towel to remove some of the vinegar. Set a good amount of pickled carrot and radish on top of the cucumber slices, followed by a row of pickled jalapenos. Stuff the cavities on the top buns, with fresh cilantro, then place a few dollops of the sauce onto the leaves. (Doing it this way holds the cilantro in place while we flip the bun and keeps it from spilling out the sides when you take a bite). Finally... carefully flip the top bun over and onto the sandwich. Done.

NOTES & SUGGESTIONS:

- **DAIKON RADISH:** Now, I totally understand that not everybody has access to these, in the produce departments of their local stores. So, here's some alternatives:
    * Red Radish: Ya'know... those little round red ones? You can slice those thin and use them instead.
    * Jicama: Peel and slice jicama. The cool thing if you use it instead of radish is, where radishes are crisp, bitter and peppery... jicama is crisp and mildly sweet.
- **JALAPEÑOS:** First off, if you are handling raw peppers, DO NOT RUB YOUR EYES!!! Also, WEAR GLOVES!!. For folks who don't like heat, once you remove the seeds and pickle them in vinegar, they pretty much lose 90% of their spiciness. TRUST ME... I think the mild sauce at Taco Bell is spicy and I was ok with this. Side note, if you can get red jalapenos, they are prettier in the sandwich.
- **THE BREAD!!!!!:** As noted, the points for my recipe DO NOT INCLUDE the points for the bread. I want you to be able to use WHATEVER brand or type of bread you want for this sandwich. Add my points to your bread's points. Easy. If you use an 8 point bun, add it to the points for 1 serving of my sandwich, boom, done.
- **WHAT I DID FOR MY BREAD:** I used a generic, store bought, 6 point 'french bread hoagie roll'. I scanned the bag and pulled it up in the app. I then scrolled down to see how many grams I'd need to remove to make it a 5 point roll, by weight. I scooped out bread from the top bun, till I hit that number on a food scale. So... I turned my 6 point roll into a 5 point roll. So on MY plan... my 1 sandwich was 5 points.
- **SAUCY:** For a huge flavor kick, drizzle some of my teriyaki sauce over the pickled veggies, before closing up the sandwich. You can also use more Sriracha, if you want.

BEEF LOK LAK STIR FRY (BÒ LÚC LẮC)

Cambodian Peppered Beef with Onions And Bell Peppers In A Savory, Smoky Sauce

Though I never really eat beef, this is one of those sentimental dishes that I'll order whenever I see it on a menu. This popular Cambodian street food, known as 'Shaking Beef', is something you might see on the menu at a Thai or Chinese restaurant and never order, because you have no idea what it is. Beef Lok Lak (or **Bò lúc lắc**) has a peppery, savory sauce, coating tender chunks of beef and vegetables. The traditional dish uses a very specific variety of black peppercorns, regional to Southeast Asia... But, my version is using regular, coarse ground black pepper, which is more widely available here in the States.

Servings Info.:

Yields: 8 cups
Servings: 8
Serving Size: 1 cup

R D
4-4

- last checked 11/21/22 -
Use your mobile device's 'Camera' App to
look at this code for nutritional info.

Ingredients:

Meat & Marinade:
- 2 pounds beef top sirloin steak, trimmed, sliced into 1" cubes.
- 1/2 tsp baking soda, dissolved into 1 Tbsp water
- 1 Tbsp oyster sauce
- 1 Tbsp reduced sodium soy sauce
- 1 Tbsp 'dark' soy sauce
- 1-1/2 tsp 0 point sweetener o' choice
- 5 medium garlic cloves, minced

Sauce:
- 2 Tbsp oyster sauce
- 2 Tbsp reduced sodium soy sauce
- 1 Tbsp dark soy sauce (I used 'sushi chef' brand)
- 1/3 cup fat free beef broth
- 1 Tbsp coarse ground black pepper
- 1 Tbsp cornstarch, dissolved in 1 Tbsp water

Additional Ingredients:
- 1 large red bell pepper, sliced into strips
- 2 large red onions, halved, sliced into thin wedges (picture 1B)
- (optional) green onions, thin sliced, for garnish

Dipping Sauce:
- 3 Tbsp lime juice
- 1/8 tsp coarse ground black pepper
- 1/4 tsp salt

Directions:

1. **(A)** Mix the sliced & trimmed beef with all the marinade ingredients. Let marinate for at least 30 minutes, though you can also marinate overnight. **(B)** Slice and prep the onions and bell peppers, set aside. **(C)** Heat a LARGE pan over High heat for 1 minute. Spray with cooking spray, then add the onions. Do NOT move the onions. Let cook, undisturbed, for 2 minutes over high heat. Toss, then cook 1 more minute. Set aside in a bowl. **(D)** Return pan to heat, spray pan again and add bell peppers. Cook over high heat, unmoved, for 1 minute. Toss, then cook for 1 minute. You want a little char to develop. Pour the peppers into the same bowl as the onions. Return empty pan to heat.

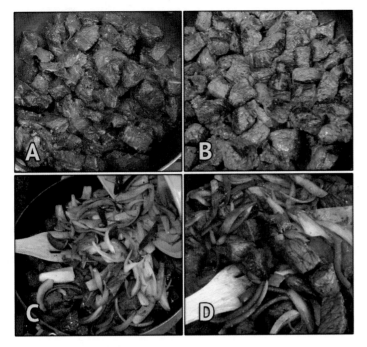

- **MARINADE:** As stated in the instructions, though you can marinate the beef for as little as 30 minutes, I marinated mine overnight.
- **BEEF/CHICKEN:** Though this dish is usually made with beef, obviously, you can make it with chicken breast.
- **OYSTER SAUCE:** If you don't like the taste of oyster sauce, you can use 'vegetarian oyster sauce', which is a thick, savory sauce, made from mushrooms.
- **DARK SOY SAUCE:** I used 'Sushi Chef' brand to calculate the points for this recipe.
- **COARSE GROUND BLACK PEPPER:** In this dish, we are using 'coarse ground' black pepper, NOT regular, finely ground black pepper you used to have in your mom and dad's little pepper shaker. You can either use a pepper mill on the coarsest setting, to grind your own... in which case, you'll end up with forearms like popeye, to get this much. Or, you can buy a container of 'coarse ground black pepper' at the grocery store, in the spice aisle. That's what I do.

2. **(A)** Spray pan with cooking spray, add marinated beef into the pan, press down into a single layer, then allow to cook for 2 minutes, over high heat, without touching it. **(B)** When the meat has seared, untouched, for 2 minutes, toss the meat in the pan. Cook for 2 additional minutes or until juuuust cooked through and no longer pink. **(C)** Return the bell peppers and onions to the pan, then toss to combine. Let the pan get back up to heat, then pour in the sauce. **(D)** Continue to cook for 2-3 minutes, or until the sauce has thickened and coats the beef in a nice, thick coating. Toss and fold the meat and vegetables till the thick sauce is evenly distributed. Serve immediately, garnish with thin sliced green onions, if desired.

3. To make the simple dipping sauce, mix the lime juice with the 1/4 tsp of salt and cracked black pepper. Done.

Beijing Chicken

My Healthier Version of 'Beijing Beef' From Panda Express, Using Chicken Instead of Beef

THIS DISH IS AWESOME!!! This sauce is absolutely fantastic and has an insanely complex flavor. It has deep savoriness from the soy and oyster sauce, sweetness from the hoisin and 'brown sugar', tang from the vinegar, and heat from the chili sauce and pepper flakes. Combine that with extremely tender, breaded chicken and crisp veggies... yeah, get ready for your happy place.

Servings Info.:

Yields: 6 cups
Servings: 4
Serving Size: 1.5 cups

MY PLAN

R D
3-3

- last checked 11/21/22 -
Use your mobile device's 'Camera' App to
look at this code for nutritional info.

Ingredients:

Chicken:
• 1-1/4 pounds boneless skinless chicken breast, or chicken breast tenderloins, cut into bite sized chunks.
• 1/2 tsp baking soda, mixed with 1 tsp water.
• 1 batch of my 'toasted breading' recipe on pg. 17.

Beijing Sauce:
• 1/2 cup fat free beef broth (YES... beef)
• 1-1/2 tsp cornstarch, dissolved into the water
• 1/2 cup 0 calorie brown sugar replacement
• 1/3 cup tomato sauce
• 2-1/2 Tbsp hoisin sauce
• 3 Tbsp reduced sodium soy sauce
• 1 Tbsp 'dark' soy sauce
• 1 Tbsp oyster sauce
• 2 Tbsp apple cider vinegar
• 2 tsp asian chili sauce (I used 'Huy Fong' brand chili garlic sauce)
• 1/2 to 1 tsp red pepper flakes, to taste

Additional Ingredients:
• 1 large onion, quartered, then sliced into strips
• 2 large red bell peppers, cut into roughly 1" pieces.
• 4 medium garlic cloves, minced

Directions:

1. Mix all of the Sauce ingredients together in a bowl, till well combined. Set aside.

2. Preheat oven to 400 degrees. Line a large pan with foil, then spray with cooking spray. Set aside.

3. **(A)** Mix chicken pieces with the baking soda solution, marinate for 20 minutes. **(B)** Dip pieces in egg mixture, making sure to allow extra egg to drip off of the chicken. You just want the pieces to be lightly covered. **(C)** Place dipped chicken, one piece at a time, into the breading and lightly coat. Do not attempt to dump it all in a bag, like shake 'n bake, you'll end up with a bag of mush. Bread these one at a time. Set breaded chicken onto pan, repeat.
(D) Spray breaded chicken with cooking spray. Bake 12 minutes, then remove from oven. Flip the chicken pieces over, then bake 4-5 more minutes, or until breading is a uniform, dark golden brown. Remove from oven.

4. **(A)** Heat a laaaarge pan for 1 minute over medium heat. Spray with cooking spray, then add the chopped bell peppers and onion. Season with salt and pepper. Crank the heat up to medium-high and cook for 4 minutes. **(B)** When the onions are starting to slightly brown at the edges, add the minced garlic. Cook for 1 more minute. **(C)** Pour the sauce into the pan, bring to a boil and cook for 3 minutes, till the sauce is noticeably thicker. **(D)** Fold in and toss the baked chicken pieces, allowing the sauce to continue thickening as it coats all of the pieces. Once all of the chicken is coated in thick sauce, serve immediately.

NOTES & SUGGESTIONS:

- *CRISPINESS:* Though this is a good, healthy alternative to restaurant style deep fried chicken breast pieces, the breading on this chicken WILL lose its crispness after being coated with the sauce for a few minutes. Just like with chicken Parmesan, once your breaded chicken begins to absorb the sauce, it will start to lose its crunchy exterior. Serve right after mixing the chicken and sauce.
- *POINTS:* You can skip the breading and simply cook the chicken pieces in the pan. If you go that route... Marinate the chicken with the baking soda, then cook it in a large pan, till just cooked through. Remove the cooked chicken from the pan, then jump to step **4A**. Best part, you'll save time and lose 1 point per serving.
- *BREAD CRUMBS INSTEAD OF RICE KRISPIES:* If you have access to 1 point per slice bread, instead of using my 'breading 2.0' recipe, for the crumbs... you can make a batch of my low point bread crumbs, from pg. 16. It makes enough real breadcrumbs to double-bread all the chicken for the same points. You'll just need an extra egg or two for the egg wash. But, the chicken will be CRAZY crunchy.
- *SWEETENER:* If you don't want to purchase 0 calorie brown sugar replacement, go ahead and use any sugar replacement you want. The color of the finished dish will end up a little lighter in color though.
- *CHILI SAUCE:* Regular recipes for this dish call for using "Asian sweet chili sauce". That stuff has points. Instead, I use 0 point Asian chili sauce. There's plenty of sweetener in this sauce already.
- *SPICINESS:* As-is, this sauce has a nice subtle heat that is present, but doesn't melt your face off. Feel free to add more chili sauce and/or red pepper flakes, to suit your own preferences.
- *EAT MOR CHIKIN!:* Yes... you can make this with beef, if you want. Use my recipe as a template, then adjust your points.
- *DARK SOY SAUCE:* My recipe's points were calculated using 'Sushi Chef' brand Dark Soy Sauce.

BIBIMBAP

A Lighter, Full Flavored Version of The Famous Korean Rice Bowl That's Taken The U.S. By Storm

Calling 'Bibimbap' a rice bowl is like simply calling Godzilla a reptile. This dish is loaded with so much flavor and varying textures, it's a culinary explosion. Putting it together is a lot of work, but luckily, you can make almost all of the different toppings days ahead of time, for convenience.

Servings Info.:
Yield: 2 BIG bowls
Servings: 2 bowls
Serving Size: errr... 1 bowl

MY PLAN

R D
2-2

*My listed points **DO NOT INCLUDE** rice! Use as much of whatever type of rice you want. Add MY points, to your rice. (see notes)

Ingredients:

Chicken: *(Mix it all together, let marinate for at least 30 mins)*
- 1 good sized boneless skinless chicken breast, sliced into thin bite sized pieces
- 1 Tbsp oyster sauce
- 1 Tbsp reduced sodium soy sauce
- 1/8 tsp baking soda, dissolved into the soy sauce

Vegetables:
- 2 cups carrots, shredded (I used bagged shredded carrot)
- 2 cups zucchini, sliced into thin matchsticks, like the carrots
- 8 oz sliced mushrooms, any variety you want
- 6 oz bean sprouts (plus 1/2 tsp fish sauce, set aside. See '2D')
- 5-6 oz baby spinach, rough chopped

Additional Ingredients:
- 2 servings (1/2 cup) of my "Gochujang" sauce, recipe in the sauces and dips section, pg 23
- 2 large eggs
- 1/2 tsp toasted sesame seeds
- additional salt and pepper, to season veggies, if desired
- Cooked rice... as much as you want. **_(see notes)_**

Directions:

1. (Do Ahead) Make a batch of my Gochujang sauce, then set aside. Can be made 1-2 days ahead of time.

2. Mix the chicken breasts with the oyster sauce/soy sauce/baking soda solution. Let rest for 30 minutes.

2. **(A)** Heat a large pan over medium-high heat for 1 minute. Spray with cooking spray, then add the carrots. Cook for 3-4 minutes, mix in 1 Tbsp Gochujang sauce, set aside. **(B)** Return pan to heat, add zucchini and cook 3-4 minutes, till tender. Stir in 1 Tbsp Gochujang sauce, set aside. **(C)** Return pan to heat, add mushrooms and splash of water. Cover, cook 5 minutes, set aside. **(D)** Put pan back over heat, cook bean sprouts for 4-5 minutes, till tender. Add 1/2 tsp fish sauce, mix well, set aside.

NOTES:

- **_THAT'S A LOT OF PREP/COOKING!:_** Actually... not really. There are 2 ways you can tackle this 'prep-time' behemoth. I personally used method 1... because I'm lazy and it let's you prep a lot of it 1-2 days in advance. Method 2, is for masochists with daddy issues. I've tried both, I'd recommend method 1, unless you have a maid.

  Method 1: Cook the different veggies, as well as the sauce separately, over the course of a few days. Store them in the fridge, till ready to eat. The day of, simply warm 'em all up, cook the chicken and egg... then boom, done.

  Method 2: The veggies all cook quickly. Use 2 or 3 pans and cook them all at the same time on your stove. You'll be done with the veggies and chicken in 15 minutes. But, your kitchen'll look like Tokyo, after a 1950's Kaiju movie.

- **_RICE:_** As stated, my listed points <u>DO NOT</u> take your rice into account. Use as much or as little as you want, then add my points to your rice. Example: In MY dish, pictured on these pages, I used 3/4 cup white rice, which is 5 points. The actual ingredients of the bowl (everything other than the rice) is 2 points for 1 serving. So, for me... my Bibimbap bowl was 7 points. 5 for the rice, 2 for the chicken, veggies and sauce.

3. **(A)** Preheat pan for 1 minute over medium-high heat, add chicken, then cook for 4-5 minutes. Set aside **(B)** Return pan to heat, add the chopped spinach, cover with a lid and cook till wilted (3-4 minutes). Set aside. **(C)** Organize all your cooked ingredients. Now... let's get crackin'. **(D)** Reduce the heat in your pan to medium. Spray with cooking spray, then add 1 egg into the center of the pan. If egg whites start spreading everywhere, use a rubber spatula to push it all in together till it stays put. Reduce heat to medium-low. Cook egg till the egg whites are JUST cooked through. Set aside, repeat with 2nd egg.

4. **(A)** Add cooked rice to the center of a large bowl or plate. **(B)** Arrange half of the vegetables and chicken, separated, around the rice. **(C)** Add the sunny-side up egg over the top of the rice. **(D)** Pour 1/4 cup of warmed Gochujang sauce over the egg and garnish with 1/4 tsp sesame seeds. Done. When ready to eat, break the egg yolk and mix the entire dish together. It sounds crazy... but it is fantastic.

BLACK PEPPER CHICKEN

Ginger Marinated Chicken Breast in a Spicy Black Pepper Sauce

My 2nd favorite dish to get at Panda Express, as far as their chicken entrees go, has always been their Black Pepper Chicken. However, I stopped getting it once I joined WW, because I'm a points hoarder. So... I've finally gotten around to making my own version. This dish is extremely simple to make, and other than fresh ginger and some rice vinegar, uses common ingredients that most everyone already has. This lightened version is extremely flavorful, with a smoky and savory sauce, that allows you to control the heat. Remember... use COARSE ground pepper, they sell it like that at the store, in the spice aisle.

Servings Info.:
Yields: 5 cups
Servings: 4
Serving Size: 1-1/4 cup

- last checked 11/21/22 -
Use your mobile device's 'Camera' App to look at this code for nutritional info.

Ingredients:

Chicken:
• 1.5 pounds boneless skinless chicken breast, or chicken breast tenderloins, cut into bite sized chunks.

Marinade:
• 2 Tbsp reduced sodium soy sauce
• 2 Tbsp rice vinegar
• 1/4 tsp baking soda (trust me)
• 1 tsp fresh ginger minced. Or you can use 1/4 tsp ground ginger, but the flavor won't be as awesome-sauce.

Black Pepper Sauce
• 5 Tbsp reduced sodium soy sauce
• 1/2 tsp 0 point sweetener o' choice
• 2-1/2 tsp 'dark' soy sauce
• 1-1/2 tsp cornstarch dissolved into 1 Tbsp water
• 1 Tbsp COARSE GROUND black pepper, to taste***

Additional Ingredients:
• 1 large onion, quartered and rough chopped (see pictures)
• 5 large celery ribs, sliced on a bias, about 1/4 inch thick
• Additional salt 'n peppa (not the 90's group), if needed.
• Green onion, thin sliced, for garnish
• Up to 1 tsp sesame seeds, for garnish

Directions:

 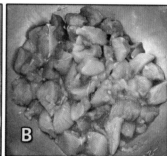

1. **(A)** Cut all of the chicken into bite sized pieces and place into a mixing bowl. Stir together the marinade ingredients, then add to the chicken. **(B)** Cover and set aside for 30 minutes.

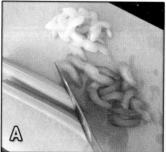 

2. **(A)** Slice the celery at a bias, keeping the slices around 1/4" thick. **(B)** Then, quarter the onion and chop it into good sized chunks. We aren't going for a fine dice. Reference the picture at the top of the page for a good visual. Set aside.

3. Preheat a large pan or wok over high heat, till a splash of water in the pan immediately evaporates.

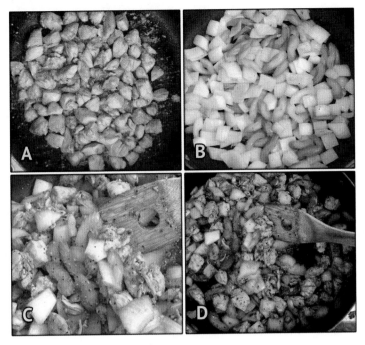

4. **(A)** Spray the pan with cooking spray, then add the chicken. Cook over high heat until just browned. In a large pan, it took 5 minutes for me, but in a wok it might be faster. **(B)** Remove chicken from the pan and set aside. Add onions and celery to the pan, and cook over high heat until slightly softened and beginning to caramelize/brown around the edges. **(C)** Add the chicken back into the pan, along with the black pepper, toss to combine. **(D)** Stir the cornstarch into the remaining 5 Tbsp of soy sauce, then pour into the pan, still cooking at high heat. The sauce should immediately begin to sizzle, reduce and thicken, turning into a thick sauce that coats the chicken. Done. Garnish with thin sliced green onions and a 0 point amount of sesame seeds.

NOTES & SUGGESTIONS:

- *VINEGAR:* If you don't have rice vinegar, you can use regular white vinegar, but add 1/4 tsp sweetener or sugar to it. Rice vinegar has a slight sweetness to it.
- *PROTEIN:* It goes without saying, for a vegetarian option, you can replace the chicken with firm tofu.
- *GLUTEN FREE:* If you have a Gluten intolerance, you can use 'Tamari' type Soy Sauce. It's available in all major super markets and walmarts. Also, cornstarch is gluten free, so you're good to go.
- *COARSE GROUND BLACK PEPPER:* Do NOT USE regular table shaker black pepper, that stuff is finely ground. You need to use pepper that's 'coarse ground', where the bits o' black pepper are larger sized granules. Also, start low on the amount of black pepper, then add more to taste. You don't want to burn the roof of your mouth off. Adust the heat to your own liking.
-- *LARGE FRYING PAN vs. WOK:* I'm using a large pan instead of a Wok, because most people don't have one. My recipes will always use common equipment in their preparations, to make the dishes as accessible as possible. Hence, why I also don't use an air fryer or grill. Not everyone has a grill, but everyone has an oven or toaster oven. Same with good ol' frying pans. Now, in the words of my Uncle... "Allez Cuisine!"
- *DARK SOY SAUCE:* To keep things consistent, I used 'Sushi Chef" brand dark soy sauce, to calculate the points for this recipe.

BULGOGI BEEF STIR FRY

My Healthier Version of The Fantastic Korean BBQ Beef, Turned Into A Stir Fry

If you've ever gone out for Korean BBQ, you know what Bulgogi Beef is. As served at restaurants, it's extremely thin sliced, tender cuts of beef, marinated in a savory, sweet, sliiiighly spicy sauce. They bring it to you on a big plate, raw... and you cook it on a big open grill in the center of your table. It... is... fantastic. Unfortunately, it's also INSANELY high in points (I call BS on the '5 points per serving', for the generic listing in the database). REGULAR Bulgogi recipes have a ton of: *sugar, sesame oil, high point Korean chili sauce, Asian cooking wine*.... Traditional recipes are 'point bombs', so, "5 points" is a lie. My version is skinnied down and made into a stir fry, just to get it to only 4 points

Servings Info.:

Yields: 6 cups, packed
Servings: 6
Serving Size: 1 cup, packed

MY PLAN R D 3-4

- last checked 11/21/22 -
Use your mobile device's 'Camera' App to look at this code for nutritional info.

Ingredients:

Meat:
- 1-1/2 pounds uncooked lean trimmed sirloin (see notes)

Marinade:
- 1/4 tsp baking soda, dissolved with 1/2 tsp water
- 15oz canned pears, no sugar added. Drain and rinse, then puree the pears. You'll end up with **1/2 cup pureed pear.**
- 6-1/2 Tbsp lower sodium soy sauce
- 2 Tbsp 'dark' soy sauce
- 3-1/2 Tbsp 0 point sweetener o' choice (I used monkfruit)
- 2 Tbsp rice vinegar
- 6 medium garlic cloves or 2 Tbsp, minced
- 1 Tbsp fresh ginger, minced
- 2 tsp Asian chili sauce (I used Huy Fong chili garlic)
- 1-1/2 tsp miso paste
- 1 tsp sesame oil
- 1/4 tsp black pepper

Additional Ingredients:
- 1 tsp toasted sesame seeds (see 3A)
- 1 large onion, quartered and thin sliced
- 1/2 cup shredded carrots (thin strips, like for coleslaw)
- 1 large red bell pepper, sliced into thin strips
- 1 bunch green onions, sliced into 2" pieces
- 1-1/2 tsp cornstarch dissolved into 1 Tbsp water, set aside

Directions:

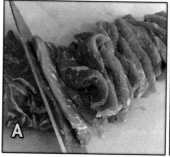
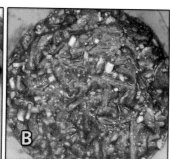

1. **(A)** Trim as much fat and gristle off of the beef as you can, then THINLY slice the beef, seriously... THIN. Really, I'm talkin' 1/8" thick. We want thin and tender meat.
   (B) Mix the marinade together, till well combined. Rub the marinade all over the meat. Marinate the meat for at least a few hours, overnight if you can.

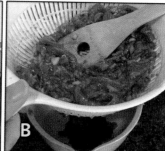

2. **(A)** When the meat has finished marinating, prep and slice all your veggies. **(B)** Just trust me on this... place the meat, in 2 batches, into a strainer over a bowl. You want to remove a good deal of the marinade. There will still be some left on the meat, but we want to sautee the meat... not braise it in a ton of liquid.

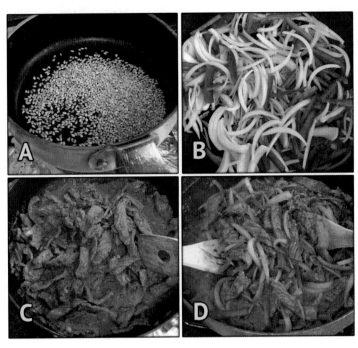

3. **(A)** Add 1tsp sesame seeds into a small pan and cook for a few minutes over medium heat, till the sesame seeds are toasted and golden. Set aside. **(B)** Preheat a LARGE pan for 1 minute over medium-high heat, then spray with cooking spray. Add the onion, carrots and bell pepper. Cook 3-4 minutes, or till they begin to caramelize and sweat. Remove veggies from pan, then return pan to the heat. **(C)** Add half of the meat to the pan *(see, there's still a fair amount of liquid)* and cook for 3-4 minutes, till just cooked through. Pour into a large bowl, then add the 2nd half of the meat. Once the second batch is cooked **(D)** add all of the meat and vegetables back into the pan, along with the green onions, the cornstarch solution and HALF of the toasted sesame seeds. Cook for an additional 1-2 minutes, till all ingredients are well coated in thick sauce. Garnish with the remaining toasted sesame seeds. Done.

NOTES & SUGGESTIONS:

-   *SIRLOIN:* We are using a VERY SPECIFIC entry in the database for our meat. When you are checking the points for this, or adding it into your database, make sure to use the entry for uncooked lean trimmed sirloin. It's 14 total points.
-   *CHICKEN:* Don't want to use beef? No problem. Use chicken breast instead. The entire platter will drop down to only 1 point per serving on both the 'regular' and 'diabetic' plans.
-   *DARK SOY SAUCE:* I used 'Sushi Chef' brand dark soy sauce, when calculating this recipe's points.
-   *SLICING IT THIN:* Slicing the meat thin is important for this dish. The colder the meat is, the easier it is to slice. If ou put it in the freezer for 20 mins before slicing, you can make super thin slices much easier than room temperature meat.
-   *PEARS:* You can peel, slice and puree fresh pears, or use unsweetened 0 point canned, drained pears like I did. I bought a 15oz can of no sugar added pears (in water), then drained, rinsed and pureed the pears. I ended up with 1/2 cup of pear puree. REGULAR bulgogi recipes use pear JUICE, which is very high in points. I'm reducing the points to 0 on the 'regular plan' by using puree instead of juice.

CHICKEN & BROCCOLI

My Leaner Version of Take-Out Beef & Broccoli. Though, Let's Be Real... Use Beef If Ya Want

One of my favorite 'veggie-heavy' dishes is regular beef & broccoli. Funny part is, I don't really care to eat the beef. My favorite part is the broccoli florets, once they begin to absorb the rich and savory sauce. My version uses a LOT less soy sauce than is in traditional 'skinny' food blogger recipes, with some using nearly 3/4 cup of soy sauce, with over 1500mg of sodium per serving. Mine has 1/3 of that, a lot less 'sugar' than normal, but still retains a great depth of flavor, thanks to the addition of our secret weapon of culinary destruction... 'DARK' soy sauce.

Servings Info.:

Yields: 9 cups
Servings: 6
Serving Size: 1-1/2 cup

MY PLAN

R D
1-1

- last checked 11/21/22 -
Use your mobile device's 'Camera' App to look at this code for nutritional info.

Ingredients:

Chicken & Marinade:
- 1.5 pounds boneless skinless chicken breast, or chicken breast tenderloins, cut into thin slices
- 1/4 tsp baking soda, mixed with 2 tsp water.

Sauce:
- 1-1/2 cups fat free beef broth (use 0 point brand)
- 2-1/2 Tbsp cornstarch, dissolved into the beef broth
- 3 Tbsp reduced sodium soy sauce
- 2 Tbsp <u>DARK</u> soy sauce (see notes)
- 1 tsp sesame oil
- 1-1/2 Tbsp oyster sauce
- 1/4 tsp red pepper flakes
- 1/8 to 1/4 tsp black pepper, to taste
- 1 Tbsp 0 point sweetener o' choice
- 4 medium garlic cloves, crushed and minced
- 1/2 tsp ginger, minced

Additional Ingredients:
- 24oz uncooked broccoli florets. I purchased (2) 12oz bags of 'Green Giant' broccoli florets. Though, you can use fresh.
- 1 tsp sesame seeds, for garnish

Directions:

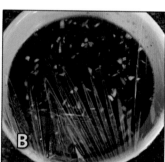

1. **(A)** Mix chicken pieces with the marinade ingredients, let sit for 20 minutes. **(B)** Meanwhile, in a separate bowl, mix the sauce ingredients together. Set aside.

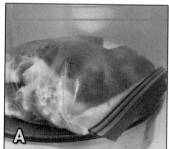
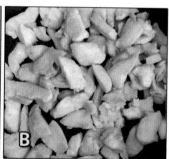

2. **(A)** Now, let's QUICK-steam the broccoli. You can either place the broccoli in 1 or 2 large ziplock bags, poke a small hole into the bag(s) with a knife, then cook for 2 minutes. Or... use the bags the florets came in, if microwave safe. 'Nuke' for 2 minutes, then remove broccoli from bags to stop them from steaming. Set aside. **(B)** Heat a large pan over medium-high heat for 1 minute. Spray with cooking spray, then place chicken into the pan. Cook for 5 minutes, or till just cooked through.

- *PROTEIN:* Though my dish uses chicken, you can definitely make this with beef, if you'd like. If you do so, remember to adjust your points. If you're going a vegetarian route, you can also use extra firm tofu. If you do, don't use the baking soda in the marinade... That'd be disgusting.
- *GLUTEN FREE:* If you have a Gluten intolerance, you can use 'Tamari' type Soy Sauce. You can also find gluten free, vegan oyster sauce, like mentioned above, as well as making a gluten free 'dark soy sauce' substitute, by adding some molasses to Tamari soy sauce. Though, it might change the points. Also, cornstarch is gluten free, so you're good to go.
- *DARK SOY SAUCE:* I used 'Sushi Chef' brand while calculating the points for this recipe. If you use a different brand, adjust your points if needed.
- *LARGE FRYING PAN vs. WOK:* I'm using a large pan instead of a Wok, because most people don't have woks. My recipes will always use common equipment in their preparations, to make the dishes as accessible as possible. Hence, why I also don't use an air fryer or grill. Not everyone has a grill, but everyone has an oven or toaster oven. Same with good ol' frying pans. Now, in the words of my Uncle... "Allez Cuisine!"

3. **(A)** When the chicken is just cooked through, increase the heat to high, then pour in the sauce, stir to combine. **(B)** Cook over high heat for 4-5 minutes, stirring while the sauce continues to reduce, thicken and coat the chicken. **(C)** Once the sauce has thickened to a good consistency, add the lightly steamed broccoli florets to the pan. Fold the broccoli into the dish, till well mixed, then cover with a lid. Reduce heat to medium-high, then cook, covered, for 1 more minute. **(D)** Turn off heat, remove lid, then toss till the broccoli and chicken are both well coated in the sauce. Pour into a large serving bowl or platter, garnish with sesame seeds.

CHICKEN JAPCHAE NOODLES

Korean 'Glass' Noodles with Chicken, Vegetables & Toasted Sesame Seeds in a Sweet/Savory Sauce

Korean food is something new to me, so I was excited to look up as many new dishes as I could. This one uses 'Glass' noodles. They are made from sweet potato starch and can be found in the Asian aisle at your supermarket. Once cooked, they are nearly translucent, with an AWESOME texture. You will absolutely love 'em.

Ingredients:

Meat:
- 1-1/2 lb chicken breast, sliced into thin, bite sized pieces
- 1/4 tsp baking soda, dissolved in 1 tsp water
- 1 Tbsp sauce, see below

Sauce:
- 3 Tbsp PLUS 1 tsp reduced sodium soy sauce
- 1 Tbsp 'dark' soy sauce
- 5 medium garlic cloves, minced
- 3 Tbsp sweetener o' choice (I used Lakanto monkfruit)
- 1 Tbsp rice vinegar
- 1 tsp sesame oil
- 1/4 tsp each: salt, and cracked black pepper

Vegetables:
- 1 LAAAARGE onion, halved, sliced into strips
- 8oz sliced mushrooms (white, shitaki, oyster, whatever)
- 1-1/4 cup carrot, 'shredded' (long strips, like for coleslaw)
- 1 large yellow bell pepper, sliced into thin strips
- 1/2 cup green onion, sliced into 2" pieces, loosely packed
- 5-7oz baby spinach, rough chopped (see notes)

Additional Ingredients:
- 8oz uncooked sweet potato 'glass' noodles (see notes)
- 1 tsp toasted sesame seeds

Directions:

1. Mix all of the sauce ingredients together. Set aside. Combine the chicken, baking soda mixture and 1 Tbsp of the sauce. Set aside for 20-30 minutes.

Servings Info.:

Yield: 12 cups
Servings: 8
Serving Size: 1.5 cups

R D
3-3

- last checked 11/21/22 -
Use your mobile device's 'Camera' App to
look at this code for nutritional info.

2. **(A)** Boil the 'glass' noodles, according to package directions. Rinse under cold water to stop the cooking process. **(B)** Use kitchen shears to snip the noodles a few times, then set aside. **(C)** In a small little pan or pot, heat sesame seeds over medium-low heat, till lightly browned. Set aside. **(D)** Heat a large pan over High heat for 1 minute. Spray with cooking spray, then add the chicken. Cook until just cooked through, then pour the cooked chicken into a bowl and return pan to the heat.

- **SWEET POTATO 'GLASS' NOODLES:** These noodles are made from the starch of sweet potatoes. You can find these in the Asian aisle of the grocery store, where they sell Asian-style noodles. My store sold them in small 3.5oz packages, so I actually had to buy 3 bags, then weigh 8oz. If you cannot find them, feel free to substitute them with spaghetti, as once cooked, the noodles are the same exact size. The texture of 'glass' noodles... is unique. For you folks who have never had them before, I HIGHLY recommend giving them a try. The noodles are nearly see-through, and have a slight chewy 'bounce' to them. It makes for a very, very unique "mouth-feel" for a noodle dish. Also, in case anyone needs to know, for tracking, my recipe uses 26 points-worth of them.
- **SHIRATAKE NOODLES:** Believe it or not, those 0 point noodles that come in sealed bags of water, are actually really good substitutions for glass noodles, in Asian dishes.
- **CARROTS:** Ok, this caused some confusion in prior recipes. When I say 'shredded carrots', I mean the bagged, shredded carrots you find in the produce department of your grocery store. The carrots are in long, very, very thin matchsticks, like you'd find in coleslaws. They aren't truly shredded, like you'd get from a hand grater.
- **SPINACH:** I'm not going to be an exact-measurment kind of guy with this. Different stores carry different sized small bags of spinach. Get anything in-between 5 to 7 ounces.

3. **(A)** Add onions to the hot pan, cook for 2-3 minutes or until just browning. Pour cooked onions into a large bowl, return pan to heat. **(B)** Add the carrots, mushrooms and a a splash of water to the pan. Cook for 2 minutes, or till the mushrooms are just browning. Pour veggies into the same bowl as the onions. **(C)** Return pan to heat, spray with cooking spray, then add bell pepper, cook for 1 minute. Add the green onions, cook for 1 more minute. Pour into the bowl with the other cooked veggies. **(D)** Return pan to heat and add spinach. Cook till slightly wilted, then add to the bowl of cooked vegetables.

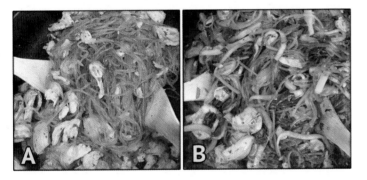

4. **(A)** Reduce heat to medium, then return the chicken to the pan, along with the sauce and noodles. Toss and toss and toss the chicken, noodles and sauce, until the sauce has been almost completely absorbed into the noodles, turning them a dark brown color. **(B)** Add the big bowl 'o vegetables to the pan, then carefully. Add all of the toasted sesame seeds into the pan, then gently fold all of the ingredients together, repeatedly. It'll take a few minutes, but keep folding and tossing the contents of the pan, till the the entire dish is a nice, dark, uniform color. Done.

SPECIAL NOTE:

The reason why so many of the veggies are being cooked separately, then added together at the end... is because there is a ton of them in this recipe. If we try to cook them all together, they'll all be piled in the pan. We don't want steamed vegetable mush.

CHICKEN MAI FUN

Thin Sesame Seasoned Rice Noodles with Chicken and Vegetables

Alright, first off... this dish actually is darker than what's pictured. For whatever reason, my pictures came out reddish in hue. But, whatevz. This is a pretty danged yummie, low point spin on a Chinese rice noodles dish. Though I use chicken in my recipe, the star of this dish is the noodles, so you can definitely swap out vegetables or protein for ingredients you prefer.

Servings Info.:

Yields: 9-1/4 cups
Servings: 7
Serving Size: 1-1/3 cup

R D
4-4

- last checked 11/21/22 -
Use your mobile device's 'Camera' App to
look at this code for nutritional info.

Ingredients:

Meat:
- 3/4 pound chicken breast
- 1/4 tsp baking soda, mixed with 2 tsp water

Sauce:
- 1/2 cup fat free chicken broth
- 2 Tbsp oyster sauce
- 2-1/2 Tbsp reduced sodium soy sauce
- 1 Tbsp 'dark' soy sauce', I used 'Sushi Chef' brand
- 1 Tbsp white wine
- 1-1/2 tsp each: rice vinegar & balsamic vinegar
- 1/2 tsp 0 point sweetener o' choice (I used lakanto monkfruit)
- 1/2 tsp salt
- 1/4 tsp pepper
- 1 Tbsp PLUS 1-1/2 tsp cornstarch

Veggies:
- 1 cup 'shredded' carrots (the bagged stuff, like for cole slaw)
- 1 large onion, quartered and thinly sliced
- 1 tsp ginger, minced (see notes)
- 1 cup thiiiinly sliced cabbage (can buy 'angel hair' cabbage)
- 1 cup green onions, cut into 2" lengths

Additional Ingredients:
- 8 oz dried vermicelli rice noodles (see notes)
- 2 tsp 'dark' soy sauce, I used 'sushi chef' brand, for noodles
- 1 tsp sesame oil
- 1 tsp toasted sesame seeds. (3/4 tsp in noodles, 1/4 tsp garnish)

Directions:

1. Combine the chicken and baking soda solution, till well mixed. Set aside for 20 minutes. Prepare the noodles according to package directions. Drain, rinse, set aside.

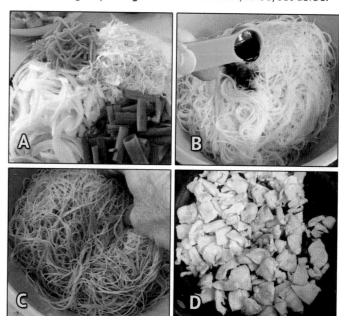

2. **(A)** Make sure that ALL of your veggies and chicken are prepped before you continue. The rest of this comes together quick. **(B)** Place the cooked, drained noodles into a large bowl, add the sesame oil and 2 tsp 'dark' soy sauce. **(C)** This will take a few minutes... but mix the noodles till they take on a dark, uniform color. Set aside. **(D)** Heat a large, high walled pan over high heat for 1 minute. Spray with cooking spray, then add the thin sliced chicken. Cook for 3-4 minutes, or until it's aaaalmost cooked through. It's ok if there's a litle pink.

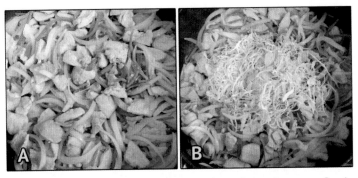

- **RICE NOODLES:** Ok folks, we're using 'vermicelli rice noodles'. They can be found in the Asian food aisle, if your store has them. They look like angel hair pasta, but are even thinner. The might be called vermicelli rice noodles... they might also be packaged as "MAIFUN RICE STICKS". Some brands ask you to boil them for 2-3 minutes, while other brands (like what I used) simply have you soak the noodles in hot water for a few minutes. Follow the package instructions for the noodles you buy, then use them in my recipe.

- **DARK SOY SAUCE:** I used "Sushi Chef" brand, when calculating the points for this recipe.

- **GINGER:** If you don't want to use fresh ginger, you can use ground ginger. However, only use 1/2 tsp ground ginger... and add it to your sauce, not the onions/carrots.

3. **(A)** Add carrots, ginger and onions into the pan. Cook over high heat for 3 minutes. **(B)** Add finely shredded cabbage, stir to mix. Cover pan with lid, cook/steam for 2 minutes.

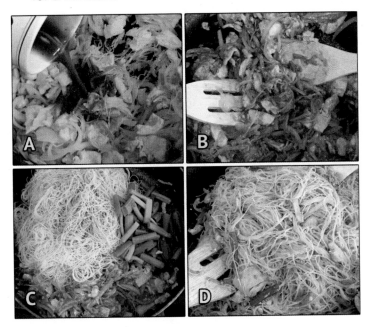

4. **(A)** Pour sauce into pan, it should start thickening almost immediately. **(B)** Stir till the sauce coats the vegetables, then **(C)** lower heat to medium and add the noodles, green onions and 3/4 tsp of the toasted sesame seeds. **(D)** Now... here's the tough part. Toss/Stir/Mix it all, till it's completely combined and the sauce is evenly distributed. "But Daniel, what's so hard about that?" If you haven't tried to mix a dish with these THIN rice noodles before... imagine pouring super glue into Rapunzel's hair, after she wakes up with it in knots.... then, trying to untangle it with kitchen utensils. THAT's about how hard it is. It'll definitely take you a few grumbling minutes to separate the noodles. By the end of it, you'll either thank me, or you'll unfollow me, out of spite. Either way though, don't give up, rice noodles are worth it.

5. Once you've managed the minor miracle of untangling and mixing the noodles... garnish by sprinkling the remaining 1/4 tsp of toasted sesame seeds on top. Then... go get yourself a drink. Done.

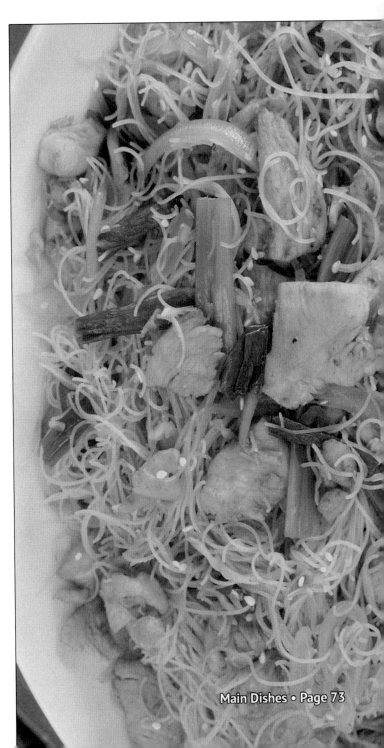

CHICKEN PANANG CURRY

Tender Chicken And Bell Peppers In A Rich, Flavorful & Spicy Coconut Curry Sauce

Panang Curry is an insanely delicious and spicy dish, typically loaded with enough fat and calories to require a triple bypass. I'm hacking it down with some pretty smart ingredient substitutions. In my recipe, I am using a very specific brand of 'panang curry paste', which I ordered online. I usually don't recommend a specific brand of an ingredient, but this brand is really good and lets you have the most, for the points. However, you can definitely use regular red curry paste as a substitute, which is available at most grocery stores. The sauce won't have the depth, but it's still good.

Ingredients:

Chicken:
- 1lb boneless skinless chicken breast, sliced into very thin strips
- 1/4 tsp baking soda, dissolved with 1 Tbsp water

Sauce 1:
- 3 cups low calorie coconut beverage (see notes!). I used 'Silk' brand Almond/Coconut milk blend. Another popular option is 'So Delicious' light coconut beverage. They are in the milk aisle.
- 1 cup fat free chicken broth
- (OPTIONAL) 1/2 to 1 tsp coconut extract (in the baking aisle)

Sauce 2:
- 2 Tbsp fish sauce (found in the Asian food aisle)
- 3 Tbsp lime juice
- 2 Tbsp powdered peanut butter
- 4 medium garlic cloves, minced
- 2 tsp ginger, minced
- 3 Tbsp PLUS 2 tsp cornstarch
- 1/4 tsp salt

Additional Ingredients:
- 1-1/2 to 2 Tbsp Panang Curry Paste *(see notes about brand!!)*
- 1 large red bell pepper, sliced into thin strips
- 1 large green bell pepper, sliced into thin strips
- 1 small onion, halved, sliced into strips
- Pam (or other brand) coconut oil cooking spray
- 1 cup fresh basil leaves, loosely packed, rough chopped

Servings Info.:

Yield: 6 cups
Servings: 4
Serving Size: 1-1/2 cups

R D
2-2

- last checked 11/21/22 -
Use your mobile device's 'Camera' App to look at this code for nutritional info.

Directions:

1. Mix together the chicken & baking soda, set aside for 20 minutes. Prepare Sauces 1 & 2, both in separate bowls/containers. Set aside.

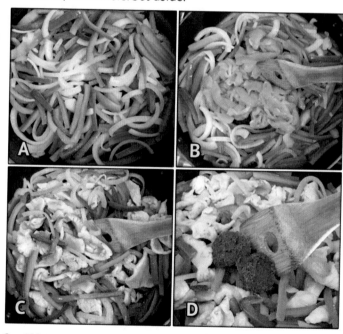

2. **(A)** Preheat a LARGE pan over high heat for 1 minute. Spray with a 0 point amount of coconut cooking spray, add bell peppers and onion. Cook till they start to sweat.
(B) Push veggies to the sides of pan, then add the chicken. **(C)** Cook over High heat, till chicken is ALMOST cooked through, then **(D)** add the curry paste. It will take a few minutes, but break up the curry paste and continue mixing till well coated.

NOTES:

- **_PANANG CURRY PASTE:_** I very very very seldomly recommend you to purchase a specific brand of an ingredient, but in this case, I'm going to. I highly recommend going online and ordering "Mae Ploy Panang Curry Paste". It allows you to have 2 Tablespoons for 1 point. Other brands, such as 'Thai Kitchen' are 1 point for a single teaspoon. The bad thing is it comes in a 14oz container, but you can easily justify it. Take 2 scoop portions of the paste and put them into little snack sized freezer bags. Freeze a few of those, then freeze the big container. Now, if you ever want panang curry, simply grab a little baggie and thaw it out, already portioned out. You'll have panang forever. When you look it up in the database... use the ingredient listing created by '_dhallakx7_'. I converted the servings to teaspoons, rather than everyone else that has it by 'servings'... because, I rock.

- **_PANANG SUBSTITUTE?:_** If you don't want to order that panang paste... no worries. You can go to your local store and purchase some 'red curry paste', located in the Asian food section. The flavor won't have the same flavor or depth, but it won't require you to order special ingredients. Also, be advised, regular red curry paste is typically a little bit spicier than panang curry paste.

- **_COCONUT BEVERAGE???:_** In my recipe, we're eliminating the high fat, high calorie, high point 'light coconut milk', and instead using "coconut beverages". In your grocery store, where they sell the almond, cashew and soy milks... they also sell lightened coconut drinks. Such as "So Delicious" brand unsweetened coconut beverage... which is pretty much coconut milk that's been filtered down to remove the fat, in the same matter as how there's skim milk vs whole milk. A more commonly available alternative is what I used in this recipe, a 'Coconut/Almond milk blend'. Most all major grocery chains, as well as walmarts carry the 'Silk' brand. Making the sauce my way, has 20 less points than regular light coconut milk.

- **_ALLERGIES:_** You can omit the powdered peanut butter.

- **_WHERE'S THE KAFFIR LIME LEAVES??:_** I'm not going to make you find kaffir lime leaves, hence the 3 Tbsp of lime juice. However, if you can get the lime leaves, use 5-6 of them instead of the lime juice. Add at step **3C**.

3. **(A)** When the curry paste is well integrated into the dish, **(B)** pour the coconut beverage/chicken broth mixture into the pan. Allow it to cook for a minute or two, until it comes to a good simmer. **(C)** Once the coconut liquid is simmering, pour in the second sauce, which contains all the snazzy ingredients. Return to a rolling boil for 3-4 minutes, stirring while it thickens. **(D)** Turn off the heat. Add the chopped basil, stir to combine, allowing the basil to wilt. Taste the sauce, add Asian chili sauce if you want it spicier.... but seriously, you shouldn't need it. Because this sauce has no actual fatty milk in it, it's spicier, with less chili used, than regular fatty curry.

"Mae Ploy" brand Panang Curry Paste was the lowest point brand I was able to find online. If you have a local Asian market nearby, it's muuuch cheaper in-store.

CHICKEN WITH BLACK BEAN SAUCE

A Quick And Delicious Dish Loaded With Vegetables With A Tremendously Savory Sauce

One of the things I really wanted to try and push myself to do, with this collection of Asian recipes, is to step out of my culinary comfort zone. Most of the 'popular' ww-friendly food bloggers all make the same exact handful of Asian dishes. Nobody really branches out to more exotic dishes. If there's one thing we know about me, I don't like to play it safe and boring. This dish accomplishes 2 things. It gives you an extremely fast and easy chicken dish, loaded with veggies and a deeply intense, savory flavor. This dish also lets you bust out the jar of 'black bean sauce' I made you get, to make my 'string bean chicken' recipe. I figured if I'm going to make you buy a jar of that stuff, I need to give you more recipes that call for using it.

Servings Info.:

Yields: 7 cups
Servings: 5
Serving Size: 1-1/3 cup

MY PLAN
R D
0-0

- last checked 11/22/22 -
Use your mobile device's 'Camera' App to
look at this code for nutritional info.

Ingredients:

Chicken & Marinade:
- 1-1/2 pounds boneless skinless chicken breast, or chicken breast tenderloins, cut into thin strips
- 1 Tbsp reduced sodium soy sauce
- 2 tsp 'dark' soy sauce (see notes)
- 1/4 tsp baking soda. Trust me, roll with the madness.

Sauce:
- 1/2 cup fat free chicken or beef broth
- 1-1/2 tsp cornstarch stirred into the broth, till dissolved
- 3 Tbsp black bean sauce *** (see notes)
- 1 Tbsp 'dark' soy sauce
- 1 Tbsp white wine (see notes)
- 1 tsp rice vinegar
- 1 tsp balsamic vinegar
- 1 tsp 0 point sweetener o' choice
- 5 medium garlic cloves, finely chopped
- 1 tsp fresh ginger, minced
- 1/4 tsp cracked black pepper

Veggies:
- 1 large onion, quartered, sliced into strips (2-1/2 cups)
- 1 large red bell pepper (2 cups), cut into bite sized chunks
- 1 large or 2 medium green bell peppers (2 cups), cut into bite sized chunks
- 4 green onions, green parts only, sliced into 1 inch lengths

Directions:

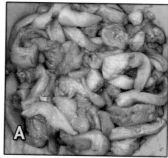

1. **(A)** In a small cup, mix together the soy sauce, dark soy sauce and baking soda. Pour over the sliced chicken breast and allow to rest for 30 minutes.
(B) In a separate bowl, add all of the 'Sauce' ingredients, till well combined. Set aside.

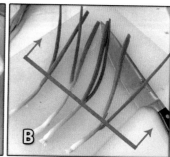

2. **(A)** Cut the bell peppers and onions, set aside.
(B) Slice the upper 'green' portions of 4 green onions (or more, if desired) into 1 inch lengths. Set aside.

3. Heat a LARGE pan over high heat for 1 minute, or until water droplets sizzle off it's surface.

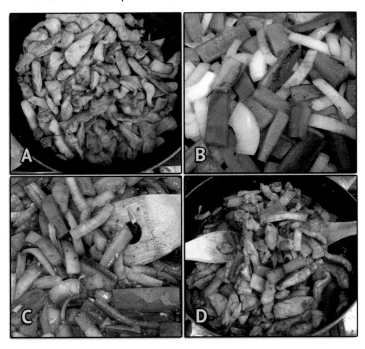

4. (A) Spray hot pan with cooking spray and add the chicken. Spread into 1 even layer, then DON'T TOUCH! Cook for 1 minute, untouched, then stir the chicken and cook again for 1 minute, untouched. Continue for 5 minutes, or till just cooked through. Remove chicken from pan, return pan to heat. **(B)** Add onion and bell peppers to pan, cooking for 4-5 minutes over high heat. **(C)** Pour in the prepared sauce and sliced green onions, stir to combine. Allow to continue cooking and thickening over high heat for 1 minute. **(D)** Add the chicken back into the pan, mix to combine, cooking until the sauce has thickened to a gravy-like consistency. Serve immediately.

NOTES & SUGGESTIONS:

- *BLACK BEAN SAUCE:* BBS Is essential for the traditional version of this dish. Check for it in the Asian food aisle of your local grocery stores. I had to check 6 stores before I found it. You can fix that by ordering some online from walmart or elsewhere. Note, different brands are different points. I used 'Kikkoman' brand, Black Bean Sauce with Garlic, which is 2 points for 3 Tbsp. If you cannot get black bean sauce, use oyster sauce, though it'll have a drastically different flavor. I highly recommend the black bean sauce, as it's also used in my String Bean Chicken.
- *WHITE WINE:* What the heck?... Well, The traditional recipe calls for an Asian sweet wine. I'm not going to tell you to buy that. Instead, we're going to make our own substitute, using regular white wine, plus some sweetener, rice vinegar and balsamic. Problem solved.
- *PROTEIN:* It goes without saying, you can replace the chicken with beef, tofu or seafood. Adjust points if needed.
- *GLUTEN FREE:* If you have a Gluten intolerance, you can use 'Tamari' type Soy Sauce. It's available in all major super markets and walmarts. Also, cornstarch is gluten free, so you're good to go.
- *DARK SOY SAUCE:* I used 'Sushi Chef' brand to calculate the points for this recipe.
- *POINTS:* This recipe lets you have up to 2 servings for 0 points on both the 'regular' and the 'diabetic' plans. However, there IS a lot of sodium, so be mindful of that.

CHOP SUEY

A Filling and Hearty Dish, Loaded With Tons of Fresh Vegetables, With A Thick Yet Mild Sauce

Let's start off by addressing the elephant in the room... Chop Suey's bad rap. It's usually considered disgusting 'strip mall' Chinese fast food that nobody orders. Or if you're like me... you were traumatized by the 'canned' chop suey back when you were a kid. REAL chop suey is fantastic. It is a wide assortment of veggies and a meat, cooked and tossed with a very light and savory sauce. You can customize this dish a million ways. Though my recipe is Chicken Chop Suey, I'm presenting it merely as 'chop suey', so you can use this as a template for your own creation.

Ingredients:

Meat:
- 1-1/2 lb chicken breast, sliced into thin strips
- 1/2 tsp baking soda, dissolved into 1 Tbsp water
- 1 Tbsp reduced sodium soy sauce

Sauce:
- 1 cup fat free beef or chicken broth
- 1-1/2 Tbsp cornstarch, dissolved into the broth
- 1 Tbsp PLUS 2 tsp oyster sauce
- 1 tsp sesame oil
- 1 Tbsp PLUS 1 tsp 'Dark' soy sauce
- 1 Tbsp white wine (see notes)
- 1 tsp rice vinegar
- 1 tsp balsamic vinegar
- 1 Tbsp 0 calorie brown sugar replacement o' choice
- 1/2 tsp cracked black pepper
- 5 medium garlic cloves, minced

Veggies:
- 1 LARGE onion, quartered and thin sliced (around 3 cups)
- 2 cups celery, sliced on a bias (around 3-4 ribs)
- 2 large carrots, sliced on a bias about 1/4" thick, then cut into strips (see picture 1A), around 2 cups.
- 2 cups green leafy vegetable, loosely packed, rough chopped. Though not traditional, I used tuscan kale. (see notes)
- 10 to 12 oz canned 'baby' corn, sliced in half, lengthwise
- 1/2 cup canned bamboo shoots or water chestnuts.

Servings Info.:

Yield: 9 cups
Servings: 6
Serving Size: 1.5 cups

- last checked 11/22/22 -
Use your mobile device's 'Camera' App to look at this code for nutritional info.

Directions:

1. Mix together the chicken with the baking soda/soy sauce. Set aside for 20-30 minutes.

2. Mix the sauce ingredients together, set aside.

3. **(A)** Slice the carrots on a bias, then slice into thin strips. **(B)** Slice all of the other vegetables as directed, minus the 'bamboo shoots', they come already sliced. Set aside. **(C)** Heat a LARGE high walled pan over medium high heat for 1 minute. Spray with cooking spray, cook chicken for 5 minutes, till just cooked through. Remove from pan. **(D)** Add carrots to pan, turn heat up to high, cook 1 minute. Add onions, cook for 2 more minutes.

4A | 4B
4C | 4D

4. **(A)** Add celery, bamboo shoots and sliced corn to the pan and cook for 1 more minute. Add the green leafy veggie, toss, cover with a lid and cook for 1 more minute. **(B)** Add the chicken back into the pan, then pour in the sauce. **(C)** Continue to cook, tossing and stirring for 2-3 more minutes, or until the sauce thickens and coats everything. **(D)** Place onto a large platter, serve immediately. As an optional garnish, you can top your platter with up to 7/8 tsp of sesame seeds for 0 points. Another nice garnish would be some thin sliced green onion.

SUBSTITUTION IDEAS:

- You can add fresh minced ginger to the sauce in addition to, or in place of the garlic.
- If you don't want to use canned bamboo shoots, you can use canned 'sliced water chestnuts'. They are pretty crunchy, so you should add them into the dish at the same time as the onions.
- This is an 'empty out your fridge' kind of dish, as far as veggies go. You can replace any of the onions, celery or carrots with whatever you have on hand. Bell peppers, small broccoli florets, broccoli rabe, green snap peas, mushrooms... pretty much anything can go in this dish. Just try to keep the same 'amount', in total, as the other veggies. Otherwise, you'll have less servings and you'll need to adjust the points.
- I used 'Tuscan Kale' for my dish because my local store was out of Bok Choy. I chose Tuscan kale over regular kale because it's a darker color and the ribs on Tuscan kale aren't as hard. Collard greens, mustard greens, regular kale (remove the ribs), or cabbage are other choices for green leafy veggies you can use in place of the tuscan kale that I used. You can ALSO use spinach.... but you'll need about 100lbs of it, considering how much spinach cooks down.
- Another common 'bulk' item in a dish like this, would be adding bean sprouts.

NOTES:

- **PROTEIN:** I'm using chicken, but you can obviously make this dish with beef, pork, or tofu. Adjust points if needed.
- **OYSTER SAUCE:** My wife HATES oyster sauce... a fact I learned after I made this dish. If you are vegetarian, or don't like the slight seafoody taste of oyster sauce, you can purchase vegetarian oyster sauce at stores. It's made from mushrooms.
- **DARK SOY SAUCE:** I used 'Sushi Chef' brand, to calculate the points for this recipe.
- **LARGE FRYING PAN vs. WOK:** I'm using a large pan instead of a Wok, because most people don't have woks. My recipes will always use common equipment in their preparations, to make the dishes as accessible as possible. Hence, why I also don't use an air fryer or grill. Not everyone has a grill, but everyone has an oven or toaster oven.
- **WHITE WINE:** Traditional recipes call for Chinese cooking wine. Because it's high in points and I don't want to make you order it, we're making an easy substitution. By mixing some white wine with a little 'brown sugar', rice vinegar and balsamic vinegar, we get a similar flavor profile with ingredients you probably already have in your pantry.
- **POINTS:** On both plans, only the first serving is 0 points. After that, you can have up to 4 servings for 1 point. Though I hiiiighly don't recommend eating 6 cups of this. 0 points doesn't mean 0 calories. Plus... you'll pop.

CHOW MEIN

A Lightened Up Take On Basic Chow Mein Noodles

There are so many variations on how to properly cook traditional Chow Mein noodles it'd make your head spin, so I'll just start off by saying, this is not traditional. This is my low calorie, low fat take on the Chow Mein from Panda Express. I use store bought 'Soba' noodles in this recipe, but you are more than welcome to use any type of noodles you want. The amount of cabbage and onion may seem like a lot, but they cook down. I tried the recipe with half the veggies, but I really preferred it using the full amount of cabbage and onion, as shown below. If you'd like this to be more of a main course, you can add chicken, shrimp, pork, beef or tofu. Doing so will add bulk to the dish, giving you even more servings, so you'll need to adjust the points.

Ingredients:

Noodles:
- 6oz package of dried Asian 'Soba' style noodles. I used 24 points worth. Different brands have different point values. They are located in the Asian food aisle.

Veggies:
- 1 large onion, halved, and thin sliced.
- 1 large head of cabbage. Core removed, slice the cabbage in half, then slice each half into (4) 1/4's *(pictured in 1A)*.

Sauce:
- 3 Tbsp reduced sodium soy sauce
- 3 Tbsp oyster sauce

Additional Ingredients:
- Green onion, thin sliced on a bias, for garnish.
- 1 tsp sesame seeds, for garnish

Servings Info.:

Yield: 6 cups
Servings: 6
Serving Size: 1 cup

- last checked 11/21/22 -
Use your mobile device's 'Camera' App to look at this code for nutritional info.

Directions:

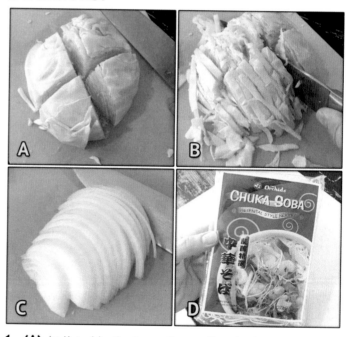

1. **(A)** As listed in the ingredients, slice the large head of cabbage in half, then cut each half into 1/4's as shown. **(B)** Slice each of the sections into roughly 1/4 inch thick strips, then chop across them all a few times. Set aside. **(C)** Slice the onion in half, lengthwise, then cut into 1/4 inch wide strips. Place the onions and cabbage into a large mixing bowl, season with some salt, toss, then set aside for later use. **(D)** I'm pretty much only including this picture, so you can see the type of 'Soba' noodles I used. As long as what you get says Soba on it, you should be fine.

2. Bring a large pot of water to a boil, then preheat a LARGE pan or a wok over high heat for 30-40 seconds.

NOTES:
- **NOODLES:** For this recipe, I used 'Soba Noodles', which are in the Asian food aisle. There are many different brands and varieties, all with varying points. The package that I bought was 6oz for a total of 24 points.
- **NOODLE SUBSTITUTIONS:** You can use any type of noodle you would like. 8oz of regular whole wheat spaghetti can be used in place of the Soba noodles, though the texture will be different. You can also use other types of Asian noodles, even the vacuum sealed soba or buckwheat noodles in the refrigerated Asian foods section. You do you. However, remember that my recipe assumes 24 points of DRIED noodles.... which expand and make a lot more pasta than 24 points of already cooked, vacuum sealed Asian noodles.

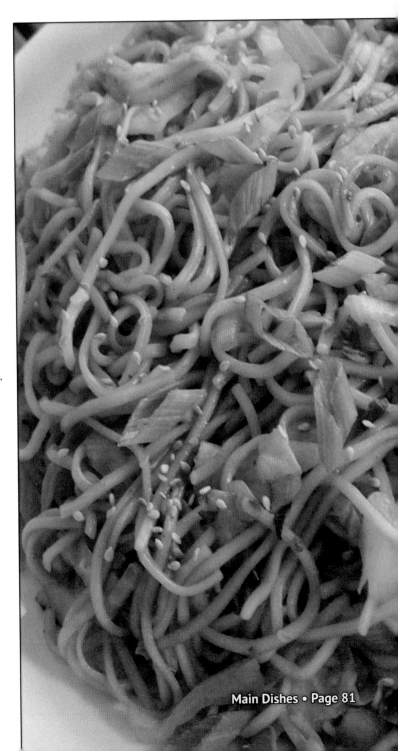

3. **(A)** Spray the hot pan with cooking spray, then add the onions and cabbage. Cook for 5-6 minutes, till the veggies start to sweat and slightly brown. **(B)** While the veggies are cooking down, add your 'Soba' noodles to the boiling water. The packaging says to cook them for 2 minutes, but we want them to be plumper, so I cook them for 6 minutes. **(C)** Drain the noodles and rinse them off with cold water to stop them from cooking and getting mushy. While they are in the colander, use scissors to snip them 2 or 3 times. "WHAT!?!?!? Cuttin the noodles!?!" We're shooting for shorter noodles, like at Panda Express. Leave them long if you want, Nancy! **(D)** Now, your veggies should have some caramelization to them. So now, **(E)** gently fold the noodles into the vegetables, to combine. **(F)** Pour in the soy sauce and oyster sauce. Fold it all together till the noodles are well coated. Done.

4. Serve hot. Garnish with thin sliced green onions, cut on a bias, along with sesame seeds.

Drunken Noodles

Despite it's funny monicker, this noodle dish is freakin' delicious. Tender chicken is tossed with sautéed mixed veggies, ginger, garlic, a rich and savory sauce, with a little spicy kick. However, what absolutely MAKES this dish is the rice noodles.

Ingredients:

Meat:
- 1.5 lbs chicken breast, sliced into thin, bite sized strips
- 1/4 tsp baking soda, dissolved in 1 tsp water
- 1 Tbsp low sodium soy sauce

Sauce:
- 2 Tbsp reduced sodium soy sauce
- 2-1/4 tsp 'dark' soy sauce
- 1 Tbsp Asian 'fish' sauce
- 2 tsp oyster sauce
- 2 tsp Asian chili sauce (I used Huy Fong Chili Garlic sauce)
- 1-1/2 tsp cornstarch, stirred in till dissolved
- 1/4 tsp sesame oil

Vegetables:
- 5-6 medium garlic cloves, sliced thin
- 1 tsp fresh ginger, minced
- 1 LARGE onion, halved, then sliced into thin strips
- 1 LARGE red bell pepper, sliced into thin strips
- 1/2 cup green onions, sliced into 2" pieces
- 10 baby corn ears, sliced in half, lengthwise
- 1 cup Thai Basil leaves OR.... 2 cups 'regular' Basil with 1 Tbsp finely chopped fresh tarragon.

Additional Ingredients:
- 8oz uncooked wide RICE noodles (see notes)

Directions:

1. Combine the chicken, baking soda and soy sauce. Set aside for 20-30 minutes. In a separate cup, mix all the sauce ingredients till smooth, cover, set aside.

Servings Info.:

Yield: 9-1/4 cups
Servings: 7
Serving Size: 1-1/3 cups

- last checked 11/22/22 -
Use your mobile device's 'Camera' App to look at this code for nutritional info.

2. **(A)** Slice and prep all the vegetables, set aside. **(B)** Cook the rice noodles according to package directions. Rinse and set aside. **(C)** Heat a large pan over high heat for 1 minute. Spray with cooking spray, add the marinated chicken. Cook until just cooked through, about 5 minutes. Remove chicken from pan, setting aside, then return pan to heat. **(D)** Spray the pan with cooking spray, then add the garlic, ginger, onion and bell pepper. Cook for 3-4 minutes, till they start to slightly caramelize around the edges.

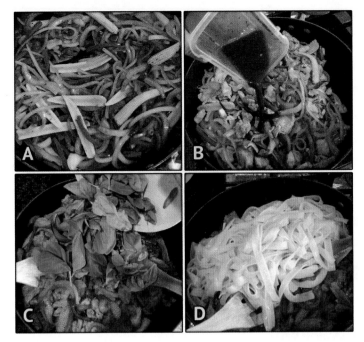

- **RICE NOODLES:** Ok folks, we're using a new ingredient your local stores may not have, mine didn't... WIDE rice noodles. They can sometimes be found in the Asian food aisle, or at Asian/Ethnic grocery stores. Honestly though, I ordered a 16oz box off of Amazon. The brand is called "A Taste of Thai, Wide Rice Noodles". With Prime, it cost me $8 to get a 16oz box delivered 'next day'. Can't beat that, considering I spent hours driving to different stores to find them, with no luck. Follow the package instructions for the noodles you buy. Some brands want you to boil the noodles for 5-6 minutes, some ask you to soak the noodles for an hour... do what your box says, but you want them 'al-dente'. If you have no desire to order the wide rice noodles, you can use fettuccini, or extra wide pappardelle pasta. However, the texture will be VERY different. It'll still be good... just, not as good. My recipe used 23 points of dried, wide rice noodles.

- **GLUTEN SENSITIVITIES:** Rice noodles are gluten free. You can also buy gluten free soy sauce, called 'tamari' soy sauce.

- **BABY CORN:** These are those funky lookin' little mini ears of corn, you used to see at salad bars. You can find them either by the canned corn or in the Asian food aisle.

- **THAI BASIL OR SUBSTITUTIONS:** Thai Basil has a stronger basil flavor than 'regular' basil. It also has a slight licorice flavor. If you can't get Thai Basil (I can't), a simple way to substitute for it is to use twice as much 'regular' basil, and add something with a licorice flavor. In this case, tarragon.

3. **(A)** Add the sliced green onions and baby corn to the pan. Cook for 1 minute over high heat, tossing to combine. **(B)** Return chicken to the pan, then pour in the sauce. Cook for 1-2 minutes, stirring/tossing till the chicken and veggies are coated in a thick, uniformly dark sauce. **(C)** Add the fresh herbs (either Thai Basil or Basil & Tarragon), toss to combine. Once the basil begins to wilt, **(D)** Add the pre-cooked rice noodles to the pan and reduce heat to medium. Toss, toss and toss it all together, until the noodles are completely coated in sauce, 1-2 minutes.

4. **(A)** Try a piece of one of the noodles. If they are still too firm, continue cooking for an additional minute or two, till the texture, like Goldilocks, is juuuuust right. **(B)** Grats, you're done. Now, to keep with the recipe's name, feel free to crack a 'cold one', then get your grub-on, Gangnam Style... Yeah, I know you just read that text bubble in-tune with the song, sexy lady.

Keep In Mind:

This is NOT a heavily "sauced" dish. It's not dripping with thick, gravy-like sauce, unlike how you might get this dish at a take-out or strip mall restaurant. The star of this dish is the thick, chewy rice noodles... NOT a quart of sauce.

GENERAL TSO'S CHICKEN

This Spicy, Savory, Sweet & Tangy Dish Is A Favorite At Chinese Restaurants Across America

General Tso's Chicken isn't a 'true' Chinese recipe. It wasn't invented in a monastery, by a Shoalin Monk... but one bite will make you think this dish's Kung Fu is strong.

Think of this as a sweet cousin to Kung Pao chicken, but breaded. It's a bit spicy, but has a good balance between spicy, sweet, savory and sour.

Servings Info.:

Yields: 6 cups
Servings: 6
Serving Size: 1 cup

MY PLAN

R D
2-2

- last checked 11/22/22 -
Use your mobile device's 'Camera' App to look at this code for nutritional info.

Ingredients:

Chicken:
- 1-3/4 pounds boneless skinless chicken breast, or chicken breast tenderloins, cut into bite sized chunks.
- 1/2 tsp baking soda, dissolved in 1 Tbsp water
- 2 large eggs, whisked together... will be used in step **3B**.

Breading:
- 2 cups rice krispies cereal, measured then lightly crushed
- 1/4 cup panko breadcrumbs
- 1-1/2 tsp flour (any type you want)

General Tso's Sauce & Glaze:
- 1 cup fat free chicken broth
- 3 Tbsp cornstarch, stirred into the broth, till dissolved
- 3 Tbsp PLUS 1 tsp low sodium soy sauce
- 1 Tbsp 'dark' soy sauce
- 4 Tbsp rice vinegar
- 1-1/2 tsp balsamic vinegar (see notes)
- 2 to 3 Tbsp Asian chili sauce (I used Huy Fong chili garlic)
- 4 Tbsp 0 point sweetener o' choice (I used monkfruit)
- 1 Tbsp no sugar added ketchup, OR tomato sauce
- 2 tsp paprika... No, really, I'm serious. (see notes)
- 2 tsp ginger, minced
- 4 medium garlic cloves, minced
- 1 tsp sesame seeds, for garnish

Directions:

1. Marinate the chicken pieces with the baking soda solution for 20 to 30 minutes.

2. Crush the rice krispies till they are the consistency of regular breadcrumbs, set aside.

3. **(A)** Heat a pan over medium heat for 1 minute, then add all breading ingredients. Toast for 3-4 minutes, or until the crumbs are a nice, uniformly golden color. Remove from pan and set aside, letting the crumbs cool to room temperature. **(B)** Place the whisked eggs into the bowl with the chicken pieces, mix to combine. **(C)** Place the toasted crumbs in a bowl, then place the chicken chunks, ONE AT A TIME, into the crumbs. Use a fork to lightly coat each chunk with the breading. **(D)** Place the lightly breaded chicken pieces onto 2 large baking pans, covered with foil and sprayed with a light coat of cooking spray.

4. Mix all of the sauce ingredients together, in a bowl, till well combined. Set aside. Preheat oven to 425 degrees.

5. **(A)** Place the chicken into the oven and bake for 15 minutes. Remove chicken from oven, flip each piece over, then return to oven. Bake for an additional 5-7 minutes, till the chicken is cooked through. Remove and let cool on counter for 5 minutes. **(B)** Heat a LARGE pan over high heat for 1 minute. Stir the sauce again, then pour it into the hot pan. Begin stirring continuously. **(C)** The sauce should begin to thicken almost immediately. Once it gets to the consistency of maple syrup. **(D)** Add the chicken into the pan and toss till completely coated. Slather it up like a cast member of Jersey Shore putting on suntan lotion. Serve immediately. Garnish with sesame seeds.

NOTES & SUGGESTIONS:

- *BREADING:* I strongly advise you NOT to dump all of the breading and chicken into a ziplock bag, then shake it all up. It does NOT work. It takes time, but you need to bread the chicken one piece at a time. It took me around 15 minutes.

- *CRISPINESS:* Though this is a good, healthy alternative to restaurant style deep fried chicken breast pieces, the breading on this chicken WILL lose its crunchiness after being coated with the sauce for a few minutes. Just like chicken Parmesan does. Once your breading begins to absorb the sauce, it'll eventually lose its crunchy exterior. For this dish, toss the chicken into the sauce and serve within a few minutes.

- *BREAD CRUMBS INSTEAD OF RICE KRISPIES:* If you have access to 1 point per slice bread, instead of using my 'breading 2.0' recipe, for the crumbs... you can make a batch of my low point bread crumbs, from pg. 16. It makes enough real breadcrumbs to double-bread all the chicken for the same points. You'll just need an extra egg or two for the egg wash. But, the chicken will be CRAZY crunchy.

- *BALSAMIC!?:* Traditional recipes call for using 'Chinkiang' vinegar. An easy substitution for it is mixing a little balsamic with a some rice vinegar. So, that's what we're doing here.

- *KETCHUP & PAPRIKA!?!?:* In order to get a dark, deep reddish color for the sauce, I'm adding a 0 point amount of no sugar added ketchup, as well as paprika. You can also use canned tomato sauce instead of the ketchup. See that deep red color in my pics? That's from the ketchup, paprika and Asian chili sauce. Without them, the sauce would be dark brown.

- *DARK SOY SAUCE:* I used 'Sushi Chef' brand, for calculating points.

- *HEAT:* You can customize the spice level of this dish by increasing/decreasing the Asian chili sauce.

HOISIN CHICKEN

Sweet, Savory, Fruity And Smoky... This Dish Features Tender Chicken & Veggies In A Rich Sauce

I realized today, other than my Beijing Chicken recipe, I really didn't have any other dishes that used Hoisin sauce. I can't expect you folks to purchase a condiment that's only used once... so the only natural thing for me to do, is make a dish that is completely dependent upon that ingredient. Hmmm... kind of reminds'ya of my Black Bean Chicken, doesn't it? Anyways...Hoisin sauce is an incredibly flavorful paste/sauce that's used in Chinese recipes. It lends a sweet, savory and slightly smoky flavor. Think of it as the base for a good Chinese style BBQ sauce. It's very tasty, but high in points, unless stretched across a large recipe.

Servings Info.:

Yields: 7.5 cups
Servings: 5
Serving Size: 1-1/2 cup

MY PLAN

R D
1-1

- last checked 11/22/22 -
Use your mobile device's 'Camera' App to look at this code for nutritional info.

Ingredients:

CHICKEN:
- 2 pounds boneless skinless chicken breast, cut into bited sized pieces
- 1/2 tsp baking soda, stirred into 1 Tbsp water

SAUCE:
- 4-1/2 Tbsp hoisin sauce
- 2 Tbsp reduced sodium soy sauce
- 2 tsp 'dark' soy sauce (optional, but makes a big difference)
- 1 Tbsp no sugar added ketchup OR canned tomato sauce
- 1/2 to 1 tsp Asian chili sauce, to taste
- 1 tsp ginger, minced
- 1/2 tsp cornstarch, dissolved with 1 Tbsp water

ADDITIONAL INGREDIENTS:
- 2 large red bell peppers, cut into 1/4" wide strips. (2 cups)
- 1 large onion, halved, then sliced into strips
- 6oz bagged fresh snow peas, trimmed (see steps 2A & B)
- (optional) Thin sliced green onions, for garnish, if desired.

Directions:

1. Mix together the chicken with the baking soda. Set aside for 20-30 minutes. While it's marinating, mix the sauce together and chop the onions and bell peppers.

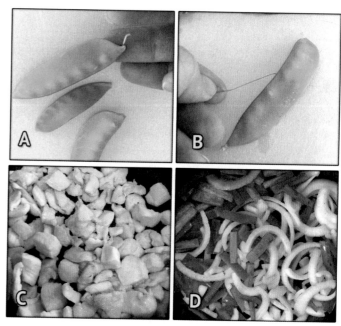

2. **(A)** To 'clean' the snow peas, pinch off the little string on one end, then **(B)** peel back to the opposite end of the pea pod. If it comes off as a long strand, awesome. If it doesn't, that's ok. The primary goal is to at least remove the little string at the end. Set aside **(C)** Heat a LARGE pan over medium-high heat for 1 minute. Spray pan with cooking spray, then add the chicken. Let cook for 2 minutes without stirring. Toss, then cook for an additional 3-4 minutes, or until just cooked through. Pour chicken into a bowl, return pan to heat. **(D)** Spray pan with cooking spray, then add the onions and bell peppers. Turn heat up to High, then cook for 3-4 mins. You want them to begin caramelizing, but still have some crunch to them.

3. **(A)** Add snow peas to the pan, toss to coat, and cook for 1 minute over high heat. **(B)** Pour in the sauce, stirring and tossing to coat, as it thickens. Once the veggies are coated, **(C)** add the chicken back into the pan. **(D)** Continue cooking as you stir/toss the contents of the pan. You want the sauce to thicken and coat the chicken in a thick, dark glaze. Pour the contents of the pan onto a large serving tray or into a serving bowl. If desired, sprinkle with thin sliced green onions, for garnish. Done.

NOTES & SUGGESTIONS:

- *SNOW PEAS:* Are NOOOOOOOT the same as 'snap peas'. Snap peas have a much tougher 'shell'. Buy snow peas. My local grocery store sells them in 6oz bags. If your store only has them in slightly larger bags... don't worry about being exact. Use what you can get.
- *DARK SOY SAUCE:* Once again... I used 'Sushi Chef' brand dark soy sauce, while calculating this recipe's points.
- *WHERE ARE THE PEPPERS?:* I am NOT going to tell you all to go find an Asian market and find/buy dried Chinese chili peppers. That's why I'm using Asian chili sauce for the slight heat in my recipe. It's at every store and it's very easy to adjust to your desired level of heat. However... if you are one of those crazy people that likes face-melty food... feel free to ratchet up the heat by adding more chili sauce. Even sliced jalapeños, spicy Thai peppers, or dried Chinese chili peppers would be an easy addition... you fire-breathing sadists.
- *HOISIN SAUCE:* Is available at ALL major grocery stores and at Walmarts, in the Asian food aisle. It is sold in jars, located near the soy sauce. It is a thick, reddish sauce, which has a rich savoriness, sweetness, and a hint of fruitiness... but must be kept refrigerated after use, or it goes bad. Kind of like *@chiafullo*... but in paste form.

HONEY GARLIC CHICKEN

My Non-Traditional, Kinda Traditional Recipe.... Which Is Both Confusing AND Delicious 😶 😐 🙄

If anyone is here looking for a typical "skinny blogger" honey chicken recipe, consisting of a little garlic, a 1/2 cup of soy sauce and enough honey to make Winnie The Pooh diabetic... sorry. I searched for a TRADITIONAL Chinese recipe, then used ingredient swaps to mimic the flavor profile, while lowering the sugar, calories and points. I also added an onion (non-traditional) to bulk up the dish and add a serving. My recipe has a lot of stuff in it, but it's worth it to have depth of flavor vs. a 1-note, sugary syrup dish.

Ingredients:

Chicken & Marinade:
- 2 lbs boneless skinless chicken breasts, sliced very thin
- 1/2 tsp baking soda... no questions... "Just do'eeeeeet!"
- 1 Tbsp lower sodium soy sauce
- 1 Tbsp white wine
- 1 tsp rice vinegar
- 1 tsp balsamic vinegar (see notes)
- 1 tsp 0 calorie brown sugar replacement
- 1/2 tsp 'dark' soy sauce

Sauce:
- 7 Tbsp fat free chicken broth
- 1-1/2 Tbsp cornstarch, whisked into broth, till dissolved
- 2 Tbsp PLUS 1 tsp lower sodium soy sauce
- 2 Tbsp 0 calorie brown sugar replacement, loosely packed
- 1 Tbsp rice vinegar
- 2 Tbsp PLUS 1 tsp honey
- 3 Tbsp sugar free syrup (pancake syrup)
- 1/4 tsp sesame oil
- 1 tsp sesame seeds
- 6 garlic cloves, crushed and minced
- 1-1/2 tsp ginger, finely minced/chopped
- 1/4 tsp salt
- 1-1/2 tsp 'dark' soy sauce

Additional Ingredients:
- 1 large red onion, quartered, sliced into thin strips
- 1/2 cups green onion, cut into 1" lengths

Servings Info.:
Yields: 6 cups
Servings: 6
Serving Size: 1 cup

MY PLAN

R D
2-2

- last checked 11/23/22 -
Use your mobile device's 'Camera' App to
look at this code for nutritional info.

Directions:

1. Place the thin sliced chicken in a large bowl, then mix together the marinade ingredients. Pour over the meat, mix, then set aside for 30 minutes.

2. **(A)** Mix the sauce together, set aside. **(B)** Heat a large pan over medium-high heat for 1 minute. Spray with cooking spray, then add the onions. Cook 3-4 minutes, remove from pan, set aside. **(C)** Spray the pan with cooking spray again, then add HALF of the chicken in a single layer. Cook for 2 minutes, without moving the meat, then **(D)** flip and cook 2 more minutes. Set the cooked chicken aside, then cook the remaining chicken for 2 minutes per side, repeating the process.

3. **(A)** When your second batch of chicken is finished cooking, return all of the chicken back into the pan, along with the sliced red and green onions. Mix to combine. **(B)** Pour in the sauce, mix, then allow it come to a simmer. **(C)** Once it begins to thicken, start mixing and tossing the pan's contents for 2-3 minutes. The sauce will continue to reduce and thicken. **(D)** When your dish is coated in a thick, sticky, gravy-like glaze, serve immediately. Garnish with additional thinly sliced green onion, if desired.

NOTES & SUGGESTIONS:

- ***SUGAR FREE SYRUP!?!?!?:*** As you all know by now, dealing with me and my recipes for 3 years (as of 2021), I am the poster child for ingredient substitutions. I barely have over 2 Tbsp of Honey in this dish, because I am adament about keeping the first serving at 2 point for this entree. By using just over 2 Tbsp of honey, mixed with 3 Tbsp sugar free syrup, we get 1/3 cup of sweet, sticky sauce, that still has a good honey flavor to it for 14 points, instead of 27. If you'd like to use more honey, BE MY GUEST... but adjust your points accordingly.

- ***THAT'S A LOT OF INGREDIENTS!:*** Most all of the popular ww-skinny-bloggers don't make a traditional-ish Honey Garlic Chicken. They make near-carbon copies of the same 'copycat' recipes, which are the Americanized 'fast food' versions of Chinese dishes. They use a ton of honey, a bunch of soy sauce, a little garlic.. and come in at 7-8 points per serving The REAL DEAL has ginger, rice vinegar, Chinese cooking wine... and a BALANCE of the honey, garlic and other flavors. What we're all used to, is 1-note, sickeningly sweet, honey-slathered chicken with no depth of flavor.

- ***BALSAMIC VINEGAR?!?:*** Traditional versions of this dish call for Chinese 'Shoaxing' cooking wine, however it's high in points. We're making a simple 0 point substitute with white wine, rice vinegar, balsamic vinegar and sweetener.

- ***DARK SOY SAUCE:*** Yup, yooooou guessed it. 'Sushi Chef'.

HUNAN CHICKEN

A Savory Dish Brimming With TONS of Fresh Vegetables In A Sweet, Savory And Spicy Sauce

First off... it's Hunan Chicken, not HUMAN Chicken!!! Sweet sassy molassy, so many people were confused when I posted this recipe online. <u>Hunan</u> is a province in China, the same one the Shaolin Temple is in, for all you Kung Fu fans. Hunan chicken is very similar to spicy Szechuan, but Hunan chicken has a TON more vegetables. Mine is on the mild side, so you can definitely amp up the heat with more Asian chili sauce, if you'd like. My recipe is a nice balance of savoriness, with a bit of sweetness and heat.

Servings Info.:

Yield: 10 cups
Servings: 6
Serving Size: 1-2/3 cups

MY PLAN

R D
1-1

- last checked 11/23/22 -
Use your mobile device's 'Camera' App to look at this code for nutritional info.

Ingredients:

Meat:
• 1-1/2 lb chicken breast, sliced into thin strips
• 1/4 tsp baking soda, dissolved into 1 Tbsp water
• 1 Tbsp reduced sodium soy sauce

Sauce:
• 4 Tbsp reduced sodium soy sauce
• 1-1/2 tsp cornstarch, dissolved into the soy sauce
• 2 Tbsp 'dark' soy sauce
• 3 Tbsp oyster sauce
• 1 Tbsp black bean sauce (see notes)
• 3 Tbsp tomato sauce
• 1 Tbsp white wine
• 1 Tbsp rice vinegar
• 1 Tbsp Asian chili sauce (I used 'Huy Fong' chili garlic sauce)
• 1 tsp sesame oil
• 3 Tbsp 0 point sweetener o' choice (I used lakanto monkfruit)
• 6 medium garlic cloves, chopped
• 1 Tbsp ginger, minced

Veggies: *(highly customizable, see notes)*
• 1 large onion, cut into large chunks, 2 cups
• 4 medium carrots, peeled, cut into 1/4" thick 'coins', 2 cups
• 4 celery ribs, sliced 1/4" thick, around 1-1/4 cups
• 1 large red bell pepper, cut into 1" pieces
• 7oz broccoli florets, 4 cups.

Directions:

1. Mix together the chicken with the baking soda/soy sauce. Set aside for 20-30 minutes. While it's marinating, mix the sauce together, cover, set aside.

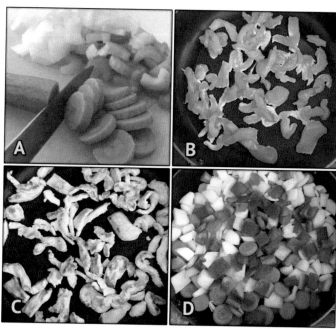

2. (A) While the chicken's marinating, prep the veggies. **(B)** Heat a LARGE pan over high heat for 1 minute. Spray with cooking spray, then add half of the chicken, arranging in 1 layer. Cook, undisturbed, for 2 minutes. **(C)** Flip the chicken, then cook for 2 additional minutes. Do not move the chicken, allow it to brown. Remove from pan, then repeat with the rest of the chicken. **(D)** When all the chicken is cooked and set aside, spray the pan, then add the onions, carrots and red bell peppers. Cook 2 minutes on high heat, without moving the pan.

3. **(A)** Toss the vegetables, then cook for 2 more minutes, without moving the pan. Pour the veggies into a large bowl, set aside. **(B)** Reduce heat to medium-high, then add the celery and broccoli florets. Add 1 Tbsp of water to the pan, then cover with a lid. Cook the broccoli and celery for 1 minute. Remove lid, toss the broccoli and celery, then cook for 1 more minute, covered. **(C)** Turn the heat back up to high and add the carrots, onions, bell peppers, chicken and the sauce. Carefully fold all the ingredients together to combine. **(D)** Cook for 2-3 more minutes, tossing till the sauce thickens and coats the dish. Pour into a large platter and garnish by sprinkling with sesame seeds and sliced green onions, if desired.

SUBSTITUTION IDEAS:

- Hunan Chicken can be compared to Chop Suey's bigger, older, more macho brother. Though both dishes make large platters full of chicken and vegetables, the big difference is the sauce. Chop Suey has a very light, somewhat thin sauce, with only a few flavors... Hunan Chicken's sauce has layer upon layer of different savory components. It also has a nice heat to it. Again, though mine is mild, with a very subtle heat... a traditional recipe would be MUCH spicier. To emulate the heat of a traditional recipe, I'd recommend upping the Asian chili sauce to 3-4 Tbsp.

- You can mix and match the veggies in this dish to better reflect your own personal preferences. Try to keep the quantities of your substitution in line with the amounts I used... otherwise your points per serving might change. Typical vegetables in Hunan Chicken can include:

* Broccoli, Carrots, Mushrooms, Bell Peppers, Snow Peas, Snap Peas, Zucchini, Celery, Asparagus, Baby corn, Edamame, Bean sprouts, Cabbage, Spinach, Bok choy, or heck... if you want to go fully legit, add Asian red chili peppers *(see notes)*.

NOTES:

- *PROTEIN:* I'm using chicken, but you can obviously make this dish with beef, pork, or tofu. Adjust points if needed.
- *OYSTER SAUCE:* If you don't like the taste of oyster sauce, you can use 'vegetarian oyster sauce', which is a thick, savory sauce, made from mushrooms.
- *LARGE FRYING PAN vs. WOK:* I'm using a large pan instead of a Wok, because most people don't have woks. My recipes will always use common equipment in their preparations, to make the dishes as accessible as possible.
- *WHERE ARE THE PEPPERS?:* I am NOT going to tell you all to go find an Asian market and buy Asian chili peppers for this dish. That's why I'm using Asian chili sauce for the heat in my recipe. It's at every store and it's incredibly easy to adjust the level of heat. However, regular Hunan Chicken uses a variety of chili peppers, from Thai chilies to Birdseye chili peppers. To make the recipe more accessible, you can use red jalapeno peppers. If you can't find red jalapenos, you can use green jalapenos or serrano peppers. If you use jalapeno peppers, you will need slightly more and if you use serrano peppers, you need far less as they are much spicier.

KOREAN GOCHUJANG CHICKEN

A Savory, Spicy and Sweet Marinated Chicken, INSPIRED BY Korean 'Gochujang' Sticky Chicken

Let's branch out a little bit and explore some new regions of Asia by diving into a few Korean dishes. My recipe for 'Korean Gochujang Chicken' is inspired by a REAL Korean recipe, but its WW-ified with creative ingredient swaps, to keep the dish as low in calories as possible. If you are Korean and you want to wave your fists in the air about how untraditional my version is... you're in good company. Have you seen what I did to my Latino amigos, with my Mexican Brown Mole' sauce? It may not be how your *Halmeoni* makes it... but your grandma wasn't as concerned about your waistline as I am.

Servings Info.:

Yields: 2-1/2 pounds
Servings: 5
Serving Size: 1/2 lb.

- last checked 11/23/22 -
Use your mobile device's 'Camera' App to look at this code for nutritional info.

Ingredients:

Chicken:
- 2-1/2 pounds boneless skinless chicken breasts, sliced across into thin 'filets'. We're going for B cup chicken breasts, not DD's.
- 3/4 tsp baking soda, stirred into 2 Tbsp water

Marinade:
- 1/2 cup low sodium soy sauce
- 1 Tbsp 'dark' soy sauce
- 1 tsp sesame oil
- 3 Tbsp rice vinegar
- 1 Tbsp white wine
- 1 Tbsp minced ginger
- 5 medium garlic cloves, minced
- 2 to 3 Tbsp Asian chili sauce (or more, to taste 😀)
- 1 Tbsp 'gochujang' fermented red bean paste *(see pg. 11)*
- 1-1/2 tsp miso paste (optional)
- 2 tsp paprika, stirred, till dissolved into the marinade

Reserved Glaze Ingredients: *(see steps 1B & 4A)*
- 1/4 cup water
- 3 Tbsp 0 calorie brown sugar replacement
- 3 to 4 Tbsp sugar free syrup (pancake syrup), to taste
- 1-1/2 tsp cornstarch, dissolved into 1 Tbsp water

Additional Ingredients:
- 1 tsp sesame seeds for garnish
- green onions, thin sliced on a bias, for garnish (optional)

Directions:

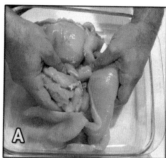

1. **(A)** Mix together the thin sliced chicken and baking soda solution till coated. Cover, set aside 30 minutes.
   (B) In a bowl, mix the Marinade ingredients. Pour 1/2 cup of the sauce into a container, then store in the fridge. THAT is going to be your glaze. <u>The remaining liquid is your marinade, which will be used in step 2B.</u>

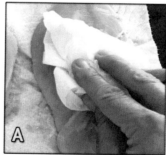
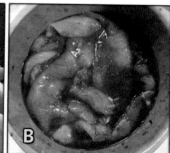

2. **(A)** Carefully rinse off the chicken breasts, then pat dry with paper towels. **(B)** Place the chicken breasts into a a large mixing bowl, or casserole dish, then pour the marinade over the chicken. Mix well, till the chicken is nicely coated. Cover, then store overnight in the fridge. The longer it marinates, the better.

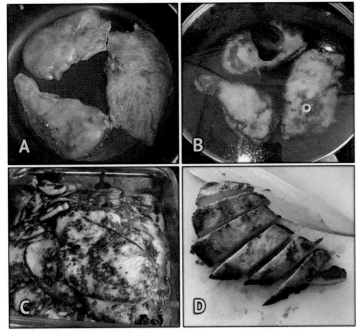

- **_HOW IS THIS KOREAN, DANIEL!??!:_** The traditional recipe for Korean spicy 'sticky' chicken calls for using "Gochujang" hot pepper paste. It's similar to regular Asian Chili Sauce, but it also has some miso and sweetness to it. Another big difference... it is VERY HIGH IN POINTS. This recipe makes a 0 point substitute by using regular asian chili sauce, adding a little bit of miso paste, plus sweetener. We just saved 5 points, by making our own.
- **_WHITE WINE?:_** The regular recipes call for rice wine. I'm using a 0 point amount of white wine, plus rice vinegar, as a 0 point ingredient substitution.
- **_PAPRIKA!?!?!:_** This dish traditionally gets its deep red color from copius amounts of red chili sauce. My recipe is milder. We're getting the dark red color from adding paprika into the sauce. You can also add more chili sauce if you want.
- **_SUGAR FREE SYRUP:_** The only thing in the world that has more points than Lard (joking), is Honey. I'm substituting syrup for honey. It's thick, it's sweet, it serves the same purpose.
- **_ASIAN RED PEPPER PASTE:_** Can be found in the Asian Food aisle of most major chain grocery stores. It might also be found as 'Gochujang' red pepper paste. Different brands of have varying point values. I used 1 Tbsp, which is only 1 point. For more info., read the description on pg. 11.
- **_COOKING METHOD:_** You can also cook the chicken on the grill, skipping steps 3A & 3B. But, you'll still need to glaze it in a pan.

3. **(A)** The following day, preheat a LARGE pan over HIGH heat for 1 minute. Spray with cooking spray, then quickly add a few of the chicken breasts. Do NOT overcrowd the pan, cook in batches. DO NOT move the chicken! Let it sear, unmoved, for 3 minutes... no touching! **(B)** Flip the chicken, cover with a lid, reduce heat to medium-high, then cook for 2 more minutes. **(C)** Place cooked chicken into a bowl or platter. Repeat process till all the chicken is cooked. Let rest for 15 minutes. **(D)** After 15 minutes, slice the cooked chicken breasts into thick strips, roughly 3/4" to 1". Set aside.

4. **(A)** Add the reserved liquid (Step 1B) and the "reserved glaze" ingredients to a small pot. Bring to a boil for 4-5 minutes, till thick. **(B)** Meanwhile, add the sliced chicken to a hot pan for 1-2 minutes, over medium heat. **(C)** Pour in the hot glaze and continue cooking. **(D)** Cook until the sauce has thickened and coated the chicken in a thick, sticky glaze. Garnish with sesame seeds and sliced green onion.

KUNG PAO CHICKEN

My Heavily Modified, Yet Incredibly Delicious Twist on a Savory and Spicy Take-Out Favorite

Kung Pao Chicken is, by far, one of the most popular Chinese dishes in the USA. It is known for it's savoriness, along with having enough heat to make Chuck Norris' beard sweat.

My recipe is a <u>HEAVILY</u> tweaked combination of a traditional Sichuan recipe and the Kung Pao chicken from PF Chang's. In an attempt to keep this dish as accessible as possible, while still keeping the flavors as true to the original as I can, I'm using some pretty interesting ingredient swaps. Just roll with it... they are all explained in the notes at the end of the recipe.

Ingredients:

Chicken & Marinade:
- 2 pounds boneless skinless chicken breast, or chicken breast tenderloins, cut into 1/2 inch chunks.
- 1 tsp fresh ginger, finely minced
- 4-5 medium garlic cloves, crushed and minced
- 2 Tbsp reduced sodium soy sauce
- 1 Tbsp white wine (see notes)
- 2 tsp 0 point sweetener o' choice
- 1/2 tsp baking soda, mixed with 2 tsp water.

Sauce:
- 1/4 cup chicken broth
- 1-1/2 tsp balsamic vinegar (just do it.... see notes)
- 1 tsp rice vinegar
- 3 Tbsp soy sauce
- 1 Tbsp <u>DARK</u> soy sauce (see notes)
- 1 tsp sesame oil
- 1-1/2 to 2 Tbsp asian chili sauce (like 'Huy Fong' brand)
- 1 Tbsp no sugar added ketchup, or tomato sauce *(for color)*
- 2 tsp paprika *(for color, trust me, see the notes)*
- 1 Tbsp cornstarch, dissolved in 1 Tbsp water

Additional Ingredients:
- 1 large red bell pepper, sliced into bite sized squares
- 4 large celery ribs, sliced on a bias, about 1/4" thick
- 1/4 cup scallions (white part of green onions), sliced into 1/4 inch rounds. *(pictured in step 1C)*
- 1/3 cup dry roasted peanuts, halved ... *(SEE NOTES)*
- 1 tsp sesame seeds, for garnish

Servings Info.:
Yields: 7 cups
Servings: 5
Serving Size: 1-1/4 cup

R D
2-2

- last checked 11/23/22 -
Use your mobile device's 'Camera' App to look at this code for nutritional info.

Directions:

1. **(A)** Mix chicken pieces with the marinade ingredients, let sit for 20 minutes. **(B)** Meanwhile, in a separate bowl, mix together the sauce ingredients, till smooth. Set aside. **(C)** Cut celery, red bell peppers, and slice the bottom 1/2 of the green onions into 1/4" slices. Set aside. **(D)** Preheat a LARGE pan (or wok) over high heat for 45 seconds. Spray with cooking spray, then quickly add the chicken and marinade into the pan. Cook over high heat until the chicken is just cooked through, about 5 minutes. Once the chicken is cooked through, take the chicken out of the pan, set aside. Return the pan to heat.

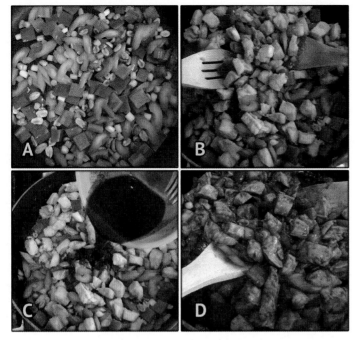

2. **(A)** Spray the hot pan with cooking spray and immediately add the bell peppers, celery and sliced scallions. Cook over High heat until just starting to get a little color, but are still firm, about 3-4 minutes. Add the peanuts and toss to combine. **(B)** Add the chicken and juices back into the pan, toss to combine. **(C)** Pour the sauce into the pan, which should still be set to high heat. Begin stirring and tossing the contents, to distribute the sauce. **(D)** The sauce will begin to thicken quickly. Continue to toss/mix for around 2-3 minutes, or until the sauce thickens to the consistency of a thick gravy, coating the dish. Done. You can garnish with thin sliced green onions and up to 7/8 tsp of sesame seeds for 0 points, if desired.

NOTES CONT.:

- **WHITE WINE??:** Traditional recipes call for using Chinese 'Shaoxing' cooking wine. I'm not going to make you go hunt down a bottle of it. Use regular white wine, it still tastes fine with the substitution.
- **BALSAMIC!?:** Again, traditional recipes call for using 'Chinkiang' vinegar. Nope. An easy substitution for it is mixing a little balsamic with a little rice vinegar. Every grocery store has those. I'm trying to make this easy on'ya.
- **PAPRIKA & KETCHUP??:** I'm sounding like a broken record at this point. In order to get a dark, deep reddish color for the sauce, true recipes get that from cooking lots of those dried little red Asian chiles in hot oil, then cooking the dish in the oil filled with disintigrated red chili peppers. In order to get that color without the chiles and without food coloring... we're stirring some paprika and ketchup into our sauce. Once combined with the Asian chili sauce and the dark soy sauce, it gives a very deep, rich red color.
- **WHERE ARE THE PEPPERS?:** I am NOT going to tell you all to go find an Asian market and buy miniature, dried Asian chili peppers for this dish. That's why I'm using Asian chili sauce for the heat in my recipe. It's at every store and it's incredibly easy to adjust your level of heat. However... if you want to go full-tilt traditional, replace the chili sauce with 8-10 dried asian chili peppers and add 2 teaspoons of whole Sichuan peppercorns. That'll melt your face off.
- **PEANUT HALVES?:** We're using 1/3 cup of roasted peanuts, which is around 56 whole peanuts. But, so they could spread through as much of the dish as possible, I chose to use peanuts that were split in half, rather than whole peanuts. Yeah, it took a couple minutes to split each peanut into 2 halves, but it's worth it. That way, instead of only having around 56 whole peanuts spread out through the entire dish, I had 112 peanut halves.
- **SPICE LEVEL:** Kung Pao chicken is supposed to be pretty spicy. My recipe uses 1-1/2 to 2 Tbsp of Asian chili sauce. HOWEVER... that's because I had to eat it. Both my wife and I have the heat tolerance of 4 year old French kids, so... feel free to add more chili sauce than I recommend. You can make this dish as spicy or as mild as you want, because even without heat, it's a really tasty dish.

LEMONGRASS CHICKEN

Vietnamese Style Chicken, Coated with Turmeric, In A Savory, Sweet, Tart & Fragrant Sauce

As I'm coming to the final dozen recipes of this book (not alphabetically, obviously), I realized that rather than sticking with the regular 'food bloggery' Asian food, ie: Chinese with a spattering of Thai... it'd be cool to branch to some not-so-common regional cuisine. So, welcome to Saigon. Rather than doing a typical Chinese lemongrass chicken recipe, I decided to take you on a trip to Vietnam. This dish uses lemongrass, which you may be able to find in your grocery store's produce department. If not, they also carry it pre-minced, in squeeze tubes. This dish is extremely flavorful, with a nice kick of savory flavors.

Servings Info.:

Yields: 6-1/4 cups
Servings: 5
Serving Size: 1-1/4 cup

MY PLAN   R D
0-0

- last checked 11/23/22 -
Use your mobile device's 'Camera' App to
look at this code for nutritional info.

Ingredients:

Chicken:
• 2 pounds boneless skinless chicken breast, or chicken breast tenderloins, sliced into thin pieces.

Marinade:
• 1-1/2 tsp ground turmeric
• 1/4 tsp salt
• 1/4 tsp pepper
• 1/4 tsp baking soda, dissolved into 2 Tbsp water (just do it)
• 1 tsp reduced sodium soy sauce

Sauce: (mix ingredients together, set aside)
• 3 Tbsp reduced sodium soy sauce
• 2 tsp 'dark' soy sauce
• 2-1/2 Tbsp asian 'fish sauce'
• 3 Tbsp 0 calorie brown sugar replacement
• 1 Tbsp rice vinegar
• 1 Tbsp lemon juice
• 1-1/2 tsp cornstarch, dissolved into 2 tsp water

Additional Ingredients:
• 1 large onion, halved, sliced into thin wedges or strips
• 1 large red bell pepper, sliced into bite sized strips
• 1/4 cup fresh lemongrass, minced (see pics 2A&B)
• 6 medium garlic cloves, minced (about 2 Tbsp)
• 1/3 cup fresh chopped cilantro, loosely packed

Directions:

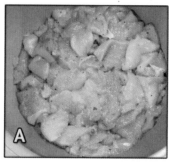 

1. **(A)** Mix together the chicken and marinade ingredients. Let rest for at least 1-2 hours. The longer it sits, the better. Then, mix the sauce together in a separate bowl. Set aside. **(B)** Slice the onion and bell pepper, set aside.

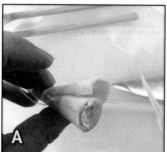 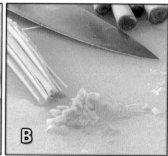

2. **(A)** Peel the firm outer layers of the lemongrass stalks, to expose the softer inner layers. **(B)** Slice the lemongrass, lengthwise, then mince. It'll take a few stalks to make 1/4 cup. Set aside.

3. Preheat a large pan or wok over high heat, for 1 minute.

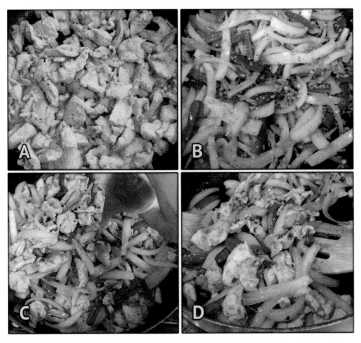

4. **(A)** Spray hot pan with cooking spray then immediately add marinated chicken. Spread across the pan and cook, without moving or stirring, for 2 minutes. Toss chicken, then cook for 2 more minutes, or until just cooked through. Remove the chicken from pan, set aside. **(B)** Return pan to high heat, then add onions, bell peppers and lemongrass. Cook for 2 minute, then add garlic. Toss to combine and cook for 2 more minutes. **(C)** Return chicken to the pan, toss to combine, then pour in the sauce. **(D)** Continue to cook, tossing and mixing, till the sauce thickens and coats the veggies and chicken. Add the cilantro to, toss to combine. Done.

NOTES & SUGGESTIONS:
- **GLUTEN FREE:** If you have a Gluten intolerance, you can use 'Tamari' type Soy Sauce. It's available in all major super markets and walmarts. Also, cornstarch is gluten free, so you're good to go.
- **TURMERIC:** The reason we're using Turmeric in this dish, is for the signature yellow color which it'll help impart.
- **FISH SAUCE:** Is a common condiment in Asian cooking. It can be found at most all major grocery stores, in the Asian food aisle, near the soy sauce.
- **LEMONGRASS:** It is becoming more and more common to find lemongrass stalks in the produce departments of grocery stores. If you can't find fresh stalks, it may be available as a paste, in the produce department. "Gourmet Garden" sells squeeze bottles of fresh herb pastes, which can often be found at grocery stores and even at Walmart. If you go that route, check the points on the tubes, as it may alter your recipe's point value. If you want more instructions on how to prepare/chop lemongrass... there's a cool website on Al Gore's invention, the internet, called "Youtube". It's all the rage, nowadays.
- **LARGE FRYING PAN vs. WOK:** I'm using a large pan instead of a Wok, because most people don't have one. My recipes will always use common equipment in their preparations, to make the dishes as accessible as possible. Hence, why I also don't use an air fryer or grill. Not everyone has a grill, but everyone has an oven or toaster oven. Same with good ol' frying pans. Now, in the words of my Uncle... "Allez Cuisine!"

MISO GLAZED SALMON

A Riff on Japanese Miso Glazed Salmon, Baked, With A Miso-Ginger Glaze. Domo Arigato, Mr. Roboto.

I love salmon. I love the rich, meaty, fatty flavor of it. I figured if I'm going to be putting an Asian cookbook together, I should throw in a couple of ways to prepare it. For this recipe, I'm tweaking a traditional Japanese recipe to make it lower in calories and sugar. A typical recipe uses up to 1/4 cup of honey. For mine, I'm using sugar free syrup (pancake syrup). I'm also subbing 'Mirin' with rice vinegar, regular white wine and a little sweetener. Though I baked mine and finished it with the broiler, you can cook yours on the grill or in a pan, if you wish.

Servings Info.:

Yields: 4 salmon filets
Servings: 4
Serving Size: 1 filet

R D
1-1

- last checked 11/25/22 -
Use your mobile device's 'Camera' App to
look at this code for nutritional info.

Ingredients:

Salmon & Marinade:
- 4 Salmon Filets (I used 6-7oz salmon filets. Thanks, Costco!)
- 2 Tbsp miso paste ***
- 2 Tbsp low sodium soy sauce
- 2 Tbsp rice vinegar
- 1 Tbsp 0 calorie brown sugar replacement
- 1/2 tsp ginger, minced
- 1 tsp sesame oil
- 2 Tbsp sugar free syrup (pancake syrup)

Glaze:
- 1 Tbsp miso paste ***
- 1 Tbsp low sodium soy sauce
- 1 Tbsp rice vinegar
- 1 Tbsp white wine
- 1 Tbsp 0 calorie brown sugar replacement
- 2 Tbsp sugar free syrup (pancake syrup)
- 1 tsp cornstarch, dissolved with 1 Tbsp water

Additional Ingredients:
- 1 tsp sesame seeds, for garnish
- green onions, thin sliced on a bias, for garnish (optional)

Directions:

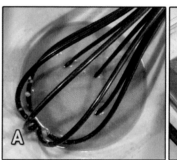 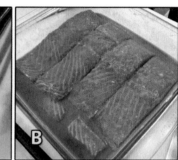

1. **(A)** In a bowl, whisk together the miso paste, soy sauce, vinegar, sweetener, ginger, sesame oil and syrup. Mix till smooth and well combined. **(B)** Place the salmon filets in a container large enough for them to lay in a flat layer. Pour marinade over the salmon and rub to cover completely. Allow to marinate for at least 1 hour.

2. **(A)** Preheat oven to 450 degrees. Line a pan with parchment paper, place salmon onto the pan and bake at 450 degrees for 12 minutes. **(B)** While the salmon is baking, add Glaze ingredients to a small pan and bring to a boil. Cook till syrup-like, set aside.

- **MISO PASTE:** Different brands of Miso paste can vary in points. For this recipe, I used 2 points of Miso paste, which is 3 Tbsp, using the 'generic' miso paste listing in the WW ingredient database. Scan the brand that you get and adjust your points if needed. You can use any type of Miso Paste that you'd like. You can find them in the Asian food section of your grocery store, as well as in the refrigerated area, near the Tofu.
- **WHERE'S THE MIRIN!!?!?:** Recipes for miso glazed salmon or chicken almost always have a good deal of Mirin. If you're wondering what Mirin is... it's a sweet rice wine, used in a lot of Asian cuisine. Because of how incredibly high in points and calories Mirin is... we're replacing it with rice vinegar, 1 Tbsp white wine and sweetener.
- **OTHER SAUCES:** You can make this same dish, but use any number of my other sauces and glazes, such as: The glazes from my orange chicken, Korean glazed chicken, sweet & sour chicken and my teriyaki sauce.
- **COOKING METHOD:** You don't HAVE to cook your salmon exactly like I do. Yes, I baked mine, then brushed it with more sauce and placed it under the broiler again.. But you don't have to. When I make this at home and I'm in a time crunch, I marinate it like normal, but I cook the salmon in a hot pan for 3-1/2 minutes per side, without moving it, so it gets a nice sear. While its cooking, I simmer the sauce, in a small pot, till thickened, then lower the heat to keep it juuust warm. When the salmon is done cooking in the pan, I cover the filets with sauce, flip them, then swirl them around the pan to coat them. A lot less time and a lot easier than messing with the broiler.

3. **(A)** When the salmon has been roasting for 12 minutes, take it out of the oven and turn on your oven's Broiler setting to High. **(B)** Coat the salmon all around with your thick glaze, till it's all used up. **(C)** Place the salmon back into your oven, on an oven rack 2 positions down from the top. Broil for 2 minutes, with the door closed. Rotate the pan, then broil for another 2-3 minutes till the top of the salmon is starting to lightly char. Keep an eye on it, so that it doesn't burn. **(D)** Remove from oven, allow to rest for 5 minutes. Garnish with sesame seeds, as well as thin sliced green onions, if desired.

MONGOLIAN CHICKEN

"It's A Meal Fit For Genghis Khaaaaaaaaaaaaaaaaaaaaaaaaaaaaan!!!!" - Captain James T. Kirk

Mongolian Chicken is the forgotten step brother of Mongolian Beef, which is a mainstay on the menus of Chinese restaurants across the country. If you've never had it before, it's a savory, sweet, mildly spicy dish, packed with fresh ginger and garlic. Though most restaurants only list Mongolian Beef on their menus, you can certainly request the chicken version. In my version, we're using chicken breast strips, rather than the more traditional chicken thighs. Feel free to bulk this up with more vegetables, if you want, which will stretch both the yield and your servings.

Servings Info.:
Yields: 6 cups
Servings: 4
Serving Size: 1-1/2 cup

R D
1-1

- last checked 11/25/22 -
Use your mobile device's 'Camera' App to look at this code for nutritional info.

Ingredients:

Chicken & Marinade:
- 2 pounds boneless skinless chicken breast, or chicken breast tenderloins, cut into thin strips
- 1 Tbsp reduced sodium soy sauce
- 1 tsp 'dark' soy sauce
- 1/2 tsp baking soda, dissolved into the soy sauce.
- 1/4 tsp sesame oil

Sauce:
- 6 Tbsp reduced sodium soy sauce (see note) ***
- 2 Tbsp PLUS 2 tsp DARK soy sauce
- 4-1/2 tsp cornstarch, dissolved into the soy sauce
- 1 Tbsp white wine *** (see notes)
- 1/2 cup beef broth
- 1/4 cup 0 calorie brown sugar replacement
- 5 medium garlic cloves, finely chopped
- 1 to 1-1/2 tsp fresh ginger, minced
- 1/4 tsp cracked/coarse black pepper
- 1-1/2 to 2 tsp (or more) asian chili sauce, to taste ***
- 2 Tbsp of the 'white part' of green onions, thin sliced into rounds. *(see the 1A picture for reference)*

Additional Ingredients:
- 1 Jumbo sized onion, quartered and sliced into thin strips
- 2 bunches of green onions. **The green parts only**, sliced into 2" long lengths *(see the 1A picture for reference)*
- 1 tsp sesame seeds, for garnish

Directions:

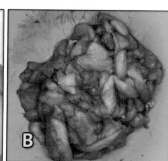

1. **(A)** Slice the white lower portions of the green onions into thin rounds, separate from the green lengths. The white parts go into the sauce. Combine the sauce ingredients, set aside. **(B)** Mix the 'Chicken & Marinade' ingredients together, then let rest for 20-30 minutes.

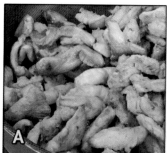

2. **(A)** Preheat a large pan over medium-high heat for 1 minute, till water sizzles on it. Coat with cooking spray then add the chicken, spreading apart into 1 layer. Let it cook, unmoved for 2 minutes. Toss/stir, then cook for 2 more minutes. Remove from pan. **(B)** Add onions to the pan, coat with cooking spray, then cook for 2 minutes.

3. **(A)** Return the chicken to the hot pan and toss to combine with the onions. Give it a second to build up some heat again, then pour in the sauce. **(B)** Stir and toss, cooking over high heat for 4-5 minutes. **(C)** Turn off the heat, then add the sliced green onions. **(D)** Gently fold/toss the green onions into the dish, for around 30 seconds. Don't let them sit for too long in the hot dish, or they go limp and flaccid. No amount of sexy cooking aprons, dirty kitchen talk, candles, or Marvin Gaye will bring them back after they wilt and go limp. Serve immediately. Garnish with sesame seeds.

FOR CONSIDERATION - SODIUM BOMB:

This particular sauce has a TON of sodium in it. It has the most soy sauce of any of my Asian dishes thus far. If you make it, plan accordingly and drink lots of water to help flush your system. There is a good probability that you'll experience temporary 'salt-bloat'. Drink your water, it'll be ok.

NOTES & SUGGESTIONS:

- **WHY THE DARK SOY SAUCE & BEEF BROTH?:** Because, I want this to look and taste more like Mongolian BEEF than Mongolian chicken. In order to have the chicken take on a darker 'beef-like' coloring, in the finished dish, I had to darken the sauce with more dark soy sauce. It made it much more visually appealing than when I made the chicken lighter in color. As for the Beef, I made this dish a few times. It had a deeper, more complex flavor when I used beef broth instead of chicken broth. Trial and error.
- **WHITE WINE:** I'm not going to tell you to go buy a fancy Asian cooking wine. Instead, we're using regular white wine in the sauce. Alternatively, you could also use Rice Vinegar.
- **PROTEIN:** It goes without saying, for a vegetarian option, you can replace the chicken with firm tofu and swap the beef broth for veggie..
- **GLUTEN FREE:** If you have a Gluten intolerance, you can use 'Tamari' type Soy Sauce. It's available in all major super markets and walmarts. Also, cornstarch is gluten free, so you're good to go.
- **CHILI SAUCE:** I used the regular 'asian chili sauce' that you find in the grocery store's "Asian Food" section. I purchased Huy Fung brand, Chili Garlic Sauce. If you'd like, you can use red pepper flakes, Sriracha, or even some of those fiery little dried asian red peppers.
- **LARGE FRYING PAN vs. WOK:** I'm using a large pan instead of a Wok, because most people don't have one. My recipes will always use common equipment in their preparations, to make the dishes as accessible as possible. Hence, why I also don't use an air fryer or grill. Not everyone has a grill, but everyone has an oven or toaster oven. Same with good ol' frying pans. Now, in the words of my Uncle... "Allez Cuisine!"
- **GREEN ONION FIRMNESS:** The first time that I tried making this, I added the green onions at the same time I added the sauce, then cooked it all together for a few minutes. Do not do that. They'll wilt into sad, limp little green strips. 4 out of 10 green onions suffer from performance anxiety.

MOO GOO GAI PAN

Chicken and a Wide Assortment of Vegetables In A Thick, Savory Sauce

Confession time! Prior to making this recipe, I have never had 'Moo Goo Gai Pan' in my entire life... which is preeeetty much on par with most of the dishes in this cookbook. :-) That being said, I will definitely order it, if I want an entree so loaded with veggies you'd mistake it for a farmer's market stall. Unlike every other Asian recipe I've made up to this point, this is the first one that doesn't have a single drop of soy sauce in it. Moo Goo Gai Pan has a thick, 'clear', gravy-like sauce, which is primarily just seasoned broth, thickened with cornstarch..

Servings Info.:
Yield: 9 cups
Servings: 6
Serving Size: 1.5 cups

R D
0-0

- last checked 11/26/22 -
Use your mobile device's 'Camera' App to look at this code for nutritional info.

Ingredients:

Meat:
• 1-1/4 lb chicken breast, sliced into thin strips
• 1/4 tsp baking soda, dissolved into 2 tsp water

Sauce:
• 1-1/4 cups fat free chicken broth
• 2-1/2 Tbsp cornstarch
• 1 tsp sesame oil
• 1 Tbsp rice vinegar
• 4 medium garlic cloves, crushed and minced
• 1/2 tsp ginger, minced
• 1/2 tsp salt
• 1 tsp 0 point sweetener o' choice (I used lakanto monkfruit)
• 1/4 tsp black pepper

Veggies: *(highly customizable, see notes)*
• 8 oz sliced mushrooms, any variety you want
• 1-1/4 cup carrots, thin sliced
• 8 oz broccoli florets
• 1 cup snow peas (not snap or sugar peas!)
• 1 large onion, halved and thin sliced
• 8 oz canned bamboo shoots, drained
• 8 oz canned water chestnuts, sliced, drained
• Toasted sesame seeds for garnish, no more than 1 tsp.

Directions:

1. Mix the sauce ingredients together, set aside.

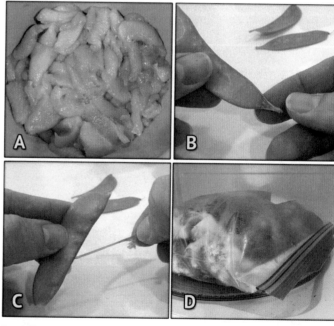

2. (A) Mix together the chicken and baking soda/water solution. Set aside for 20-30 minutes. **(B)** Now let's start prepping the veggies. Take your snow peas and grab the one hard, pointy side with your finger nails. **(C)** Pinch, to JUST break off the hard tip, then pull back and up, along the length of the snow pea. You'll pull off a hard little string. Those strings go in the trash. **(D)** Place the broccoli florets in a large ziplock bag with a splash of water. Poke a tiny hole in the bag, then microwave for 1-1/2 minutes. Remove broccoli from bag, set aside.

3. Let's get cookin'! Get out a LARGE, high walled pan and put it over medium-high heat, for 1 minute. Spray the pan with cooking spray, then immediately...

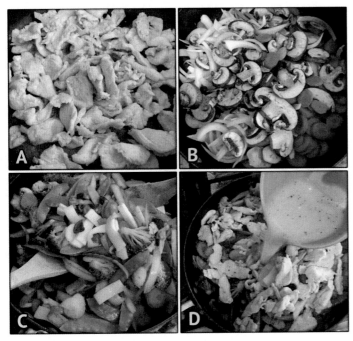

4. **(A)** Add the chicken to the hot pan and cook over medium-high heat for 5 minutes, or till just cooked through. Remove from pan, set aside. **(B)** Return pan to heat, ,spray with cooking spray, then add the carrots, mushrooms and onions. Cook for 4-5 minutes, or till the onions and mushrooms just start to soften and brown. **(C)** Add the snow peas, par-cooked broccoli, canned bamboo shoots and sliced water chestnuts. Toss and cook for 1-2 minutes. **(D)** Return the cooked chicken back to the pan, then pour in the sauce. Cook for 4-5 minutes, or until the sauce thickens and coats all of the ingredients in a thick, gravy-like sauce. Garnish with sesame seeds.

NOTES:

- **PROTEIN:** I'm using chicken, but you can obviously make this dish with beef, pork, or tofu. Adjust points if needed. If you use tofu... don't use the baking soda... obviously.

- **LARGE FRYING PAN vs. WOK:** I'm using a large pan instead of a Wok, because most people don't have woks. My recipes will always use common equipment in their preparations, to make the dishes as accessible as possible. Hence, why I also don't use an air fryer or grill. Not everyone has a grill, but everyone has an oven or toaster oven.

- **VEGETABLE SUBSTITUTIONS:** You can obviously use whatever veggies you want for your dish, using my recipe as a template. No matter what veggies you swap in or out try to keep the measurements the same, so that the servings and points will remain the same. Don't like water chestnuts? Fine, add some thin sliced celery. Want to swap out the bamboo shoots with more carrots or a different filler? Be my guest. I'm not a recipe snob. Use what'cha got, baby! ;-)

- **SODIUM.:** As I've mentioned, this is the only dish in this entire book which doesn't call for any soy sauce. As a result it's the most 'sodium friendly', for folks on a sodium restrictive diet. The only real noteworthy amount of salt in this dish, comes from the chicken broth. But, remember to look at the nutritional info at the back of the book, to get an accurate approximation of the sodium per serving for this dish.

- **POINT INFO.:** I feel that I always need to mention this: Though a serving of this is 0 points on both plans, that's only the first serving. I put this recipe together to be as light and healthy as possible. As a result, you can have up to 3 servings for only 1 point, on both plans. HOWEVER... just because you CAN have a lot of servings, doesn't mean you should. I wouldn't recommend eating 4.5 cups of this stuff "just because it's 1 point! woohoo!" That would completely negate the reason we're cooking like this. That'd be like saying "It's healthy to eat 10 low point Lean Cuisine dinners in one night, because I have the points for it!" No, no it isn't.

MUSHROOM CHICKEN

Chicken Breast With Onions, Garlic, Ginger, Zucchini And More 'Shrooms Than A Pink Floyd Concert

This dish is a testament to the peril I will put myself in to make a dish for you all. My wife hates mushrooms... my wife hates ginger... this entree contains both, in large quantities. This dish uses thin sliced chicken breast in a thick, earthy, ginger garlic sauce. The chicken's pan seared, then tossed with sauteed onions, sliced zucchini... and loaded with so many mushrooms, you'll think you've gone back to the 70's to see the 'Spirit World'.

Servings Info.:

Yields: 6 cups
Servings: 6
Serving Size: 1 cup

MY PLAN

R D
0-0

- last checked 11/26/22 -
Use your mobile device's 'Camera' App to
look at this code for nutritional info.

Ingredients:

Chicken:
- 1.5 pounds boneless skinless chicken breast, or chicken breast tenderloins, cut into thin slices.

Marinade:
- 1 Tbsp reduced sodium soy sauce
- 1 Tbsp white wine
- 1 tsp rice vinegar
- 1/2 tsp 0 point sweetener o' choice (I used lakanto monkfruit)
- 1/4 tsp baking soda, dissolved into 1 tsp water

Sauce:
- 5 Tbsp fat free chicken broth
- 1 Tbsp cornstarch, stirred into the broth, till dissolved
- 2 Tbsp PLUS 1 tsp low sodium soy sauce
- 1-1/2 tsp 'dark' soy sauce'
- 1 Tbsp PLUS 2 tsp oyster sauce
- 1 tsp sesame oil
- 1-1/2 tsp balsamic vinegar (see notes)
- 3 garlic cloves, crushed and minced
- 1 tsp ginger, finely chopped/minced

Additional Ingredients:
- 1 small onion, quartered and thin sliced (around 2 cups)
- 2 medium zucchini, sliced across, horizontally, then cut into half circles
- 16 oz sliced mushrooms, any variety you want. I'm not a mushroom snob. I bought pre-sliced, packaged mushrooms.
- 1 tsp toasted sesame seeds, for garnish

Directions:

1. Mix the chicken with the marinade, set aside for 30 minutes. In a separate bowl, mix the sauce, set aside.

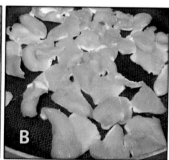

2. **(A)** Slice/chop the onion, zucchini, ginger and garlic, set aside. **(B)** Heat a LARGE pan over medium-high heat for 1 minute, then add HALF of the chicken. Spread into a single layer, uncrowded. DO NOT MOVE THE CHICKEN! Let cook, unmoved, for 2-1/2 minutes.

3. **(A)** Flip chicken and cook 2-1/2 minutes on other side. Pour into a large bowl, then cook the 2nd half of the chicken in the same way. Set aside with the cooked chicken. **(B)** Spray pan with cooking spray, add onion and zucchini. Cook for 4-5 minutes.

4. Pour the cooked onions and zucchini into the same bowl as the cooked chicken. Return pan to heat.

5. **(A)** Add mushrooms to the pan, with 1 Tbsp water. Cover and let cook/steam for 2 minutes. Remove cover, add another 1 Tbsp water, cover with lid, cook 2 more minutes. **(B)** Stir the sauce, then pour into the pan, over the 'shrooms. It'll take 1-2 minutes, but let the sauce start simmering. Let cook for an additional minute, till the sauce begins to thicken. **(C)** Once the sauce is thick and coating the mushrooms, return the chicken and cooked vegetables to the pan. Toss to combine. **(D)** Cook the dish for an additional 2-3 minutes, or until the sauce has become very thick and all of the ingredients are well coated. Done. Garnish with up to 1 tsp toasted sesame seeds.

NOTES & SUGGESTIONS:

- *BALSAMIC VINEGAR?:* Traditional recipes call for 'chinese black vinegar'. I'm not going to make you guys order it for this one dish. Use balsamic vinegar, it'll work just fine.
- *WHITE WINE?:* Traditional recipes call for Chinese cooking wine, which is an extremely salty and dark rice wine. It's also pretty high in points, so we're doing a 0 point substitution. 1 Tbsp white wine with some rice vinegar. Just roll with it. Ya'know... be flowy, like Tai Chi.
- *ONIONS:* If you don't like onions, replace them with 2 additional cups of zucchini or any veggie you want. You do you, Boo.
- *DARK SOY SAUCE:* Yup, 'Sushi Chef'. I'm like a broken record.
- *WHAT IF I DON'T LIKE MUSHROOMS?:* Are you serious?... Pick a different dish... "No 'shrooms for'ju!"
- *TYPES OF MUSHROOMS:* Unlike most food bloggers and cookbook authors... I am NOT going to mandate that you use a certain type of mushrooms. You won't get "Buy 1lb of humanely harvested, organic Shitake mushrooms" from my recipes... use what you can get. For this dish, I bought the inexpensive, pre sliced 8oz packages of 'white mushrooms' at the grocery store. It still turned out fantastic.
- *LARGE FRYING PAN vs. WOK:* I'm using a large pan instead of a Wok, because most people don't have one. My recipes will always use common equipment in their preparations, to make the dishes as accessible as possible. Hence, why I also don't use an air fryer or grill. Not everyone has a grill, but everyone has an oven or toaster oven. Same with good ol' frying pans. Now, in the words of my Uncle... "Allez Cuisine!"
- *SERVINGS:* On both plans, 1 serving is 0 points, while you can have up to 4 servings for 1 point. Just because something is low in points doesn't mean you should gorge on it. Having 4 cups of this stuff iiiiiiisn't something I'd recommend.

ORANGE CHICKEN

My Sweet, Savory and AWESOME Take On Traditional Orange Chicken

Like most of the human race, I love Panda's orange chicken, but what I don't love is that it's such a 1-note entree. Other than sweet, the dish has no nuance. Where most bloggers are happy to simply make a copycat Panda Express version, I wanted to make a low calorie/fat version, based off of an actual Chinese restaurant's recipe. With orange peel, fresh ginger, & chili garlic sauce, mine's got flavor and depth without the calories.

Servings Info.:

Yields: 4 cups
Servings: 4
Serving Size: 1 cup

MY PLAN

R D
2-2

- last checked 11/27/22 -
Use your mobile device's 'Camera' App to look at this code for nutritional info.

Ingredients:

Chicken:
- 1-1/4 pounds boneless skinless chicken breast, or chicken breast tenderloins, cut into bite sized chunks.
- 1/4 tsp baking soda, dissolved with 2 tsp water
- 1 batch of my 'low point breading', recipe on pg. 17

Orange Sauce & Glaze:
- 1/3 cup orange juice, some pulp.
- 7 Tbsp cup water (1 less Tbsp than 1/2 cup)
- 1-1/2 tsp cornstarch, dissolved into the water
- 2 Tbsp PLUS 2 tsp reduced sodium soy sauce
- 1-1/4 tsp 'dark' soy sauce
- 1/4 cup 0 calorie sugar replacement (I used lakanto)
- 3 medium garlic cloves, minced
- 1 Tbsp orange zest/peel, finely chopped (Yes... go buy an orange, Nancy.)
- 1 tsp fresh ginger, finely chopped/minced
- 2 tsp Asian chili sauce (I used Huy Fong chili garlic sauce)
- 1 Tbsp PLUS 1 tsp sugar free syrup (pancake syrup)
- 1/4 tsp black pepper

Additional Ingredients:
- 1 tsp sesame seeds, toasted, for garnish.

Directions:

1. Marinate the chicken pieces with the baking soda solution for 20 to 30 minutes.

2. Gather all the ingredients to make a batch of my toasted breading recipe.

3. **(A)** Heat a pan over medium heat for 1 minute, then add all breading ingredients. Toast for 3-4 minutes, or until the crumbs are a nice, uniformly golden color. Remove from pan and set aside, letting the crumbs cool to room temperature. **(B)** Place the whisked eggs into the bowl with the chicken pieces, mix to combine. **(C)** Place the toasted crumbs in a bowl, then place the chicken chunks, ONE AT A TIME, into the crumbs. Use a fork to lightly coat each chunk with the breading. **(D)** Place the lightly breaded chicken pieces onto 2 large baking pans, covered with foil and sprayed with a light coat of cooking spray. **(E)** Pre-Heat oven to 400 degrees.

4. Bake the chicken for 12 minutes. Remove from oven, flip the pieces, then bake for 4-5 more minutes. Remove from oven, set aside as you make the sauce.

5. **(A)** Heat a laaaarge pan for 1 minute over medium heat, then pour the sauce into the pan. **(B)** Crank up the heat to medium-high and bring the sauce to a rolling boil for 1 minute, or until it begins to thicken. Stir with a cooking utensil to ensure it doesn't burn. **(C)** Once the sauce thickens to the consistency of maple syrup (it'll take a few minutes of boiling), add all of the baked chicken breast pieces to the pan. **(D)** Gently toss and stir the chicken around the pan, till well coated in a thickened glaze. Garnish with sesame seeds and SERVE IMMEDIATELY! Seriously, I'm not just saying that. The breading will start to absorb the sauce and it'll begin to lose its crunch in about 5 minutes. This is baked, not deep fried.

NOTES & SUGGESTIONS:

- **BREADING:** I strongly advise you NOT to try dumping all of the breading and chicken into a ziplock bag, then shake it all up. It does NOT work. It takes time, but you need to bread the chicken one piece at a time. It took me around 12 minutes.

- **CRISPINESS:** Though this is a good, healthy alternative to restaurant style deep fried chicken breast pieces, the breading on this chicken WILL lose its crispness after being coated with the sauce for a few minutes. Just like chicken Parmesan, once your breading begins to absorb the sauce, it will eventually lose its crunchy exterior. For this dish, toss the chicken into the hot sauce right before serving, to ensure the crisp texture lasts for as long as possible.

- **BREAD CRUMBS INSTEAD OF RICE KRISPIES:** If you have access to 1 point per slice bread, instead of using my 'breading 2.0' recipe, for the crumbs... you can make a batch of my low point bread crumbs, from pg. 16. It makes enough real breadcrumbs to double-bread all the chicken for the same points. You'll just need an extra egg or two for the egg wash. But, the chicken will be CRAZY crunchy.

- **VEGGIES:** This only makes 4 cups of breaded and glazed orange chicken. That's fine, but I'd highly recommend plating it with steamed or sauteed veggies, to 'stretch it out'. I steamed a 1-1/2 lb bag of broccoli florets and served it all as a large, restaurant style platter, which increases the number of servings you can get out of the recipe, as well as the size of the servings. Besides, unlike Panda, where you get a giant scoop of this stuff on its own, when you order orange chicken at a restaurant it's ALWAYS served on a big bed of steamed broccoli.

- **POINTS:** The regular "Orange Chicken" entree at Panda Express is 18 points for one serving. My version is 2 points on both the 'Regular' and the 'Diabetic' plans. Let this be yet another example of how you can eat absolutely ANYTHING on-plan, without any regret. It just requires cooking a little differently than you used to.

PAD THAI

My Waaaaay Healthier Version of The Most Popular Thai Noodle Dish In The World

Rice noodles with a tangy, sweet and savory sauce, loaded with chicken, shrimp, a ton of veggies and topped with cilantro and crushed peanuts. It's their most popular dish for a reason.

Ingredients:

Proteins:
- 3/4 lb chicken breast, sliced into thin strips
- 1 tsp soy sauce
- 1/4 tsp baking soda, dissolved in 1 Tbsp water
- 1/2 lb medium shrimp (41-50 count) peeled, tail off, deveined)

Sauce(s):
- 4 Tbsp rice vinegar OR distilled white vinegar
- 2-1/2 Tbsp fish sauce
- 1 Tbsp lower sodium soy sauce
- 2 tsp powdered peanut butter
- 3 Tbsp 0 calorie brown sugar replacement
- 1-1/2 tsp cornstarch
- 1/2 to 1 tsp asian chili sauce (I used Huy Fong chili garlic)

Tamarind Paste Substitute: (below ingredients)
- 1 Tbsp lemon juice
- 2 tsp worcestershire sauce
- 1 tsp lower sodium soy sauce
- 1 Tbsp no sugar added ketchup OR canned tomato sauce
- 2 tsp 0 calorie brown sugar replacement
- 1/4 tsp molasses (see notes)

Veggies & Additional Ingredients:
- 8oz Pad Thai rice noodles (I used Thai Kitchen rice noodles). Weigh noodles dry, cook to package directions. Set aside.
- 1 large onion, quartered and thin sliced (around 2-1/4 cups)
- 2 cups 'shredded' carrots, (the bagged coleslaw type)
- 5 medium garlic cloves, minced
- 1-1/2 tsp ginger, minced
- 1/2 large head of cabbage, sliced into strips (5 cups)
- 2 cups bean sprouts
- 1 large egg
- 1/2 cup thin sliced green onions
- 1-1/2 oz peanuts, weighed then chopped/crushed
- Cilantro, finely chopped, to garnish

Servings Info.:

Yield: 10 cups
Servings: 8
Serving Size: 1-1/4 cups

R D
4-4

- last checked 11/27/22 -
Use your mobile device's 'Camera' App to look at this code for nutritional info.

Directions:

1. Combine chicken, soy sauce & baking soda mixture. Set aside 20-30 minutes. In one bowl, mix together all the sauce & 'tamarind paste' ingredients. Set aside.

2. **(A)** Heat a LARGE pan over medium high heat for 1 minute. Using cooking spray, cook the chicken till just cooked through, around 4 minutes. Set chicken aside. **(B)** Add shrimp to pan, cook till just cooked through, around 2 minutes per side. Remove from pan. **(C)** Add onions, carrots, garlic and ginger, turn heat up to High. Cook for 3 minutes, then **(D)** add the cabbage and bean sprouts. Toss to combine.

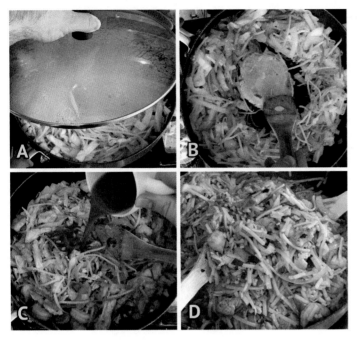

- *RICE NOODLES:* You can find 'pad thai style rice noodles' in the Asian food aisle of most major grocery stores. They may also be called 'stir fry rice noodles'. They look similar in shape and size to linguine however, they are white inside of their packaging. Cook according to package directions, then set aside. The brand I used gives 8oz dry noodles for 23 points.
- *CARROTS:* Ok, this caused some confusion in prior recipes. When I say 'shredded carrots', I mean the bagged, shredded carrots you find in the produce department of your grocery store. The carrots are in long, very, very thin matchsticks, like you'd find in coleslaws. They aren't truly shredded, like you'd get from a hand grater.
- *TAMARIND PASTE SUBSTITUTE:* Traditional Pad Thai uses Tamarind Paste to greatly enhance the flavor of the dish. Unfortunately, it's very high in points and is actually difficult to find at most grocery stores. Most food bloggers get around it by simply using ketchup as a substitute... which is a sucky and lazy substitute. I found 'my' substitute on an obscure Thai Cooking resource. It is a pretty decent substitute for the flavor profile that you'd get from the real stuff. If you don't want to use my Tamarind substitute, go the lazy route and use ketchup... but who wants lazy, when you can have delicious.
- *MOLASSES:* Tamarind paste has a very unique flavor. Above, I mention a couple of the ingredients used in my substitute for it, in this recipe. One that I wanted to give special mention to is Molasses. Molasses has a very tart, deep flavor, which is similar to Tamarind. Along with the soy sauce, ketchup, brown sugar substitute and lemon juice... this little bit of molasses in the recipe also helps round out the flavors and give a taste much closer to a REAL Pad Thai, than you'll find it regular 'skinny blogger' recipes, which all call for simply using plain ol' Ketchup for the Tamarind substitute.

3. **(A)** Cover with a lid, then cook the veggies on high heat for 2 minutes. Tossing/stirring once or twice, letting the cabbage wilt a bit. **(B)** Use a spoon to push all veggies to the side, creating a 'well' in the center of the pan. Spray with cooking spray, then crack an egg into the center. Scramble the egg, till cooked, in the center of the pan. Once the egg is cooked, stir the broken bits into the vegetables. **(C)** Add the chicken and shrimp back into the pan, along with the green onions. Toss to combine. Pour in the sauce and the tamarind paste substitute. Cook for 2 minutes or so, tossing till all ingredients are well coated. **(D)** Add the cooked rice noodles into the pan, toss and fold, till the noodles are thoroughly coated and dark with the sauce. Pour onto a platter, garnish with chopped peanuts and fresh chopped cilantro.

PANCIT SOTANGHON

An AWESOME Filipino Noodle Dish, Filled with Shrimp, Chicken & Veggies With Thin Rice Noodles

Pancit is an amazing Filipino noodle dish, loaded to the gills with everything good. If you'd like a comparison, think of it like a huge platter of chow mein, loaded with meat and veggies, but even BETTER, because of the thin, slightly chewy rice noodles. My WW sister from another mister, *@mariarachael12*, shared her mother's recipe with me. This is my WW-ified version.

Servings Info.:

Yield: 12 cups
Servings: 8
Serving Size: 1.5 cups

R D
3-3

- last checked 11/28/22 -
Use your mobile device's 'Camera' App to look at this code for nutritional info.

Ingredients:

Meat:

- 3/4 lb chicken breast, sliced into thin strips
- 1/4 tsp baking soda, dissolved in 1 Tbsp water
- 1 tsp 'dark' soy sauce (optional, for color)
- 3/4 lb medium shrimp (41-50 count) peeled, tail off, deveined

Sauce:

- 1-1/2 cups fat free chicken broth
- 2 Tbsp <u>PLUS</u> 2 tsp soy sauce
- 1 tsp 'dark' soy sauce
- 1 Tbsp fish sauce (see notes)
- 1 Tbsp lemon juice
- 2 tsp paprika (for color)
- 1-1/2 tsp cornstarch

Vegetables:

- 3 cups sliced onion, loosely packed, 1/4" wide strips
- 1-1/4 cups celery, sliced on a bias, 1/4" thick
- 1-1/4 cups carrots, "shredded" (see notes)
- 6 medium garlic cloves, chopped
- 1/2 head green cabbage, chopped, loose packed (5 cups)
- 1/2 cup sliced green onions, or more, to taste

Additional Ingredients:

- 8oz uncooked vermicelli RICE noodles (see notes)

Directions:

1. Combine the chicken, baking soda/water and dark soy sauce. Set aside for 20-30 minutes. In a separate bowl, mix all the sauce ingredients till smooth, cover, set aside.

2. **(A)** Slice and prep all the vegetables, set aside. **(B)** Place the dried rice noodles into a large mixing bowl, then cover with warm (not hot) water. **(C)** Let the noodles soak according to package directions, till they are pliable, with the feel of regular 'al dente' pasta. Drain and set aside. **(D)** Heat a large pan over medium-high heat for 1 minute. Spray with cooking spray, then add the chicken. Cook until just cooked through, then pour the chicken into a bowl and return pan to the heat.

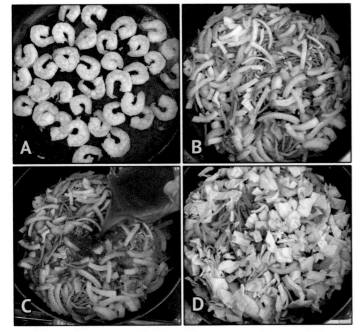

3. **(A)** Spray the pan with cooking spray, then add the shrimp. Cook for 2 minutes, toss, then cook for another 2 minutes. Place shrimp into the same bowl as the chicken, then return your pan to the heat again. Turn up heat to High. **(B)** Spray with cooking spray, then add the onions, carrots, celery and garlic. Cook over high heat for 2 minutes, till onions and celery are starting to sweat. **(C)** Pour the sauce into the pan and bring to a rolling boil. **(D)** Add the cabbage to the pan and cook, uncovered, for 4 minutes. The cabbage will begin to wilt with the sauce boiling under it.

4. **(A)** Add the chicken, shrimp and green onions to the pan, cook for 1 minute. **(B)** Mixing this much pasta together in one pan is extremely difficult, because of how fine the rice noodles are. I STRONGLY suggest that you do this like I did. Divide the pan's hot contents between itself and a 2nd large mixing bowl. Once divided, add half of the noodles into each of them. Toss till all ingredients are well combined. This will take a minute or two, but it's SO MUCH EASIER to mix it together, divided in half, because there is so much ultra fine, tangly noodles. Be patient. Once both batches are mixed well, combine them back into the pan. Turn the heat back on to medium-high, and cook for 1-2 minutes, re-warming the dish, while also helping the noodles absorb a little bit of the sauce as they heat through... Pour out onto a large platter and serve. Garnish with thin sliced green onions.

NOTES:

- **RICE NOODLES:** Ok folks, we're using a new ingredient your local stores MIGHT not have... 'vermicelli rice noodles'. They are found in the Asian food aisle, if your store has them. They look like angel hair pasta, but are even thinner. Some brands ask you to boil them for 2-3 minutes, while other brands (like what I used) simply have you soak the noodles in water for a few minutes. Follow the package instructions for the noodles you buy and use THOSE directions for steps *2B & 2C*, unless you find a type that calls for soaking, like mine did.

  If, however, you are unable to find vermicelli rice noodles at any of your nearby stores... you can make this recipe with angel hair pasta, cooked to 'al dente'. The texture will not be the same, but it will still be a really tasty platter of noodles.
- **FISH SAUCE:** You can find it in the Asian food aisle, near the soy sauce.
- **CARROTS:** Ok, this caused some confusion in prior recipes. When I say 'shredded carrots', I mean the bagged, shredded carrots you find in the produce department of your grocery store. The carrots are in long, very, very thin matchsticks, like you'd find in coleslaws. They aren't truly shredded, like you'd get from a hand grater.
- **HALVE THE RECIPE:** This baby makes a HUGE platter of pancit. As such, you can deeeeefinitely make a half batch. It'll make Step 4B unecessary. You'll be able to mix it all in just the one large pan.

SESAME CHICKEN

A low fat, low calorie version of the traditional Chinese staple

As far as 'sit-down' Chinese food is concerned, I have 2 dishes that are my comfort food. Singapore Noodles and Sesame Chicken. Hence, why they're both in this book. My version is less sweet than at most restaurants, and has a bit more savory depth. I reduced the sweetness, increased the 'umami' with a bit of oyster sauce, along with more sesame oil than is traditional. Personally, I like this version better.

Servings Info.:

Yields: 4 cups
Servings: 4
Serving Size: 1 cup

R D
3-3

- last checked 11/28/22 -
Use your mobile device's 'Camera' App to look at this code for nutritional info.

Ingredients:

Chicken:
- 1-1/4 pounds boneless skinless chicken breast, or chicken breast tenderloins, cut into bite sized chunks.
- 1/2 tsp baking soda, dissolved in 2 tsp water
- 1 batch of my 'toasted breading', recipe on pg. 17

Sesame Sauce & Glaze:
- 3/4 cup fat free chicken broth
- 1 Tbsp sesame oil (toasted sesame oil is best)
- 1-1/2 Tbsp oyster sauce
- 3 Tbsp lower sodium soy sauce
- 2 tsp 'dark' soy sauce
- 1/2 tsp minced fresh ginger (or 1/4 tsp ground ginger)
- 1 medium garlic clove, minced
- 3 Tbsp 0 calorie brown sugar replacement
- 1/4 tsp coarse ground black pepper
- 2 Tbsp rice vinegar
- 1 Tbsp PLUS 1 tsp cornstarch, dissolved with 1 Tbsp water
- 2 tsp Huy Fong Asian chili garlic sauce

Additional Ingredients:
- 1 tsp toasted sesame seeds, for garnish
- 1 green onion, thin sliced at an angle, for garnish

Directions:

1. Mix all of the Sauce ingredients together in a bowl, till well combined. Set aside.

2. Mix the chicken breasts pieces with the baking soda solution. Let marinate for 30 minutes.

3. **(A)** Heat a pan over medium heat for 1 minute, then add all breading ingredients. Toast for 3-4 minutes, or until the crumbs are a nice, uniformly golden color. Remove from pan and set aside, letting the crumbs cool to room temperature. **(B)** Place the whisked eggs into the bowl with the chicken pieces, mix to combine. **(C)** Place the toasted crumbs in a bowl, then place the chicken chunks, ONE AT A TIME, into the crumbs. Use a fork to lightly coat each chunk with the breading. **(D)** Place the lightly breaded chicken pieces onto 2 large baking pans, covered with foil and sprayed with a light coat of cooking spray. **(E)** Pre-Heat oven to 425 degrees.

4. Allow the chicken to rest for a few minutes, after it comes out of the oven. Then heat a good sized pan, or wok, for 1 minute over medium-high heat.

5. (A) Lightly spray the hot pan with cooking spray, then add the baked chicken pieces. Give the pan a few seconds to get back up to heat, then pour in the sauce. **(B)** The sauce will immediately begin to bubble, simmer and thicken. **(C)** Use 2 of your kitchen tools o' choice to quickly, yet gently, fold the chicken pieces with the sauce till well coated. Continue simmering and tossing until the sauce thickens. **(D)** Serve immediately. Garnish with sesame seeds and thin sliced green onions.

NOTES & SUGGESTIONS:

- **BREADING:** I strongly advise you NOT to try dumping all of the breading and chicken into a ziplock bag, then shake it all up. It does NOT work. It takes time, but you need to bread the chicken one piece at a time. It took me around 12 minutes.
- **CRISPINESS:** Though this is a good, healthy alternative to restaurant style deep fried chicken breast pieces, the breading on this chicken WILL lose its crispness after being coated with the sauce for a few minutes. Just like chicken Parmesan, once your breading begins to absorb the sauce, it will eventually lose its crunchy exterior. For this dish, toss the chicken into the hot sauce right before serving, to ensure the crisp texture lasts for as long as possible.
- **VEGGIES:** This only makes 4 cups of breaded and glazed sesame chicken. That's fine, but I'd highly recommend plating it with steamed or sauteed veggies, to 'stretch it out'. I usually eat it with steamed broccoli florets on the side, or sauteed broccolini/broccoli rabe, cooked with a little soy sauce and garlic.
- **POINTS:** If you'd like to lower this by 1 point per serving, do not bread the chicken. After the chicken marinates with the baking soda, simply cook the chicken in a hot pan, with cooking spray. Once the unbreaded chicken is cooked through, toss it with the sauce, just like in steps 5A, B & C.
- **BREAD CRUMBS INSTEAD OF RICE KRISPIES:** If you have access to 1 point per slice bread, instead of using my 'breading 2.0' recipe, for the crumbs... you can make a batch of my low point bread crumbs, from pg. 16. It makes enough real breadcrumbs to double-bread all the chicken for the same points. You'll just need an extra egg or two for the egg wash. But, the chicken will be CRAZY crunchy.

SHRIMP WITH LOBSTER SAUCE

A Deliciously Creamy and Savory Gravy-Like Sauce, Loaded with Ground Meat and Plump Shrimp

Ok... this is one of those 'bait and switch' dishes. For you folks thinking that you're about to get a dish full of Lobster... SURPRISE sucka! There isn't a single drop, bite, or molecule of lobster in this dish. This sauce is traditionally made, in China, for lobster, not shrimp. However, here in the good ol' US of A, Chinese cooks realized shrimp is a whole lot less expensive. Luckily, it's still an amazingly delicious entree with shrimp. This dish is typically served over rice, making it a very hearty, though light meal. As an added bonus, it is pretty low in sodium, as far as Asian dishes go.

Servings Info.:

Yields: 7 cups
Servings: 7
Serving Size: 1 cup

MY PLAN

R D
1-1

- last checked 11/28/22 -
Use your mobile device's 'Camera' App to
look at this code for nutritional info.

Ingredients:

Meat:
- 2 pounds shrimp (size 16-21ct), peeled, deveined, tail off
- 1/2 pound batch of my 'Asian' seasoned ground turkey, recipe on pg. 19 *(with 2 cups of reserved water.... for 1A)*

Sauce:
- 2-3/4 cups fat free chicken broth
- 1 Tbsp white wine
- 1 Tbsp rice vinegar
- 1 tsp sesame oil
- 1/2 tsp 0 calorie sugar replacement o' choice
- 1/2 tsp salt
- 1/4 tsp pepper
- 3 Tbsp PLUS 2 tsp cornstarch, dissolved into 1/4 cup water

Additional Ingredients:
- 2 garlic cloves, minced *(for use in step 2D)*
- 1 cup frozen peas
- 1/4 cup thin sliced green onion
- 1 large egg. Yup... an egg. Sounds crazy, but it's awesome.

Directions:

1. Mix together the 1/2 pound batch of my 'Asian' seasoned ground turkey. Set aside 20-30 mins. Mix the sauce ingredients together, set aside.

2. **(A)** Ok, this next part is going to be preeeetty weird... but just roll with it. In a large pan, bring 2 cups water to a boil, then add in the ground turkey. **(B)** Begin breaking apart the meat into smaaaall little pieces, as it cooks. Now, it gets even weirder. **(C)** Pour all of the meat into a strainer and rinse it off under cool running water. Set aside. **(D)** Heat a large, high walled pan over medium-high heat for 1 minute. Add the rinsed/drained ground turkey, 2 minced garlic cloves and the shrimp. Cook for 3-4 minutes, or until shrimp turns a light reddish-pink. Turn up the heat to High.

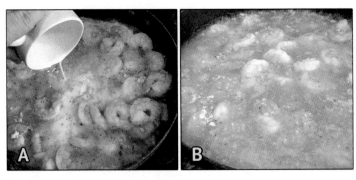

3. **(A)** Add all of the Sauce ingredients to the pan and bring to a boil. **(B)** Cook for 3-4 minutes at a rolling boil, allowing the sauce to begin thickening.

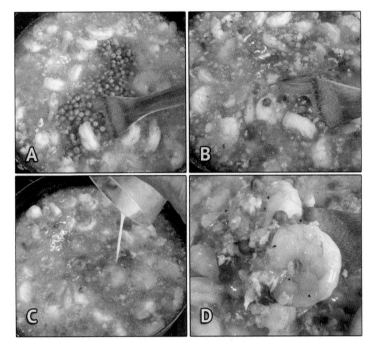

4. **(A)** Add the frozen (or thawed... you do you) peas into the sauce. Return to a rolling boil, cook for an additional 1-2 minutes, so the sauce thickens a little bit more. **(B)** Stir in the thin sliced green onions, stir to distribute, then immediately **(C)** pour in the beaten whole egg. **(D)** Begin stirring the raw egg into the pan. It will cook very quickly and will break apart into a gazillion... yes, a gazillion, fine little white threads o' egg, which will also help thicken the sauce even more, while adding a rich creaminess to the dish. This dish is typically eaten over rice. Use white or brown rice, it's up to you. You can even use that yuckie, chopped up, cauliflower stuff. Just... don't call it cauliflower rice, or I shall shun you and brandeth thee a heretic. It isn't rice!!

If desired, garnish with additional fresh sliced green onions and toasted sesame seeds.

SPECIAL MENTION:
Though I mention this dish is meant to be served over rice, my recipe does not include it, or the points for it. Use as much rice as you want, be it white, brown, or even that cauliflower heresy... but adjust your points accordingly.

NOTES (cont.)
- *WHITE RICE vs BROWN vs CAULIFLOWER:* Again... this dish is meant to be served over rice. Use whatever you want.
- *I DON'T LIKE SHRIMP, WAAAAAA!!:* Honestly, Susie... use chicken. I haven't tried it personally, but other people have told me they make it with diced chicken breast instead of shrimp and they love it.
- *WHITE WINE!?!?!:* The traditional recipes call for chinese cooking wine, however, it's very high in points. Rather than using 2 Tbsp of that hard to find Asian wine, which will 'up' the points... I'm using 1 Tbsp white wine and 1 Tbsp rice vinegar. It's 0 points and still tastes fantastic.
- *POINTS:* On both the regular and the diabetic plans, you can have up to 2 servings for 1 total point.
- *GROUND MEAT IN WATER? WTH, DANIEL!?!?!?:* Yeah, yeah, yeah... I know it's weird, but it works. The reason it's done like this is to ensure that the 99% fat free ground turkey cooks and breaks up into FINE pieces. This works, roll with it. The reason we are rinsing the cooked meat off, is the finished sauce is supposed to be 'clear' and light in color. Traditional recipes follow this same process... this isn't one of those 'crazy dhallak' things. Cooking the ultra lean ground turkey with added water is the only way to make it break into FINE grounds, like fatty ground meat would.

SHRIMP WITH SNOW PEAS

Tender Shrimp in a Light Soy, Wine, Ginger Sauce, With Crispy Snow Peas and a Subtly Vietnamese Twist

This simple recipe will be a new favorite for any of you shrimp lovers in the house. It's delicious, light, and surprisingly healthy, when you leave out the oil it's normally cooked with. This dish takes a little bit of time to prep, because of the snow peas, but once you start cooking, it all comes together in 10 minutes.

Servings Info.:

Yields: 7-1/2 cups
Servings: 5
Serving Size: 1-1/2 cups

MY PLAN R D **0-0**

- last checked 11/28/22 -
Use your mobile device's 'Camera' App to
look at this code for nutritional info.

Ingredients:

Shrimp:
- 2lbs raw shrimp, fresh or frozen. Peeled, deveined, tails removed. I used size 16-20 *"Extra Jumbo"* shrimp, you can use smaller shrimp if you want.
- 1 Tbsp water
- 1/2 tsp baking soda & 1 tsp sweetener, dissolved in the water.

Sauce:
- 3 Tbsp low sodium soy sauce
- 1/2 tsp 'dark' soy sauce
- 2-1/2 Tbsp oyster sauce
- 3 Tbsp 0 calorie sugar replacement (I used lakanto monkfruit)
- 1 Tbsp white wine (or use water if you want)
- 1/2 cup chicken broth OR clam juice
- 3 Tbsp lime juice
- 1 tsp rice vinegar
- 1 tsp fresh ginger, minced
- 1/8 to 1/4 tsp black pepper, to taste
- 1-1/2 Tbsp cornstarch, stirred into sauce, till dissolved

Additional Ingredients:
- 1.5lbs (24oz) fresh snow peas. I purchased (3) 8oz bags from my local grocery store.
- 1/2 cup green peas, fresh or frozen

Directions:

1. Combine the shrimp, water, dissolved baking soda and sweetener in a bowl. Set aside for 20 mins.

2. Mix together the sauce ingredients, set aside.

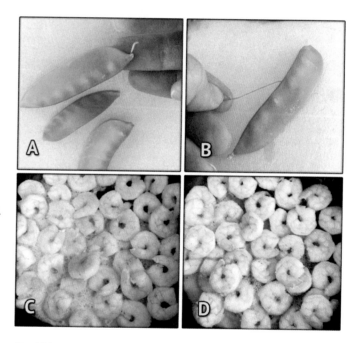

3. **(A)** To 'clean' the snow peas, pinch off the little string on one end, then **(B)** peel back to the opposite end of the pea pod. If it comes off as a long strand, awesome. If it doesn't that's ok. The primary goal is to at least remove the little string at the end. Set aside **(C)** Heat a LARGE pan over medium-high heat, for 1 minute. Spray pan with cooking spray, then add the shrimp. Let cook for 2 minutes without stirring. **(D)** Stir/toss the shrimp then cook for an additional 2-3 minutes, till they look pink and look just cooked through. Remove from pan, set aside.

4. Turn the heat up to high. Heat pan for 1 minute, or till water droplets dropped into the pan immediately sizzle and evaporate.

5. **(A)** Spray with cooking spray, then add the snow peas. Do NOT stir the snow peas! Let cook for 1-1/2 minutes, without mixing/tossing. You want them to slightly char. **(B)** Toss the snow peas, then cook another 1-1/2 minutes, without tossing. **(C)** Pour in the sauce, which will start to thicken quickly. As soon as the sauce thickens a little, toss and stir to coat the snow peas, then add the shrimp back into the pan, along with the additional peas. Mix to combine. **(D)** Cook for another minute, or until the sauce is thick and coats the dish. Done.

NOTES & SUGGESTIONS:

- *SHRIMP SIZE:* I like larger shrimp for my entrees. When you are buying shrimp, whether fresh or frozen, there are numbers listed with it. Example: 41-50 count, 21-25 count, or in this case, 16-20 count. That's how many shrimp you get per pound. I bought a bag of frozen, peeled, deveined, tail on 16-20 count "extra jumbo" shrimp. The larger the numbers per pound, the smaller the shrimp. For this recipe you can use any sized shrimp you want, just use 2 pounds worth. Also, smaller shrimp will cook quicker than larger shrimp, obviously. Adjust your cook times accordingly. PS: I bought 'tail-on' shrimp, because I wanted to remove the tails myself, so I could use them later for stock.
- *PEELED/DEVEINED:* I buy the shrimp that already have the shells removed and are already 'deveined'. For you folks new to shrimp… that means that the string of dark… um… 💩 has been removed. It's worth the couple of extra bucks to buy shrimp like this, otherwise YOU have to peel off all the shells and clean that 'waste' track out yourself.
- *WHITE WINE:* Obviously, this isn't traditional. But I'm using 1 Tbsp of white wine here, instead of Asian cooking wine, because I'm not going to make you go hunt down some 'shaoxing cooking wine', when you can get an inexpensive mini bottle of white wine at 7/11 for $2.
- *OYSTER SAUCE:* You can find oyster sauce in the same area of your local grocery store (or walmart) where you'd see soy sauce. If you don't like the briny 'ocean' flavor of oyster sauce, you can substitute it with 'vegetarian oyster sauce'. It has a kind of similar flavor… but is made from mushrooms.
- *BROTH/CLAM JUICE:* You can use chicken or vegetable broth for this dish. However, if you'd like it to have an even richer seafood flavor, you can substitute the broth with some 'clam juice'. It's found in the store, next to the canned tuna and sardines, typically.
- *SNOW PEAS:* Are NOOOOOOOT the same as 'snap peas'. Snap peas have a much tougher 'shell'. Buy snow peas.

SINGAPORE NOODLES

Singapore 'Mei Fun' is a Delicious Noodle Dish of Meat, Shrimp, & Veggies In A Peppered Curry Sauce

Singapore Noodles is a "dry" noodle dish, very light on sauce, with lots of curry and spices that are spread throughout. Loaded with shrimp, chicken and veggies, this is a very non-typical noodle dish to see on a menu. Servers are always surprised when I order it. Especially if you're a 'Guailo', like me.

Ingredients:

Meat & Veggies:
- 1/2 lb chicken breast, sliced into thin strips
- 2 tsp paprika mixed with 2 Tbsp water (for chicken)
- 1/2 tsp 'dark' soy sauce (optional, for color)
- 1/8 tsp baking soda (trust me)
- 1 lb large shrimp (16-20 count)
- 2 large red bell peppers, sliced into strips
- 1/2 cup shredded carrot
- 1/2 medium onion, sliced into strips
- 1/2 cup sliced green onion

Curried Noodle Sauce:
- 1/4 cup chicken broth
- 1/4 cup rice vinegar
- 1 Tbsp white wine ***
- 1/4 cup reduced sodium soy sauce
- 1-1/2 to 2-1/2 Tbsp curry powder, to taste. I used 2-1/2. The curry powder should be a strong flavor in this dish. This is a 'dry' noodle dish, not saucy, due to the powders.
- 1 Tbsp ground turmeric
- 1 tsp black pepper
- 1 tsp 0 calorie sugar replacement o' choice
- 1 tsp ginger root, minced
- 4 cloves garlic, chopped
- 1/2 tsp salt

Additional Ingredients:
- 1 large egg
- 8oz dry thin vermicelli RICE noodles. Cook according to package directions, then set aside. (see notes)
- 1 tsp sesame seeds, toasted in a hot pan till fragrant.
- additional thin sliced green onion, for garnish.

Servings Info.:
Yield: 11 cups
Servings: 7
Serving Size: 1.5 cups

MY PLAN R D 4-4

- last checked 11/29/22 -
Use your mobile device's 'Camera' App to look at this code for nutritional info.

Directions:

1. **(A)** Slice the chicken breasts into thin strips. **(B)** Mix the paprika, baking soda/water and dark soy sauce into a paste, then mix with the chicken. Set aside for 30 mins. **(C)** Whisk the egg until the egg and yolk are well mixed. Spray a pan with cooking spray and cook to form a flat, round omelette. **(D)** Remove from pan, roll the egg into a cigar shape, then slice thin. Set the sliced egg aside.

2. Combine the sauce ingredients in a bowl, set aside.

3. Toast the sesame seeds in a hot pan, till lightly brown and fragrant. Set aside.

NOTES:

- *RICE NOODLES:* Ok folks, we're using a new ingredient your local stores MIGHT not have... 'vermicelli rice noodles'. They are found in the Asian food aisle, if your store has them. They look like <u>SUPER THIN</u> angel hair pasta. Some brands ask you to boil them for 2-3 minutes, while other brands simply have you soak the noodles in hot water for a few minutes. Follow the package instructions for the noodles you buy. My recipe uses 26 points of thin vermicelli rice noodles.

  If, however, you are unable to find vermicelli rice noodles at any of your nearby stores... you can make this recipe with angel hair pasta, cooked to 'al dente'. The texture will not be the same, but it will still be a really tasty platter of noodles.

- *WINE:* Once again, we're subbing in some regular white wine in place of the higher point Asian cooking wine.

- *PAPRIKA CHICKEN? WTH, DAN?:* This is more for looks than anything. The REGULAR version of this dish you'd get at a Chinese restaurant, has thin sliced, ultra reddish bbq pork. To mimic the look of the bbq pork which I am obviously not including in this dish... I've using the paprika and dark soy sauce to give our sliced chicken a reddish color, once cooked. It makes the dish look closer to the real deal.

4. (A) Heat the biggest pan that'ya have, over medium heat, for 1 minute. Spray with cooking spray, then cook the chicken breast until just cooked through. Set aside. (B) Add shrimp to the pan, cover, and cook for a few minutes, till the shrimp is cooked through and pink. Set aside. (C) Admire all your prepared veggies, then crank up the heat to medium high. (D) Spray the pan with cooking spray and add the onions, red bell peppers, green onions and carrots. Cover and cook for 4 minutes, till starting to soften.

5. (A) Pour the sauce into the pan and cook uncovered for 2 minutes at a hard boil, stirring so that it doesn't burn. (B) If ALL of the liquid has evaporated, add a little water. Turn off the heat and add all of the cooked pasta into the pan. (C) Take your time and fold all of the pasta into the pan, to distribute the veggies and sauce. The pasta will be lightly coated and take on a yellow hue. (D) Add the egg, chicken and shrimp, gently fold till well mixed. Plate, then garnish with extra green onion and toasted sesame seeds.

String Bean Chicken

Yet another slimmed down version of a traditional Chinese recipe

I know that as far as Chinese fast food goes, the String Bean Chicken at Panda Express is pretty low-ish in calories and points already... but I can't leave well enough alone. My wife requested this dish because it's her favorite chicken entree on Panda's menu. Rather than simply making a copycat fast food recipe, which is what ALL the skinny bloggers do, I actually visited the website of a famous Chinese Chef, based in Taiwan, then modified his personal recipe.

Servings Info.:

Yields: 9 cups
Servings: 6
Serving Size: 1-1/2 cup

MY PLAN

R D
0-0

- last checked 11/29/22 -
Use your mobile device's 'Camera' App to
look at this code for nutritional info.

Ingredients:

Chicken & Marinade:
- 1-1/4 pounds boneless skinless chicken breast, or chicken breast tenderloins, cut into thin strips
- 1 Tbsp reduced sodium soy sauce
- 1/4 tsp sesame oil
- 1/2 tsp baking soda. Trust me, roll with the madness.

Sauce:
- 2 Tbsp reduced sodium soy sauce
- 3 Tbsp black bean sauce *** (see notes)
- 2 tsp 'dark' soy sauce
- 1 Tbsp white wine *** (see notes)
- 1/2 cup chicken broth
- 1 Tbsp 0 calorie sugar replacement o' choice
- 1 Tbsp cornstarch dissolved into 2 Tbsp water
- 4 medium garlic cloves, finely chopped
- 1/2 tsp fresh ginger, minced
- 3 green onions, sliced thin on a bias
- 1/4 tsp cracked black pepper

Additional Ingredients:
- 1 onion, quartered and sliced into thin strips
- 1-1/2 lb bag (24oz) fresh green beans, ends trimmed off. Cut into 1-1/2 to 2 inch lengths.
- 1 tsp sesame seeds, for garnish, if desired

Directions:

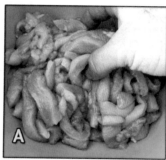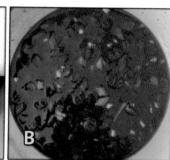

1. **(A)** Add the sliced chicken to a bowl. Stir together the soy sauce, sesame oil and baking soda, then coat the chicken with the mixture. Allow to rest for 30 minutes.
   (B) In a separate bowl, combine the 'Sauce' ingredients. Set aside.

2. **(A)** Prepare the onions and green beans, set aside.
   (B) Heat a large pan over medium-high heat for 1 minute. Spray with cooking spray, then add the marinated chicken. Cook for 4-5 minutes, or till the chicken is just cooked through.

3. Once the chicken is cooked through, remove it from the pan, set aside, then return pan to the heat.

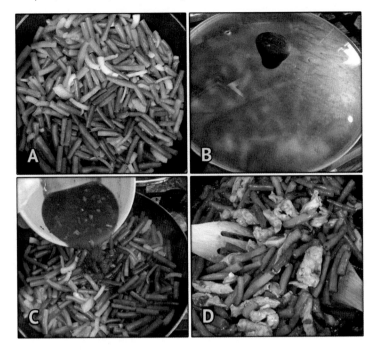

4. (A) Give the pan a few seconds to get back up to heat, then turn it up to High heat. Add the green beans and onions, spread them around the pan, then LEAVE THEM ALONE for 1 minute. Seriously, don't even shake the pan. After 1 minute, stir the contents, then let it sit again, untouched, for 1 more minute. Sear them babies! **(B)** Pour 1/4 cup water into the pan and cover with a lid. Lower the heat to Medium and steam the veggies for 4 minutes. **(C)** Remove the lid and pour the sauce over the veggies. Cook for 2 minutes, or until the sauce just begins to start thickening. **(D)** Add the chicken back into the pan, stir to combine, cook until the sauce has thickened and has slathered the dish in awesome-sauce. Try one of the green beans. If you'd like them a little softer, cook till desired doneness. Garnish with sesame seeds.

NOTES & SUGGESTIONS:

- **BLACK BEAN SAUCE:** BBS Is essential for the traditional version of this dish. Check for it in the Asian food aisle of your local grocery stores. I had to check 6 stores before I found it. You can fix that by ordering some online from walmart or elsewhere. Note, different brands are different points. I used 'Kikkoman' brand, Black Bean Sauce with Garlic, which is 2 points for 3 Tbsp. If you cannot get black bean sauce, use oyster sauce as a replacement, though it'll be a drastically different flavor. I highly recommend the black bean sauce.
- **WHITE WINE:** What the heck?... Well, The traditional recipe calls for an Asian sweet wine. I'm not going to tell you to buy that. Instead, we're using regular white wine plus some sweetener, in the sauce. Problem solved.
- **PROTEIN:** It goes without saying, for a vegetarian option, you can replace the chicken with firm tofu.
- **GREEN BEANS:** For the love of Jackie Chan, please use fresh green beans for this. They sell bags of them in the produce aisle, all you need to do is trim the ends and cut to length. I suppose you COULD use frozen green beans... but your dish will end up a sad, soggy, mushy mess. Bleh.
- **LARGE FRYING PAN vs. WOK:** I'm using a large pan instead of a Wok, because most people don't have one. My recipes will always use common equipment in their preparations, to make the dishes as accessible as possible. Hence, why I also don't use an air fryer or grill. Not everyone has a grill, but everyone has an oven or toaster oven. Same with good ol' frying pans. Now, in the words of my Uncle... "Allez Cuisine!"
- **GREEN BEAN FIRMNESS:** Again... use my cook time for the final dish as a base. If you want your green beans to be a little softer, let it cook longer. The chicken WILL NOT DRY OUT. That baking soda trick works wonders for the texture of the chicken breast pieces.

SWEET & SOUR CHICKEN

Sweet And Savory With A Sour Kick... Just Like Me, Without Coffee

Sweet & sour chicken is a staple at Chinese take out places across the country. Crispy, tangy, sweet and savory, with big chunks of crispy chicken, bell peppers, onions and pineapple. It's usually battered chicken fried in oil, mine is breaded and baked, then dressed in a sugar free sweet & sour sauce. It's a lot lower in calories, sugar and fat than any restaurant version.

Servings Info.:

Yields: 9 cups
Servings: 6
Serving Size: 1.5 cups

MY PLAN
R D
1-2

- last checked 11/29/22 -
Use your mobile device's 'Camera' App to
look at this code for nutritional info.

Ingredients:

Chicken:
- 1-1/4 pounds boneless skinless chicken breast, or chicken breast tenderloins, cut into bite sized chunks.
- 1/4 tsp baking soda, mixed with 1 Tbsp water
- 1 batch of my 'low point breading', recipe on pg. 17

Sweet & Sour Sauce / Glaze:
- 3/4 cup + 2 Tbsp water
- 3/4 cup rice vinegar
- 3/4 cup 0 calorie sugar replacement o' choice
- 2 Tbsp tomato sauce
- 1 Tbsp garlic, chopped or minced
- 1 Tbsp ginger, finely chopped or minced
- 2 Tbsp cornstarch, dissolved in 2 Tbsp water

Additional Ingredients:
- 1 jumbo onion (or 2 large onions), diced, roughly 1" pieces.
- 1 large red bell pepper (or 2 medium), cut into 1" pieces.
- 1 large green bell pepper (or 2 medium), cut into 1" pieces.
- 2 cups fresh pineapple, cut into bite sized pieces
- 1 green onion, thin sliced at an angle, for garnish.

Directions:

1. Place the chicken breast pieces into a large bowl. Mix together with the baking soda solution. Set aside for 20-30 minutes.

2. Line 2 large oven sheet pans with foil. Spray with cooking spray, set aside.

3. **(A)** Heat a pan over medium heat for 1 minute, then add all breading ingredients. Toast for 3-4 minutes, or until the crumbs are a nice, uniform, golden color. Remove from pan and set aside, letting the crumbs cool to room temperature. **(B)** Place the whisked 'egg wash' into the bowl with the chicken, mix to combine. **(C)** Place the toasted crumbs in a bowl, then place the chicken chunks, ONE AT A TIME, into the crumbs. Use a fork to lightly coat each chunk with the breading. **(D)** Place the lightly breaded chicken pieces onto 2 large baking pans, covered with foil and sprayed with a light coat of cooking spray. **(E)** Pre-Heat oven to 425 degrees.

4. Combine all of the sauce ingredients in a small sauce pot stir to combine, then bring to a boil. Boil for 3-4 minutes, till it thickens, then set aside.

5. Put the breaded chicken into the preheated oven. Bake at 425 degrees for 15 minutes. Remove from oven, flip the pieces, then bake for 4 more minutes. Remove from oven, set aside. It's ok, you want the chicken to cool a little..

6. (A) Heat a large pan for 1 minute over medium-high heat. Spray with cooking spray, then add the bell peppers and onion. Cook for 4-5 minutes, **(B)** then reduce heat to medium and add pineapple chunks. Cook for 3-4 minutes, till pineapple starts to slightly caramelize. **(C)** Add the cooked chicken and sauce to the pan. **(D)** Gently toss till all ingredients are coated in thick sauce. Garnish with thin sliced green onions. Done.

NOTES & SUGGESTIONS:

- *CRISPINESS:* Though this is a good, healthy alternative to restaurant style deep fried chicken breast pieces, the breading on this chicken WILL lose its crispness after being coated with the sauce for a few minutes. Just like chicken Parmesan. Once your breaded chicken begins to absorb the sauce, it will eventually lose its crunchy exterior. For this dish, toss all of the ingredients together right before serving to ensure the crisp texture lasts for as long as possible.

- *POINTS:* The regular "Sweet & Sour Chicken" entree at Panda Express is 13 points per serving. Mine, is 1-2, depending on which plan you're on. This is a great example of how once you figure out the basics of hacking recipes using the builder... it will make your head spin. You can make a healthier, low point version of almost anything you miss eating.

- *BREAD CRUMBS INSTEAD OF RICE KRISPIES:* If you have access to 1 point per slice bread, instead of using my 'breading 2.0' recipe, for the crumbs... you can make a batch of my low point bread crumbs, from pg. 16. It makes enough real breadcrumbs to double-bread all the chicken for the same points. You'll just need an extra egg or two for the egg wash. But, the chicken will be CRAZY crunchy.

- *SWEETENER:* For dishes like this that use a lot of 0 point sweetener, instead of sugar, I personally prefer to use Lakanto monkfruit, though it's a bit pricier. You can also use Stevia, Truvia, Splenda, or others, depending on your dietary restrictions. However, take note that some sweeteners do add points after certain amounts are used.

- *SPICY VERSION:* This sauce is my Sweet & Sour sauce, from the Condiments & Dips section. If you want to make a spicy Thai variation, add 1 Tbsp soy sauce, 3 tsp red pepper flakes and 1 Tbsp sugar free peach preserves/jam. You'll have essentially turned this sauce into a double batch of my Thai Sweet Chili sauce.

SWEET FIRE CHICKEN

This Dish Combines Crunchy Breaded Chicken With A Sweet & Spicy Pineapple Sauce

My favorite entree at Panda is Sweet Fire Chicken. It's similar to their crispy orange chicken, except instead of orange, it's a pineapple glaze, with chunks of pineapple, onions, red chilis, and red and green bell peppers. It's sweet, spicy and saucy, just like me. In order to "skinny" the dish, I decided rather than deep frying the chicken, we're breading and baking the chicken, till crispy.

Servings Info.:

Yields: 9 cups
Servings: 6
Serving Size: 1.5 cups

MY PLAN — R D 2-2

- last checked 11/30/22 -
Use your mobile device's 'Camera' App to look at this code for nutritional info.

Ingredients:

Chicken:

- 1-1/4 pounds boneless skinless chicken breast, or chicken breast tenderloins, cut into bite sized chunks.
- 1/4 tsp baking soda, dissolved into 1 Tbsp water
- 1 batch of my 'low point breading', recipe on pg. 17

Sweet & Spicy Pineapple Sauce & Glaze:

- 1/2 cup pineapple juice (see additional ingredients).
- 3 Tbsp reduced sodium soy sauce
- 4 Tbsp 0 calorie sugar replacement o' choice
- 2 medium garlic cloves, minced
- 1 tsp ginger root, finely chopped/minced
- 3/4 to 1 tsp red pepper flakes (or more, to taste).
- 1 Tbsp cornstarch, dissolved in 2 Tbsp water.
- 1 Tbsp PLUS 1 tsp sugar free syrup (pancake syrup)
- 1/4 tsp black pepper

Additional Ingredients:

- 1 jumbo onion
- 1 large red bell pepper (or 2 medium)
- 1 large green bell pepper (or 2 medium)
- 2 cups fresh pineapple, cut into bite sized chunks.
- 1 tsp sesame seeds, toasted, for garnish.
- 2 green onions, thin sliced at an angle, for garnish.

Directions:

1. In a bowl, mix together the chicken breast chunks with the baking soda solution. Set aside for 20 mins.

2. Mix all of the Sauce ingredients together in a bowl, till well combined. Set aside.

3. **(A)** Heat a pan over medium heat for 1 minute, then add all breading ingredients. Toast for 3-4 minutes, or until the crumbs are a nice, uniformly golden color. Remove from pan and set aside, letting the crumbs cool to room temperature. **(B)** Place the whisked eggs into the bowl with the chicken pieces, mix to combine. **(C)** Place the toasted crumbs in a bowl, then place the chicken chunks, ONE AT A TIME, into the crumbs. Use a fork to lightly coat each chunk with the breading. **(D)** Place the lightly breaded chicken pieces onto 2 large baking pans, covered with foil and sprayed with a light coat of cooking spray. **(E)** Pre-Heat oven to 425 degrees.

4. Bake the chicken for 14 minutes. Remove from oven, flip the pieces, then bake for 4-5 more minutes. Remove chicken from the oven, then set it aside.

5. (A) Heat a <u>large</u> pan for 1 minute over med.-high heat. Spray with cooking spray, then add bell peppers and onions. Crank the heat up to High and cook for 4 minutes. **(B)** After 4 minutes on High, add the sauce and pineapple to the pan, toss to combine. Continue cooking for 2-3 more minutes, or until the sauce thickens. **(C)** Gently fold in the baked chicken pieces. **(D)** Toss/fold until well combined and coated in thick sauce. Done. Serve immediately. Garnish with sliced green onions and sesame seeds.

NOTES & SUGGESTIONS:

- *CRISPINESS:* Though this is a good, healthy alternative to restaurant style deep fried chicken breast pieces, the breading on this chicken WILL lose its crispness after being coated with the sauce for a few minutes. Just like chicken Parmesan. Once your breaded chicken begins to absorb the sauce, it will eventually lose its crunchy exterior. For this dish, toss the chicken into the hot sauce and vegetables right before serving to ensure the crisp texture lasts for as long as possible.
- *SPICINESS:* Feel free to add more red pepper flakes, or even to toss in some dried asian chilis, to make this dish as spicy as you'd like. Your goal is for a sweet and spicy sauce. But you should definitely have a little spicy kick.
- *BREAD CRUMBS INSTEAD OF RICE KRISPIES:* If you have access to 1 point per slice bread, instead of using my 'breading 2.0' recipe, for the crumbs... you can make a batch of my low point bread crumbs, from pg. 16. It makes enough real breadcrumbs to double-bread all the chicken for the same points. You'll just need an extra egg or two for the egg wash. But, the chicken will be CRAZY crunchy.
- *PINEAPPLE:* You can use either fresh or canned pineapple. However, if you use canned chunked pineapple, the dish will 100% not taste as good. Trust me, I've made it both ways to try it out. If available, use fresh pineapple, it makes a huuuuuge difference. Canned pineapple is soggy and squishy, but it's definitely convenient and cheap. So, you do you.
- *PINEAPPLE JUICE:* Here's one where you get to pick your poison, so to speak. Well.. unless you're on the diabetic plan, then yeah... pineapple juice pretty much is. 🙀 You can choose to buy a can o' pineapple 'in pineapple juice' and simply use 1/2 cup of that liquid. Or, buy a bottle o' pineapple juice. Either way, 1/2 cup is 3 points.

TERIYAKI CHICKEN

My Teriyaki Recipe Is Awesome, But Is Sooooooo Non Traditional It'd Make A Samurai Commit Seppuku

Ok, we ALL know what Teriyaki Chicken is. Everyone has had it at Chinese take-out, or have had it while eating a teriyaki bowl. I'm not going to go through a long description of what it is, other than saying it originates from Japan. However, 'fast food' or even dine-in Teriyaki is typically a RIDICULOUS amount of points and calories. We're so used to it being coated in an extremely thick and sugary sauce, it's often one of the highest calorie dishes on a menu. My version uses a LOT of ingredient substitutions to make it fat free, and sugar free, with the exception of the teeny bit of wine (0.1g sugar).

Servings Info.:

Yields: 4 chicken breasts
Servings: 4
Serving Size: 1 breast

MY PLAN

R D
0-0

- last checked 11/30/22 -
Use your mobile device's 'Camera' App to look at this code for nutritional info.

Ingredients:

Chicken:
• 4 good sized boneless skinless chicken breasts (see notes)

Marinade:
• 1 Tbsp low sodium soy sauce
• 1 tsp 'dark' soy sauce (optional, primarily for color)
• **3/8 tsp** baking soda, dissolved with 1 Tbsp water

SAUCE: (mix together, set aside)
• 2 Tbsp PLUS 1 tsp low sodium soy sauce
• 1-1/2 tsp 'dark' soy sauce (optional, primarily for color)
• 1 Tbsp no sugar added ketchup (**No arguing!!** *see notes*)
• 2 Tbsp rice vinegar
• 1 Tbsp white wine
• 1-1/2 Tbsp 0 point sweetener o' choice (I used monkfruit)
• 1/2 to 1 tsp fresh ginger, minced (to taste)
• 1-1/2 tsp cornstarch, dissolved with 1 Tbsp water

• **Additional Ingredients:**
• 2 Tbsp water (*for braising, step 2B*)
  1/2 cup water (*for sauce, set aside for step 3B*)

RECIPE NOTES:
Though my recipe calls for 4 chicken breasts... you might notice that my pictures only show 2. Well... that's because, like an uncoordinated panda, I dropped 2 of them.

Directions:

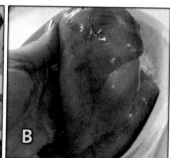

1. **(A)** Use a kitchen mallet, or summon Thor's hammer, then lightly flatten <u>the thickest area</u> of your chicken. Try to make them a uniform size, without pulverizing them. **(B)** Mix the marinade together, rub/smear it all over the chicken, then set aside for at LEAST 30 minutes.

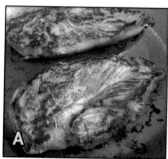
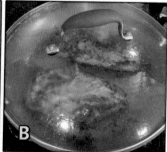

2. **(A)** Heat a LARGE pan over High heat, for 1 minute, then spray with cooking spray. Add the chicken breasts into the hot pan, smooth sides down. Let them sear, unmoved, for 2 minutes. Flip the chicken and sear 2 more minutes. **(B)** Pour 2 Tbsp water into the pan and immediately cover with lid. Reduce heat to medium, cook for 5 minutes, covered.

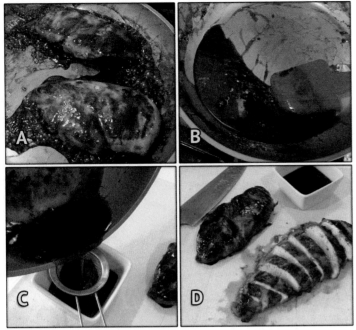

3. **(A)** Remove the lid and turn the heat up to medium-high. Stir the sauce again, making sure to get the cornstarch off the bottom, then pour the sauce into your pan. Cook the chicken in the sauce, flipping occasionally, until the sauce thickens and almost all of the liquid evaporates. Remove chicken from pan, set aside to rest. **(B)** Turn the heat up to High, then add an additional 1/2 cup of water to the pan. Mix the water and thickened bits o' sauce, till they are once again 'mostly' smooth, and cook till reduced down a bit more. **(C)** When the sauce has thickened slightly, pour it through a wire strainer, to remove any leftover bits. You want a flavorful and smooth sauce. **(D)** Now that your chicken has rested, you can serve it however you'd like. Serve it as whole breasts, or sliced, with sauce drizzled on top. If you want to serve it a little more Chinese-style, you can slice the chicken, then add it to the pan during step 3B. Then, the sliced chicken will be coated with sauce. If you go that route, you can skip steps *3C & D*.

NOTES & SUGGESTIONS:

- *CHICKEN:* For my recipe, I'm using good sized, large, thick chicken breasts.
- *COOK TIME:* The cook times for my recipe take into account using large, thick chicken breasts. Seriously, I used Dolly Parton sized Costco chicken breasts. If you are using 'thin sliced' chicken breasts, do NOT sear them on high heat for as long as I did, then braise them for 5 minutes in the water, they'll taste like shoe leather. If you use thin breasts, I'd try searing on high heat for 1 minute per side, then braise for maybe 2 minutes per side. Remember... after cooking, covered, they still get cooked for a few more minutes in the sauce. Nobody likes dry chicken, shoe leather chicken breasts.
- *THIS ISN'T A TRADITIONAL RECIPE!!!!!:* Ya'don't say, Nancy?
- *RICE VINEGAR???:* Traditional teriyaki recipes call for using a good amount of 'Mirin', which is a sweetened rice wine vinegar. Well, Mirin has points. Instead, we're using 0 point rice vinegar, then adding some sweetener. Boom, problem solved. (I used lakanto monkfruit)
- *WHITE WINE!!?!:* Again.... it's a lower point ingredient swap. Regular teriyaki uses Sake, which is a Japanese rice alcohol. Sake, being hard liquor, has a good deal of points. I'm substituting 1 Tbsp of white wine because it's 0 points. Combined with the rice vinegar and sweetener, it's a good and viable substitute for no added points.
- *DARK SOY SAUCE:* Gives the finished dish it's dark, rich looking coloring. Without it, the chicken will be pale.
- *RED HUE:* I know you guys are scratching your head, wondering "WHAT THE HECK IS HE THINIKING..... KETCHUP?!?!" Well, I'm including it because I'm used to fast food teriyaki chicken, which we ALL know has a red coloring to it A lot of fast food places add red food dye to their sauces. Instead, I'm adding that tiny, 1 Tbsp of no sugar added ketchup. That little bit will give a very slight reddish hue to the sauce. However, if you don't want to include it, skip it. Or, if you want to use it but don't want to go buy a bottle of ketchup, use 1 Tbsp of tomato sauce.

THAI BASIL CHICKEN

This Incredible Dish Is Bursting With Flavors. If You've Never Had It Before, It'll Be A New Favorite.

I have to be fully honest and up front. I'm one of those people, who has gone my entire life not knowing what to order at Thai restaurants. I have no idea what ANY of that stuff is on the menus, which is why I am having so much fun making this new cookbook!!! I'm getting to try out so many new dishes! I... absolutely... LOVE this. Today, making this dish, was the first time in my life I've ever had it. The sauce is extremely complex, with a deep, silky, nearly gravy like sauce to it. It has a nice sweetness, a bit of heat (which you can ratchet up)... and oh, my, staaars... then the basil comes along and karate chops your taste buds.

Servings Info.:

Yields: 6 cups
Servings: 4
Serving Size: 1-1/2 cup

R D
0-0

- last checked 11/30/22 -
Use your mobile device's 'Camera' App to look at this code for nutritional info.

Ingredients:

CHICKEN:

- 1-1/2 pounds boneless skinless chicken breast, cut into small bited sized pieces
- 1/2 tsp baking soda, stirred into 1 Tbsp water

SAUCE:

- 3 Tbsp <u>PLUS</u> 1 tsp low sodium soy sauce
- 2 Tbsp oyster sauce
- 2-1/2 tsp 'dark' soy sauce
- 1 Tbsp Asian chili sauce (I used Huy Fong, chili garlic)
- 2 Tbsp 0 calorie sugar replacement o' choice
- 1/4 tsp cracked black pepper
- 1-1/2 tsp cornstarch

ADDITIONAL INGREDIENTS:

- 2 large red bell peppers, cut into 1/2" pieces. (2-1/2 cups)
- 2 medium (or 1 LARGE) onion, rough chopped. (3 cups)
- 6 medium garlic cloves, minced
- 1 tsp sesame seeds, for garnish

THAI BASIL (and substitute)

- - Use either 2 cups of Thai Basil leaves... *OR*.....
  - Use 3 cups of 'regular' Basil leaves, like you use for Italian dishes. In addition to that, add 1 Tbsp finely chopped tarragon *(SEE NOTES)*

Directions:

1. Mix together the chicken with the baking soda. Set aside for 20-30 minutes. While it's marinating, mix the sauce together, cover, set aside.

2. **(A)** Chop, prep and set aside veggies and herbs.
   (B) Heat a LARGE pan over high heat for 1 minute. Spray with cooking spray, then add all of the chicken to the pan. Cook for around 5 minutes, or till just cooked through. Remove chicken from pan, set aside, return empty pan to heat. **(C)** Add the bell peppers, onions and garlic. **(D)** Cook over high heat till onions are starting to caramelize around the edges.

3. **(A)** Return chicken to the pan and mix with the veggies. Pour in the sauce, toss to mix. **(B)** Continue to cook over high heat. Let the dish sit for 10-15 seconds, then toss to combine. Repeat that process for a minute or two, so the sauce can thicken. Once the chicken is well covered in a nice, dark coating of sauce, **(C)** turn off the heat and immediately add the fresh herbs. **(D)** With the heat off, toss and mix the chicken and vegetables with the herbs, allowing them to wilt in the residual heat of the dish. Serve immediately. If you'd like, you can garnish the dish with a 0 point amount (up to 7/8 tsp) of sesame seeds, though it's optional.

NOTES & SUGGESTIONS:

- *THAI BASIL OR SUBSITUTIONS:* Ok... this is going to be a bit of a read, so bear with me. This dish is called "thai basil" chicken. As such... it is highly recommended that you use real thai basil. However... acknowledging the fact that not everyone has access to it, I wanted to present you with a viable substitution with common ingredients. Every single snootie food blog will tell you:

    "... if you can't find real Thai basil, use regular basil, but it won't taste as good. But unfortunately, regular basil lacks a licorice flavor that's present in Thai basil."

    Well, those food snoots aren't using common sense. Use regular basil... but ADD ANOTHER INGREDIENT that will give it a slight licorice flavor. In my recipe, I'm choosing to use a little bit of additional fresh tarragon. You can also try using some anise, or maybe a little fennel. This isn't rocket science. Most bloggers don't experiment with ingredient substitutions. So... yes, use 1.5x as much regular basil as you would Thai basil. BUT... also, try adding an additional ingredient that gives the missing flavor. Have fun experimenting on what you could use. Tarragon worked for me.

- *DARK SOY SAUCE:* No, it is not regular soy sauce. It is a darker, slightly thicker soy sauce, mostly used to enhance the richness and dark color of sauces. If you buy it online, look for 'sushi chef' brand. It lets you have the most for 0 points. Additionally... DO NOT GET 'Mushroom Flavored' dark soy sauce... it's disgusting.

- *WHERE ARE THE HOT PEPPERS?:* I'm NOT going to make you go find an Asian market and buy Thai chili peppers. That's why I'm using Asian chili sauce for the heat in my recipe. It's at every store and it's incredibly easy to adjust your level of heat. However... if you want to go <u>full-tilt</u> traditional, replace the chili sauce with 8-10 Thai chili peppers. You can also use some sliced red jalapeños. But seriously... ya'll are crazy. That'll melt your face off.

Thai Sweet Chili Shrimp

Sweet and Spicy Shrimp With Lemon Zest, Lime Juice, Chili Sauce and Cilantro

I figured I'd take a little departure from the Chinese themed dishes I've been doing lately, to mix it up with some Thai food. The flavor profile of this dish runs the gamut from spicy to savory, from salty to sweet, and then there's the lime juice that sneaks up and punches you in your hoobajoob. It's like hitching a ride on the Orient Express, with your tongue on the tracks.

Servings Info.:
Yields: 5 cups
Servings: 5
Serving Size: 1 cup

R D
0-0

- last checked 11/30/22 -
Use your mobile device's 'Camera' App to look at this code for nutritional info.

Ingredients:

Shrimp:
- 2lbs raw shrimp, fresh or frozen. Peeled, deveined, tail on. Get size 16-21 count shrimp (see notes)
- 1/4 tsp baking soda, dissolved with 2 tsp water
- 1 tsp 0 calorie sugar replacement o' choice (I used lakanto)
- 1-1/2 Tbsp cornstarch
- 1-1/2 tsp flour
- 1-1/2 tsp plain breadcrumbs

Sauce:
- 3 Tbsp low sodium soy sauce
- 2 Tbsp asian chili sauce (I used Huy Fong chili garlic sauce)
- 3 Tbsp 0 calorie sugar replacement o' choice
- 3 Tbsp lime juice
- 1 Tbsp white wine (or use water if you want, sissy)
- 2 tsp fish sauce (see notes)
- 2 tsp fresh ginger, minced
- 4-5 medium garlic cloves, minced
- 2 tsp minced lemon zest (2 medium lemons should do it)
- 1 Tbsp PLUS 1 tsp sugar free syrup (pancake syrup).

Additional Ingredients:
- 1 large red bell pepper, slice into long 1/2" thick strips, then cut the long strips in half.. so you get shortened thick strips.
- 3 Tbsp cilantro, finely chopped

Directions:

1. Combine the shrimp, water, dissolved baking soda & sweetener in a bowl. Set aside for 20 mins.

2. Mix together the sauce ingredients, set aside.

3. **(A)** When ready to cook, add the cornstarch and flour into the bowl with the shrimp. **(B)** Mix to combine, coating the shrimp with a thin batter. **(C)** Heat a large pan over medium heat, till water dropped onto it immediately sizzles and evaporates. Spray pan with cooking spray, then place half of the shrimp in the pan, so you don't crowd them. Cook them for 2 minutes, without moving them. Spray tops of shrimp with more cooking spray, then flip. **(D)** Cook for an additional 2 minutes, then set aside to rest on a plate. Repeat till all shrimp are cooked. Set aside.

4. Return the pan to medium-high. heat Once water droplets sizzle on the pan, it should be hot enough for the veggies. The pan should be just about as hot as you ladies find Ryan Gosling holding a baby kitten.

5. **(A)** Spray the pan with cooking spray, then add the bell peppers. Cook for 3-4 minutes, without moving them, till they are lightly charring. **(B)** Pour the sauce into the pan and allow it to cook down slightly. **(C)** Once the sauce begins to thicken/reduce, return the cooked shrimp to the pan and toss till well coated. **(D)** Add fresh chopped cilantro to the pan and toss till well mixed. Done. If desired, you can garnish with some thin sliced green onions, additional fresh cilantro and 1 tsp sesame seeds.

NOTES & SUGGESTIONS:

- *COATING:* Though I made the thin batter for my shrimp, you can choose to skip the step. If you leave the cornstarch, and flour out of the recipe, this <u>entire</u> dish goes down to 0 points on both plans. I do still recommend cooking the shrimp in batches, like I did. If you 'crowd your pan' with shrimp, they won't sear... they'll steam. Remember, 2 minutes per side on a preheated pan. You don't want rubbery shrimp.

- *SHRIMP SIZE:* I like larger shrimp for my entrees. When you are buying shrimp, whether fresh or frozen, there are numbers listed with it. Example: 41-50 count, 21-25 count, or in this case, 16-20 count. That's how many shrimp you get per pound. I bought a bag of frozen, peeled, deveined, tail on 16-20 count "extra jumbo" shrimp. The larger the numbers per pound, the smaller the shrimp.

- *PEELED/DEVEINED:* I buy the shrimp that already have the shells removed and are already 'deveined'. For you folks new to shrimp... that means that the string of dark... um... 💩 has been removed. It's worth the couple of extra bucks to buy shrimp like this, otherwise YOU have to peel off all the shells and clean that 'waste' track out yourself.

- *WHITE WINE:* Obviously, this isn't traditional. But I'm using 1 Tbsp of white wine here, instead of Asian cooking wine, because I'm not going to make you go hunt down some 'shaoxing cooking wine', when you can get an inexpensive mini bottle of white wine at 7/11 for $2.

- *FISH SAUCE:* Fish sauce is A MAJOR food flavoring in Thai cuisine. It can be found at grocery stores or walmarts, in the 'Asian food' aisle, next to the soy sauce. It's a very pungent sauce that adds a LOT of depth to Thai dishes. However, you should note that on it's own, if you just open up a bottle and take a whiff, it stiiiiiiinks by itself. It IS pretty much anchovy water, after all, so I wouldn't use it to take shots, if I were you.

TORIKATSU (KATSU CHICKEN)

Miso Marinated Chicken, Baked With Panko Breadcrumbs, Served With Japanese Katsu Sauce

Katsu Chicken, or 'Torikatsu', is one of the dishes I swore up and down I wasn't going to make. Let's face it, Katsu chicken is simply chicken, breaded with panko breadcrumbs, then deep fried or baked. Meh. But then a friend challenged me to try and 'fancy it up'. So, I marinated the chicken with miso paste, which we already have from the Miso Glazed Salmon. My intent was to give it a solid punch of umami flavor, rather than just standard salt and pepper. I also reworked my Katsu Sauce recipe. Regular katsu sauce is RIDICULOUSLY high in points, mine allows you to have up to 1/4 cup for 0 points. "**Dōitashimashite,**" mis amigos.
(You're Welcome, in Japanese)

Servings Info.:

Yields: 4 chicken breasts
Servings: 4
Serving Size: 1 breast

MY PLAN
R D
3-3

- last checked 11/30/22 -
- SPECIAL NOTE -
The actual Katsu Chicken in this recipe is only 2 points on both plans. I'm adding 1 additional point, for 1 serving of my Katsu sauce, which takes it up to 3 per serving

Ingredients:

Chicken:
• 4 large, boneless skinless chicken breasts (see notes)

Marinade:
• 3/8 tsp baking soda, dissolved with 1 Tbsp water
• 2 tsp lower sodium soy sauce
• 1-1/2 tsp miso paste

Breading:
• 1 cup PLUS 2 Tbsp Rice Krispies cereal. Measured, then lightly crushed in a ziplock bag
• 7 Tbsp unseasoned panko breadcrumbs
• 2 large eggs, beaten like a disloyal Yakuza
• 1 tsp all purpose flour
• 1 tsp cornstarch

Additional Ingredients &ThingieMcjigs:
• 1 batch of my Katsu sauce, recipe on pg. 22
• a fine wire mesh strainer (for dusting). Just roll with it.

Directions:

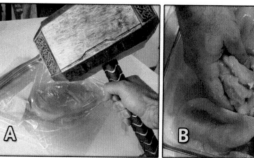
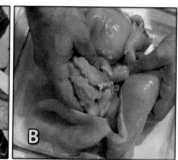

1. **(A)** Use a kitchen mallet to lightly flatten the thickest area of your chicken, to make each piece a uniform thickness. **(B)** Mix the baking soda, water, soy sauce and miso paste together. Rub over the chicken breasts. Set aside and allow to marinate for at least 30 minutes.

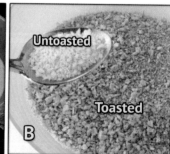

Untoasted

Toasted

2. **(A)** Combine the crushed rice cereal and panko crumbs together in a pan, over medium heat. Stir/toss every 30 seconds, till the breading has become a uniformed golden brown (about 4-5 minutes). Set aside. **(B)** This picture shows the difference between regular panko breadcrumbs vs toasted crumbs.

3. Preheat oven to 400 degrees. Line a baking pan with foil, place a wire rack OVER the pan (as seen in picture 4D).

Wire rack resting on top of the pan

4. **(A)** Place chicken breasts onto a plate, then gently scoop flour and cornstarch into a fine wire strainer. Holding the strainer over each chicken breast, lightly tap, dusting each piece in a coating of flour. Flip the chicken, to dust both sides. **(B)** In a large bowl, place your beaten eggs, then dip each piece of chicken into the egg wash, one at a time. **(C)** Place the egg-dipped chicken into a bowl with the toasted crumbs. Coat both sides, then place onto the wire rack, on the baking pan. **(D)** Spray chicken with cooking spray, then bake at 400 degrees for 35-40 minutes (for THICK chicken breasts). Less time will be required for thin chicken breasts. Done. Serve each piece with a 1/4 cup scoop of my Katsu sauce and a 1/4 tsp of sesame seeds.

NOTES & SUGGESTIONS:

- **COOK TIME:** The cook times for my recipe take into account using large, thick chicken breasts. If you use thin breasts, reduce the time to prooobably 20-25 minutes. If you aren't sure if it's done, pierce the thickest part of 1 breast with a knife. Turn the knife slighty and look inside. If it's pink.. keep cookin'. Chicken sashimi is NOT 'good eats'.
- **RICE KRISPIES???:** Normal recipes use straight panko breadcrumbs. I personally prefer a combination of panko and regular consistency crumbs. The Panko gives the crunch and body, the smaller crumbs fill in the spaces. Also, the reason I'm using rice cereal... 1-1/4 cup, crushed, gives 1/2 to 2/3 cup of crumbs for 5 points. While 1/2 cup of panko crumbs are 6 points. By combining the 2, we get a better finished texture (in my opinion, anyways), for less points than using straight panko.
- **POINTS FOR KATSU SAUCE!:** My katsu sauce is 1 point per 1/4 cup serving on both plans. As mentioned on the previous page, the actual breaded and baked chicken of this recipe, by itself, is only 2 points per breast. I'm adding 1 additional point (for 3 total points) per serving, to account for the sauce.

VEGETABLE & SHRIMP FRIED RICE

This Incredible Dish Is Bursting With Flavors. If You've Never Had It Before, It'll Be A New Favorite.

This is the second dish, I swore up and down, I would never attempt to make for this cookbook. I was convinced there was no way imaginable you could make it low in points, while still ONLY USING REAL RICE... none of that riced cauliflower nonsense! First things first, I needed to stretch the rice with as many vegetables as possible. I searched online and found an actual Chinese restaurant's recipes for both vegetable, as well as their shrimp fried rice. Then, I hacked the recipes down and combined 'em into one super dish.

Servings Info.:

Yields: 11 cups
Servings: 11
Serving Size: 1 cup

MY PLAN

R D
2-2

- last checked 12/01/22 -
Use your mobile device's 'Camera' App to
look at this code for nutritional info.

Ingredients:

Shrimp:
- 1-1/2 pound shrimp (size 41-50ct), peeled, deveined, tail off
- 1/4 tsp baking soda, dissolved with 2 tsp water
- 1/2 tsp paprika, for color

Vegetables:
- 1-1/2 cups diced onion
- 1 large red bell pepper, diced (around 1-1/3 cups)
- 3/4 cup diced carrots
- 5 oz mushrooms, diced/chopped into bite sized pieces.
- 2 medium garlic cloves, chopped
- 3/4 cup green peas, fresh or frozen
- 1 cup fresh bean sprouts
- 1/2 cup green onions, sliced thin

Sauce:
- 1 Tbsp PLUS 1 tsp 'dark' soy sauce
- 3 Tbsp reduced sodium soy sauce
- 1/2 tsp ground turmeric
- 1/2 tsp salt

Additional Ingredients:
- 4 cups cooked white rice. Precooked, leftover, cold rice. Preferably left in the fridge overnight UNCOVERED.
- 2 large eggs, beaten <u>with 1 Tbsp white wine</u>
- 1 tsp toasted sesame seeds, for garnish

Directions:

1. Mix together the shrimp, baking soda/water solution and paprika. Let rest for 20 minutes.

2. **(A)** Prep and chop all the vegetables, set aside. Whisk the eggs and white wine, set aside. **(B)** Take your day old rice out of the fridge. Measure 4 cups and place into a mixing bowl. Sprinkle with a little water and break up the rice. Big clumps bad! Set aside. **(C)** Heat a LARGE, high walled pan over medium-high heat, for 1 minute. Spray with cooking spray, add the shrimp and cook till just cooked through, around 4-5 minutes. Set aside. **(D)** Spray pan with cooking spray and add the eggs. Scramble till just cooked through, set aside.

3. **(A)** Spray the pan with cooking spray, then add the onions, carrots, mushrooms, bell peppers and garlic. **(B)** Cook 4-5 minutes, or until the vegetables are starting to soften and color.

4. **(A)** Add the leftover rice (still cold) into the pan, along with the peas. Toss to combine for 1 minute, to start warming up the rice. Pour in the sauce, toss and toss and toss, till the rice takes on a uniform color. **(B)** Add the bean sprouts and green onions, toss to combine. **(C)** Add the shrimp and the scrambled eggs back into the pan. Toss/mix to combine. **(D)** Continue to cook and toss for an additional 1-2 minutes, until the rice is completely heated through and the entire dish has a dark golden hue. Garnish with sesame seeds, as well as additional thin sliced green onion, if desired.

NOTES & SUGGESTIONS:

- **LEFTOVER vs. FRESH RICE:** Ok... my recipe calls for leftover white rice. Why's that? Because it's already cooked... but it's dried out. When we stir it back into this big pan o' hot stuff, the rice is going to get steamed for a few minutes. If we were to have fresh cooked, fluffy rice.. then add it into this pan and continue to steam it EVEN MORE... it'll turn out mushy. If you want to use fresh cooked rice, make sure to cook it with a little less water than normal, so that it still has a little bit of bite to it. Ever boiled rice with too much water? We're trying to avoid that gruel.

NOTES (cont.)

- **WHITE RICE vs BROWN vs CAULIFLOWER:** You can use brown rice if you want, but the texture will be different. You can also use 'Lie-Rice'... I mean... riced cauliflower, STOP CALLING IT CAULIFLOWER RICE, IT'S NOT RICE!!!! It's small nuggets of farty sadness!!
- **I DON'T LIKE SHRIMP, WAAAAAA!!:** Honestly, Susie... use chicken, beef or tofu. I can't do all the thinking for'ya :-) Also... though I used size 41-50 shrimp... you can use whatever size you'd like.
- **TURMERIC?!?!?:** If you'd like this rice to have a regular brownish color, then leave out the turmeric. However, it really gives it a fancy, restaurant quality look, having that golden hue to it. If you'd like to keep the turmeric, but have the brown more prominent... easy, dial the turmeric down to 1/8 tsp. Boom, done.
- **VEGGIE SUBSTITUTIONS:** It goes without saying, you don't have to use the exact veggies that I did. If you want to sub any of them out for a vegetable of your own liking, be my guest. The only thing I'd recommend is for you to try and match the amount of the veggie you're removing. IE: If you want to use zucchini instead of red bell peppers, replace the 1-1/3 cup of bell pepper with an equal amount of zucchini. That way, you keep the same number of servings and don't have to recalculate the points.

YAKI UDON STIR FRY

Thick, Chewy and Delicious Japanese Wheat Noodles in a Thick and Savory Sauce

This is my favorite of all the 'savory' noodle dishes that I've made so far, for this cookbook... and considering this is the 36th dish I've made, that says somethin'. Udon noodles are utterly awesome and are a favorite at most Japanese restaurants. Rather than making a typical soup/hot pot with them, I wanted to make a stir fry. This way, we could stretch the points/servings, while also ensuring all but one Asian region, represented in this book's recipes, has a noodle dish (sorry, Cambodia *shrug*).

Ingredients:

Meat:
- 1-1/2 lb chicken breast, sliced into thin, bite sized pieces
- 3/8 tsp baking soda, dissolved into 1 Tbsp water

Sauce:
- 2 tsp rice vinegar
- 1-1/2 tsp balsamic vinegar (see recipe notes)
- 2 tsp 0 calorie sugar replacement (I used lakanto monkfruit)
- 2 Tbsp 'dark' soy sauce (I used 'sushi chef' brand)
- 3 Tbsp lower sodium soy sauce
- 2-1/2 Tbsp oyster sauce

Veggies: *(highly customizable, see notes)*
- 8 oz sliced mushrooms, any variety (I used baby bella)
- 1 medium onion, thin sliced
- 1/2 cup green onions (scallions), sliced into 1" pieces
- 8 oz canned bamboo shoots, drained (see notes)
- 4 baby bok choy. Bottom 1" trimmed off, leaves/stems rinsed, sliced in half, lengthwise (watch a youtube video, if needed)

Noodles:
- 8 oz by weight, dried udon noodles (makes 3-3/4 cups cooked), cooked according to package directions. Drain, rinse under cold water, set aside.

Servings Info.:
Yield: 10.5 cups
Servings: 7
Serving Size: 1.5 cups

- last checked 12/01/22 -
Use your mobile device's 'Camera' App to look at this code for nutritional info.

Directions:

1. Mix the sliced chicken with the baking soda and water mixture. Set aside for 20-30 minutes.

2. Mix the sauce ingredients together, set aside.

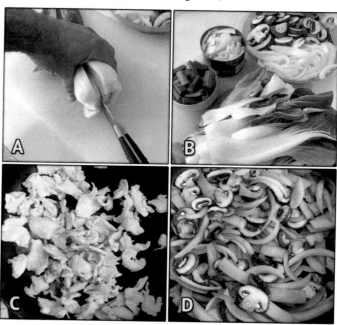

3. **(A)** Slice the washed bok choy in half, set aside.
   (B) Prep all your veggies before getting ready to cook.
   (C) Heat a LARGE high walled pan over medium high heat for 1 minute. Spray pan with cooking spray, then cook chicken for 5 minutes, till just cooked through. Remove from pan. **(D)** Spray pan, then add onions, mushrooms and bamboo shoots. Cook 4-5 minutes, set aside.

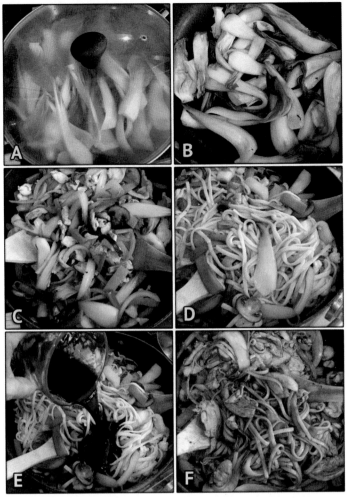

NOTES:

- *MUSHROOMS:* Though I used inexpensive, sliced baby bella mushrooms, you can use any variety you wish. Traditional recipes would call for Shitake mushrooms. Well, I don't know about ya'll... but this Cook's on a budget.
- *OYSTER SAUCE:* My wife HATES oyster sauce... a fact I learned after I made this dish. If you don't like the slight seafoody taste of oyster sauce, you can purchase vegetarian oyster sauce at stores. It's made from mushrooms and has a slightly different flavor profile.
- *LARGE FRYING PAN vs. WOK:* I'm using a large pan instead of a Wok, because most people don't have woks. My recipes will always use common equipment in their preparations, to make the dishes as accessible as possible. A frying pan won't get as hot as a wok, which is why my cook times and methods are different than traditional recipes.
- *BALSAMIC??:* In this recipe, I'm substituting balsamic vinegar for Chinese/Japanese black vinegar. It's easier to find and it works in a pinch, without ordering special ingredients.
- *RICE VINEGAR AND SWEETENER:* The traditional recipe for this dish calls for using "mirin", which has points. I'm subbing it out with rice vinegar and sweetener. It's a legit ingredient swap.
- *UDON NOODLES:* I am using <u>dried</u>, packaged udon noodles in my recipe. However... in the refrigerated aisle of your store, where they sell tofu and other cold Asian ingredients, they sell already cooked, vacuum sealed udon noodles. If you choose to use those, simply set them in some hot water for a minute, to warm them... then stir them in, the same as you would with step **4D**. Note: My dried udon noodles are 21 points for 3-3/4 cups of cooked noodles. If you use vacuum sealed noodles, check the points, and measure the noodles out. Adjust your points accordingly, if necessary.

SUBSTITUTION IDEAS:

- You can use chopped cabbage, broccoli florets, snow peas, zucchini, or any other green vegetable that you'd like, in place of the bok choy.
- If you don't want to use canned bamboo shoots, you can substitute them for thin sliced carrots or celery, though carrots will need to cook longer to soften.

4. **(A)** Return the pan to heat, ,then add the sliced bok choy and a spoonful (1 Tbsp) of water. Cover and steam for 4 minutes. Remove lid every minute and add another 1 Tbsp of water. **(B)** After 4 minutes, the bok choy should be just starting to brown. **(C)** Add the onions, mushrooms, bamboo shoots, chicken and sliced green onions to the pan. Toss to mix. **(D)** Add the cooked/rinsed noodles to the pan and toss to combine. Cook for 2 minutes. **(E)** Pour in the sauce, then **(F)** cook for an additional 3-4 minutes, mixing and tossing the entire time. Cook until the sauce begins to thicken and starts to coat the noodles. The coating will get darker as the sauce reduces. Done.

FOCUS, DANIELSAN!

Daniel Khan - 2nd Great Khan of the Mongol Empire
1215 - 1248 • Painted by: Zhu Da, early Qing Dynasty (1648)

Honestly... five!!?! Five cookbooks now? I know I say this every time, but I never would have thought I'd be here. Back when you all convinced me to start working on my original little 85 page cooking guide, back in 2018, I saw it as a monumental undertaking. I figured there's no way I could ever fill up 85 pages with tips, tricks and recipes. Boy, ya'll sure pushed the proverbial boulder down a hill, didn't you? See what you all started?

Making THIS cookbook was hard.... really hard. My wife and I never go out for Chinese food, I mean, c'mon, the last time we went out for Asian food regularly, is back when we were dating, 15 years ago! When we did go out, we were creatures of habit and ALWAYS ordered the same 3 dishes every time: Sesame Chicken, Singapore Noodles and occasionally Wor Wonton Soup. That's it. We never strayed from those 3 dishes. When we'd go to get Thai food, it was the same thing. We never tried new things. We'd only order Chicken Satay, Pad Thai and my wife would get Chicken Panang. I was too scared to try any new dishes. Of the 50+ entrees and sauces in this book, I'd never had 3/4 of them.

The hardest part about making all these recipes is I've STILL never actually gone to a restaurant and had them. I still have no idea what the 'real' dishes actually taste like. All I could do was research, research, research. I went online and looked up famous Asian Chefs like **Ming Tsai**, **Iron Chef Morimoto**, **Jet Tila** and others, to look up their recipes and see how I could hack them down. I also started taking inspiration from Asian cookbook authors & recipe bloggers, like: '**Omnivores Cookbook**', '**Drive Me Hungry**' & '**The Woks of Life**'. I learned so much about how to prepare traditional Asian food from reading their tips and watching their videos. However, the fun part was trying to take what THEY do... and merge it with what I do... modifying recipes with ingredient swaps.

I was really nervous at first, posting my WW-ified versions of traditional Asian food. I wasn't sure if I was making the recipes too complicated or not. Were my written instructions too inimidating? Would people accept a lighter version of the traditional dishes they missed? Thankfully, they were all well received and I have been blown away by the responses all of these dishes have gotten. I'm constantly being tagged by people who have made my Thai basil chicken, potstickers, black pepper chicken, or any of the other dishes. Tons of folks, saying how they made the recipes for their skeptical families.. who loved it! They all say how great it made them feel to make an Asian dish, themselves, then have their families actually clean their plates and get seconds.

Doing this recipe hacking, calorie droppin' craziness is so much fun for me. As a stay at home dad, THIS is my creative release. This is the one thing I have that's 'for me'... and the awesome part is, my 'for me' thing, actually helps people. It is an amazing, fulfilling feeling. I get complete and utter happy contentment out of this. Yeah... money is nice, but that's not my focus. If all I cared about was the Benjamins, I wouldn't let'ya all have these books for free on my website, now would I? It is such a wonderful, wonderful feeling, getting to know that in some small way, you're making a difference in the lives of 206,000 people who 'follow' you. *(as of 12-03-22)*

I hope the way I have made these recipes and laid out the pages of this book, make the thought of cooking Asian food a bit less intimidating for you. I hope you folks don't mind stepping out of your comfort zones and are willing to try cooking something totally outside of your wheel-house. Most importantly, I hope when you try it, you actually like the results. I can completely empathize with how scary it is cooking an entirely new type of cuisine. But once you get the hang of it, it's worth it. There's freedom in knowing you CAN prepare a lot of different dishes to fit into your healthier lifestyle.

I gotta tell you though, after pretty much cooking noooothing but Asian food, for the past 8-10 months, it's going to be a long time before I eat Asian food again after this, lol. Thankfully, the next cookbook is going to be Mexican food, so... hold on to your sombreros, mis amigos... we're going to kick **#TacoTuesday** up a couple notches. VIVA LOS TAMALES!! *pew pew*

ACKNOWLEDGEMENTS

I'd like to thank the Academy...

Well, here we are again... and again. Seeing that we're at the end of the book, now's as good a time as any to mention a few of the folks who have poked, prodded and tricked me into making what's probably the first full fledged, LEGIT, Weight Watchers-focused Asian cookbook. There are tens of thousands of you who have been extremely supportive, encouraging and helpful with this book over the past 9-10 months. But, there's no way I can possibly mention all of you, so I apologize if you don't see your name in here.

Let's start with the non-Weight Watchers people. More than any of you realize... a huge reason I was able to put this Cookbook together was because of all the Behavioral Therapists at '**California Psych Care, Santa Clarita**.' Yup... just like Cookbook 3, I couldn't have done this without them. These wonderful young women, come to my house, nearly every single day, to help my kids with their therapies. While they are working with my kiddos, that's when I was able to have a small window of time, which allowed me to start putting pages together. A special thanks to, **Jennifer**, **Stephanie 1**, **Stephanie 2**, **Kendal, Lisa & Melissa.**

Now... onto the Weight Watchers/Social Media folks. There are a bunch of people, especially in Weight Watchers 'Connect', I want to single out and thank. I won't be able to mention everyone, because there are so many of'ya. But I do have to call out a few. C'mon... there's 200,000+ of you following me right now. (between Connect, IG, YouTube & FB).

I have to start off with **@69gabygal**... the poor lady who is my digital best friend. She's essentially like having a retired, crabby, Jiminy Cricket, hovering around and texting me at all hours of the day. Other than dealing with my horrific grammar and typos... she spends her time trying to make me FINALLY open Pinterest links (which I won't!), making food suggestions, does her best to steer me away from Dairy Queen binges... and <u>WILL NOT</u> leave me alone with requests for pistachio recipes!

@Mariarachael12 for always offering advice on picture layout for my recipe pages, as well as sharing her mother's Pancit recipe with me. Thanks again, Kaibegen!!. **@Rbberens**, and **@mfitch**, for being my 2 local WW homies who I could occasionally drop off some of my creations to, for feedback. You folks who are happy with some of these dishes need to thank Rbberens. Because, my original versions sucked, before her feedback. **@AliciawMccauley** for letting me rant in texts, from time to time, thanks hippie! **@Bizzybee85**, who gave me a lot of suggestions for dishes, ESPECIALLY the Korean Bibimbap. That dish is 100% only in this book, because of her. Hey, Bizz... I'm still waiting for that house warming invitation. Just sayin'. **@Chiafullo**... my 'Frenemie', thank's for making Connect fun again, you almond hating Nonna!

Also, thank you to a few folks who I'm going to pull off the top of my head, at 12:30am, without opening my phone: **kimberly_jack, jan0443, pyrophage, ericaossiramos, lappelba, jazigirl01, chasing1durland, steve_burns, sailorgal329, jfo_shizzle, mnewp416, mayaski18, rosina8769, mikinp48, olahou, spockme, awfoster0105, lindaluper, exerciseforyou, poopstar** *(years later and I still laugh whenever I see your name)***, anna-demon, faithisfat, strongandhealthyme7, priyanthi_p2, margohery, rdmays2, mhertoghe** *(and your danged lemon bars!!)***, fittabe, amybethh66, libertylake2017, msneetu**... Seriously, there are too many of you to list, so I'm sorry that I can't name more of you. Amazon charges by the page, folks.

A special, unexpected shout out to my former employer, the gang at *Lee's Decorative Showcase*. Thank you for taking a chance and hiring a totally underqualified web/graphics guy. Thank you, *Jay* & *Julie*, for pushing me to constantly try and learn new ways to do graphic layout & page design... and for being the reason I had to go back to school and take night classes. It's because you guys took a chance on me, I ultimately learned the skills I'd need to put these books together, years later. Making your product catalogs, it turns out... isn't that different from laying out a cookbook. It was a good, hard, stressful job, but it changed the course of my life. Thank you.

Aaaaaaand lastly, once again... my wife. For having to put up with me for yet another cookbook. All my late nights on the computer... and your having to share me with Connect. I'd like to think that the process gets slightly more bearable with each passing Cookbook... I hope. Look at the bright side, hun... put down the chancla, Mexican food's next!

NUTRITIONAL VALUES

One of the biggest reasons for cooking and preparing meals like I do, is because I want to eat amazingly snazzy food, without having to reduce my portions. Most popular food bloggers, "skinny" cookbook authors, and celebrity chefs, usually have tiny, toddler sized portions. That's how they say their food is healthy. Of course, it is. You're being served an entree from the kids menu. In equal amounts, my recipes are usually around 1/2 (or less) of the points, fat and calories of everyone else'. Wanting to lose weight doesn't mean that you have to eat 'diet' sized kiddie portions.

SAUCES & DIPS	SERVING SIZE	CALORIES	FAT (grams)	CARBS (grams)	SUGAR (grams)	PROTEIN (grams)	SODIUM (milligrams)	PAGE #
Cambodian Pepper Lime Dip	1/4 cup	25	0	1.4	1.8	0.9	1,445.8	22
'Duck' Sauce	1/4 cup	37.9	0.1	14	5.4	0.4	163.4	22
Hoisin Dipping Sauce	Entire 1/2 cup	108.5	0.8	31.8	8.1	1.9	1,218.8	22
Katsu Sauce	1/4 cup	48	0.1	16.6	6.5	1.6	1,074.1	22
Korean Bibimbap Sauce	1/4 cup	40.3	0	19.7	3.2	0.6	778.5	23
Orange Ginger Glaze	Entire 1/2 cup	108.8	0.3	82.3	5.5	3.4	1,691.7	23
Soy Glaze & Dipping Sauce	Entire 1/2 cup	168.2	1.3	50.6	16.9	3.8	2,853.3	23
Sweet & Sour Sauce	1/4 cup	51.8	0	36.7	10.2	0.1	500.2	23
Szechuan Peppercorn Sauce	1/4 cup	16	0	19.5	0	0.3	114.3	24
Teriyaki Sauce	1/4 cup	15.4	0	9.3	0.4	0.8	529.2	24
Thai Peanut Sauce	1/4 cup	59.9	2.2	11.6	1	4.4	254.7	24
Thai Sweet Chili Sauce	1/4 cup	56.5	0.2	38.2	8.9	0.4	528.7	25
Vietnamese Dipping Sauce	1/4 cup	11.5	0	13.9	2.3	1	1,517.2	25
Vietnamese Ginger Chili Sauce	1/2 cup	60	0.1	37.1	4.8	4.7	5,791.3	25
Yum Yum Sauce	1/4 cup	41	0.4	7.2	3.7	4.7	314.5	25

DIM SUM & SOUPS	SERVING SIZE	CALORIES	FAT (grams)	CARBS (grams)	SUGAR (grams)	PROTEIN (grams)	SODIUM (milligrams)	PAGE #
Char Siu Bao	1 bun	154.3	1.5	27	1.8	12.3	322.6	28-29
Chicken Satay Skewers	1 skewer	26.1	0.5	1.6	0.5	4.6	149.4	30-31
Gyoza Potstickers	1 dumpling	32.2	0.2	5.0	0.1	2.5	98.9	32-33
San Choy Bow (meat filling)	3 Tbsp scoop	34.5	0.5	2.1	0.5	8.2	260.4	34-35
Shumai Dumplings	1 dumpling	47.4	0.4	5.1	0.2	5.6	114.1	36-37
Spring Rolls	1 spring roll	*(The macros for your spring roll will depend entirely on your filling)*						38-41
Sweet & Sour Meatballs	1 meatball	18.7	0.3	2.6	0	2.6	91	42
Vietnamese Meatballs	1 meatball	17.9	0.3	0.4	0	3.2	116	43
*** SOUPS ***								
Egg Drop Soup	1-1/4 cup	110.5	4.7	8	0	7	1,171	44-45
Hot & Sour Soup	1-1/3 cup	146.2	4.2	13.2	2.2	15.8	643.6	46-47
Wonton Soup	1-1/3 cup	174.3	1.6	21.6	0.3	11.3	1,205.8	48-49
Wor Wonton Soup	1-1/2 cups	212.1	2.6	18	3	29.1	1,939.7	50-51

HOLY SODIUM-BOMB, BATMAN!

Most cookbooks don't include Sodium when they list their nutritional information. However, I'm making this book with all of my WW-amigos in mind. The honest truth is, there are a lot of members who are 'up there' in years and are on heart medications or have dietary restrictions for how much sodium they can consume... which is why I've chosen to include the sodium numbers.

These numbers sound insanely high, however, for you folks that aren't on a sodium restrictive diet, it's not a big deal. Note that there IS a very good chance that you will see a temporary gain at the scale if you have a very high sodium dish. THIS IS NORMAL. Consuming a lot of sodium makes your body retain water Don't worry... just drink lots of water and cut back on your sodium intake for a day or two after you have a high sodium meal... and it'll all come off. C'mon... I was like a walking Yo-Yo the entire time I was working on this cookbook ,with my weight fluctuating more than a Politician's promises during an election year.

So, I just wanted to post this as a reminder for the people out there who might make one of these dishes, then see a gain. Don't stress... just drink water and like the mighty Mississippi... the weight will flow on out. It's honestly crazy how high in sodium all of these are. Especially when you consider that I only use reduced sodium soy sauce and try to limit it to no more than 3 Tbsp in most of these dishes. Imagine how much sodium is in the regular Asian food you always order. *whistles*

MAIN DISHES	SERVING SIZE	CALORIES	FAT (grams)	CARBS (grams)	SUGAR (grams)	PROTEIN (grams)	SODIUM (milligrams)	PAGE #
Adobo Chicken	1 breast	178.5	3.7	19.2	8.2	24.9	786.7	54-55
Banh Mi Chicken Sandwich	1 sandwich	358.6	8.1	41.0	7.6	34.4	1,718.4	56-57
Beef Lok Lak Stir Fry	1 cup	262.9	9.1	6.7	2.6	35.7	731.4	58-59
Beijing Chicken	1-1/2 cup	258.9	3.1	50.6	7.7	31.8	1,373.3	60-61
Bibimbap w/Gochujang	1 rice bowl	485	8.3	98.8	36.4	40.4	3,272	62-63
Black Pepper Chicken	1-1/4 cup	231.9	4.2	12.3	3.9	37.6	1,550.9	64-65
Bulgogi Beef Stir Fry	1 cup, packed	323.1	12.3	20.4	6.7	37.6	1,042.3	66-67
Chicken & Broccoli	1-1/2 cup	175.2	3.5	12.6	2.7	22	908.9	68-69
Chicken Japchae Noodles	1-1/2 cup	228	3.2	35.9	2.9	19.6	524.8	70-71
Chicken Mai Fun Noodles	1-1/3 cup	155.9	2	23.4	2.5	15.6	714.9	72-73
Chicken Panang Curry	1-1/2 cup	235.1	5.4	20.2	7.2	27	1,868.6	74-75
Chicken w/Black Bean Sauce	1-1/3 cup	231.5	3.5	22.2	8.6	31.2	876	76-77
Chop Suey	1-1/2 cup	168.3	3.4	12.7	3	25.2	837	78-79
Chow Mein Noodles	1 cup	97.5	0.9	20.6	7.8	5.2	356.7	80-81
'Drunken' Noodles	1-1/3 cup	245.7	2.5	34.2	1.9	21.4	722.6	82-83
General Tso's Chicken	1 cup	234.2	3.9	28.7	6.1	29.7	1,197.8	84-85
Hoisin Chicken	1-1/2 cup	248	4.6	15.2	7.3	39.3	865.5	86-87
Honey Garlic Chicken	1 cup	222	3.8	20.3	10.9	31.9	963.1	88-89
Hunan Chicken	1-2/3 cup	204.7	4.0	26	6.8	27.2	1,087.7	90-91
Korean Gochujang Chicken	1/2 lb meat	279.3	6.4	18.2	5.3	48.1	1,997.5	92-93
Kung Pao Chicken	1-1/4 cup	292	10.3	13.7	4	41.4	1,300.7	94-95
Lemongrass Chicken	1-1/4 cup	231.1	4.2	18.4	4.6	38.8	1,319.5	96-97
Miso-Ginger Glazed Salmon	1 filet	302.2	12.8	12.5	4.8	35.5	1,096.5	98-99
Mongolian Chicken	1-1/2 cup	296.1	5.7	27.6	2.4	48.8	1,924.5	100-101
Moo Goo Gai Pain	1-1/2 cup	217.9	3.7	26.2	8.4	24.9	731.9	102-103
Mushroom Chicken	1 cup	231.7	3.8	11.9	4.4	27.1	766.7	104-105
Orange Chicken	1 cup	231.7	4.3	25.7	2.5	36.2	948.5	106-107
Pad Thai Noodles	1-1/4 cup	270.3	4.1	44.7	9.2	21.2	856.8	108-109
Pancit Sotanghon Noodles	1-1/2 cup	240.1	2.3	34.2	4.6	22	784.1	110-111
Sesame Chicken	1 cup	269.3	7.6	24.7	3.5	36.3	1,350.9	112-113
Shrimp with Lobster Sauce	1 cup	254	3	10.6	2	44	1,467.7	114-115
Shrimp with Snow Peas	1-1/2 cup	267.1	4.4	20.2	4.4	42.6	1,063.9	116-117
Singapore Noodles	1-1/2 cup	274.8	2.9	40.4	5.1	23	932.9	118-119
String Bean Chicken	1-1/2 cup	164.9	3.3	15.5	4.9	22.8	829.3	120-121
Sweet & Sour Chicken	1-1/2 cup	239	3	45	18.3	24.6	931.3	122-123
Sweet Fire Chicken	1-1/2 cup	242.5	3.2	55.6	18.8	25.3	624.4	124-125
Teriyaki Chicken	1 breast	188.3	3.8	8.2	2.5	35.6	1,067.8	126-127
Thai Basil Chicken	1-1/2 cup	240	4.6	20.6	4.3	38	1,384.5	128-129
Thai Sweet Chili Shrimp	1 cup	224.6	2.1	15.3	2.8	39.1	1,087.6	130-131
Torikatsu with Katsu Sauce	1 breast	296.1	5.4	28.7	8.1	39.1	1,535.6	132-133
Vegetable & Shrimp Fried Rice	1 cup	184.3	1.8	26.7	3.2	14.8	682.7	134-135
Yaki Udon Noodles	1-1/2 cup	238.4	2.3	37.2	2.4	22.6	1,091.9	136-137

** *All recipes which call for "0 point sweetener o' choice", were calculated using **Lakanto Monkfruit 'classic'** or 'Truvia Sweet Complete Brown' sugar and brown sugar replacements. Because, hey... they're my sweeteners o' choice. But, you do you, boo-bear.*

🤔 CARBOHYDRATE CONUNDRUM 🤔

I know I mentioned it right above this paragraph... but it REALLY needs to be explained in more detail. For most all of these listed nutritional values, the numbers for the carbs are misleading. I'm mentioning it, because I honestly have no idea how to truly address it in the macros. Every single one of my recipes that would regularly require sugar, instead uses Lakanto monkfruit, or some other brand of "ERYTHRITOL-based" sweetener, because that's my personal preference.

Erythritol sweeteners are natural sweeteners derived from sugar alcohols. They are NON GLYCEMIC, meaning that their carbs (and they contain a lot of carbs) ARE NOT ABSORBED INTO YOUR BLOOD STREAM. They are 0 calorie and their carbs aren't absorbed and converted to sugar. Unfortunately, I still have to include all of those carbs, from the erythritol, into the nutritional macros... even though your body does not absorb them. A great example is my **Sweet & Sour Sauce**, which would be listed as having 213 grams of carbs in a 2 cup batch of sauce. However... 192 of those shouldn't count, because they are Non-Glycemic carbs your body isn't going to absorb. However, I still have to list them in the nutritional totals. This makes the total carb count seem incredibly high on a lot of these dishes. FYI: Erythritol sweeteners have a ZERO glycemic index score.

BOOK INDEX

Crouching Tiger Hidden Recipes

Hiking The Great Wall of China

Exploring Thailand

Visiting Hoboken, New Jersey

Made in the USA
Middletown, DE
31 March 2023

27995181R00080